The View from

No. 13

People's Street

The View from
No. 13
People's Street

Aline Mosby

 Random House, New York

Fourth Printing

© Copyright, 1962, by Aline Mosby

All rights reserved under International and
Pan-American Copyright Conventions. Published in New York by Random House, Inc.,
and simultaneously in Toronto, Canada, by
Random House of Canada, Limited.

Library of Congress Catalog Card
Number: 62-8466

Manufactured in the United States of
America by The Book Press

To
Ludmilla and Henry Shapiro
and
Robert J. Korengold

Contents

Foreword   ix

1   From Montana to Moscow   3

2   No. 13 People's Street   20

3   The Censor Who Never Was   36

4   Keeping a Marxist House   56

5   Some Observations on Russian Men   75

6   In My Merry MGA   91

7   The Great Invasion   106

8   Miss Moscow   125

9   The New Soviet Dog   141

10   The Private Life of a Muscovite   154

11   The Comradely Arts   171

12   Alice in Wonderland   192

13   The Party Line   215

14   Just the News That's Printed to Fit   232

15   The Powers Trial   256

16   The Case of the Forbidden Painting   272

17   Around the World in 89 Minutes   291

Foreword

This is not a book on Soviet politics, nor a definitive study of the people of the U.S.S.R. Many books have been written on those subjects. Studying the Soviet Union is a serious business, as I know after helping cover top political stories in Moscow for nearly three years as a UPI correspondent.

I have chosen instead to tell my experiences as a woman reporter in Moscow, to give glimpses of the human and personal side of the Soviet people, and of how foreign correspondents work and live and play in the Soviet capital.

Everything I have written happened. Everything attributed to Soviets was said by them. Only their names have been changed, to spare them any difficulties.

The View from
No. 13
People's Street

1

From Montana to Moscow

The way to Boris Pasternak's house wound through the suburbs with their clusters of stolid new apartment houses.

Then across a bridge, past files of clattering trucks, and we passed with relief from city to country. It made me smile to see the olive-green wooden peasant houses with their teal-blue carved shutters like lacework, and the open faces of the country people who crowded the edge of the two-lane paved highway.

In front of a water pump a little girl held her blue parasol over a white goat as if to shade him from the bright summer sun. A black baby goat nibbled on a clump of grass near by.

We passed groves of tall, tall pines and white and black birch trees. Peasants with little wagons peddled kvass, a drink made of fermented bread and, I knew, tasting that way. A peasant woman, her head wrapped in a printed kerchief, led a cow home past a sign that urged, "Surpass America in Milk Production!"

White chickens scratched in private vegetable plots next to some collective-farm houses. A pipe banged back and forth in the back of a gigantic truck that rattled by.

Then we were off the highway and heading down a dirt road. A policeman stopped our car: foreigners usually not allowed. When we said where we were going he saluted us on.

Scenes flashed through the car window. A pale yellow grocery store with carved white eaves. Nearly hidden among the pines, a pale green wooden sanitorium, once a nobleman's country home. A child with big white organdy bows flopping on her pigtails as she ran through the forest. A man in black boots and bloomer-like trousers sitting on a roadside bench. A soldier and his girl walking down the road . . .

We made two left turns on another dirt road, and finally we saw his fence, the garden in front, the old sheep-dog barking and running, the white curtains quiet at the windows of the two-story wooden house.

Pasternak lay inside in his coffin, his face like stone. The floor was heaped with pine boughs brought from the forest behind the house.

The PEN Club of America had asked my office, United Press International (UPI), to take flowers in its name. Another UPI correspondent, Henry Shapiro, and I lugged the wreath from the car and carried it up the driveway. We leaned it against the veranda steps.

I had met Boris Pasternak in Moscow in 1959. He had come to Tschaikovsky Hall to hear the New York Phil-harmonic orchestra. During the first intermission he walked backstage to congratulate Leonard Bernstein, and I noticed that his face wore an expression almost of ecstasy as he embraced the conductor.

Then, overflowing with words, the writer talked, emo-tionally, dramatically. We correspondents pressed into Bernstein's dressing room, taking photographs and plying Pasternak with questions; but the conductor was anxious for us not to upset him, and we left.

Pasternak did not shun the attention, however. At the

second intermission he walked backstage again to talk to Leonard Bernstein. Remembering the questions I had asked earlier, he sought me out near the dressing room, gesturing to me over the heads of the milling musicians. He gave me a piece of notebook paper on which he had scrawled, in spidery handwriting, in English, the answers to my questions. When I asked more, he talked to me in halting English, smiling and warm and, I felt, with a touch of gallantry because I was a woman.

I saw Pasternak's house for the first time the following spring. I had driven to the home in suburban Peredelkino to inquire after his condition when he became ill. His brother, looking like the writer's twin, came down the driveway to discuss the medical bulletins.

After that I made many trips to Peredelkino. At first the police stopped foreign correspondents near the village, as the area was not open to foreigners. But when they learned our purpose they relaxed the rules. One evening Pasternak's son came out of the house to tell us about the blood transfusions which marked the writer's losing battle with cancer. The son stood looking out across the fields at a little church on a hill and shook his head in hopelessness.

By midnight Pasternak was dead; and when the correspondents hurried to the house, his brother stood weeping on the porch. I returned to Peredelkino the next day. The family never seemed to mind the presence of reporters, and even on that day I sat on a bench in the yard for an hour, talking with Pasternak's brother, his wife, and his son. Friends arrived to talk and walk about the lawn.

And then, later, the people came, by every means, for the funeral. Students in slacks and shirts who had never met him, walking the mile from the suburban train across the fields. Diplomats and correspondents in their foreign cars, parking for a mile down the shady road. Writers and artists and musicians, not officials from the Writers' Union or the Party, but his friends, some arriving by taxi, others on foot from surrounding country homes.

An elderly man in a white linen duster hanging to his ankles, a straw hat clamped straight on his head, walked with a cane slowly up the driveway, a shadow of Chekhov. Men in their best suits, stout women in print dresses. Young people looking intense and believing and determined to be there.

The people shifted about on the lawn and the porch and walked, serious-faced, by his bed. I stood in the hallway, watching the line. In a back room, Svyatoslav Richter, Russia's great pianist, played emotionally, his head swaying.

Then the mourners moved into the procession, in ancient Russian style, the open coffin held above the heads, winding across the fields to that little hilltop church with its blue onion-shaped dome that Pasternak used to see from his bedroom window.

Some of the women who had been dear to him stood in a semicircle around the grave: his wife, in a black dress with a white round collar, her dark brown permanented hair parted low on one side; another woman, a handsome blonde, almost theatrical-looking, wept.

This day is another Russia, I thought. These, too, are the people and the land. It's not always as the newspapers say, like the red banners or the slogans.

We did not guess it then, but three months later the police entered the house of the blonde woman. They found hidden rubles, and Olga Ivinskaya went to prison. I heard some Russians whisper after the trial that her real sin had been to spirit some Pasternak letters and writings out of Russia.

This, too, was Russia.

And I was there to see it.

Some days it isn't quite so poignant to be an American woman working in Moscow. Some days it's frustrating. The day customs confiscated our TV film and my visa for Leningrad was issued so late that I missed the train, somebody brought me a copy of an American magazine. I started to cry. It was such a homesick-making remembrance of "decadent" capitalist life on the other side of the world!

But I remember many happy moments. Watching grandmothers bringing white Easter cakes, decorated with fat red paper roses, to be blessed by priests in the timeless churches. Or being spellbound by the dreamlike poetry of the fragile ballerina Galina Ulanova dancing *Giselle*. There have been thrilling times, as when Yuri Gagarin soared into space as mankind's first cosmonaut. And frightening days, such as the afternoon a rock whizzed past my head in an anti-American demonstration.

Whatever the experiences, the nearly three years I've lived in Moscow have been the most interesting and, yes, exciting years of my life.

I am probably the world's only working girl with a Russian policeman guarding my front door and Tass teletypes near my bedroom.

A block's walk to the Moskva River and I can look down the muddy water to the glistening gold domes and the turrets and towers of the Kremlin, one of the most beautiful sights I have seen.

Moscow! Sometimes I can scarcely believe I am there.

It's a long way, and not just in miles, from Moscow to Missoula, Montana, where I was born, grew up, and was graduated from the university.

Moscow is even farther from Hollywood, where for years as a correspondent for United Press I lived in an apartment with a swimming pool and interviewed Ava Gardner in a bathtub and Jerry Lewis by the Las Vegas dice tables. It was Hollywood's own glittering, insulated world that interested me until I went to Brussels in the summer of 1958 to cover the World Exposition.

Like many Americans, the pavilion I most wanted to see was the Soviet pavilion. The guides the Soviets sent to work at the fair, many of whom were getting their first glimpse of the outside world, were eager to talk to Americans, particularly females. I had no trouble making friends.

The first Russian I ever met was a handsome man named Anatoly. He was a devout member of the Communist party, and his was an example of a mind molded by Soviet education and propaganda. One time we got on the subject of psychiatry. He had never heard of Freud and psychoanalysis, both frowned upon under the Soviet system. I tried to explain them to him.

"But we are taught the individual and his problems are less important than the needs of the state," he said. "Why would anyone go to a doctor because of his personal problems?"

Many other observations of his perplexed me. During a political argument he announced he did not approve of elections "because too many factors can enter into them. They are not reliable." One day he wrinkled his brow wistfully when he looked at a Brussels apartment house. "They have their apartment problems solved. We don't," he said. Then he added defensively, "But, after all, Brussels is a very old city. Our country is only forty-one years old!" Like many Russians, he talked as if Moscow had been created at the time of the 1917 Bolshevik revolution, and as if the country had made not one inch of progress before that.

Now and then, though, I thought I glimpsed a patch of humanness beneath the layers of Soviet indoctrination. The day Russians stoned the American Embassy in Moscow to protest the U.S. marine landing in Lebanon, I dropped in at the Soviet pavilion for some reactions. The first Soviet acquaintance I saw wasn't the least concerned with the American landing. With a grin he explained, "Imagine a crowd stoning an embassy! I think our authorities are relaxing a bit."

Later I showed another Russian a *Reporter* magazine article claiming that Soviet rulers could be classified as left-wing Stalinists, right-wing non-Stalinists, etc. In an effort to be friendly, he said, "I'm a right-wing non-Stalinist. Does that make me too far from American Democratic party voters?"

When another Russian friend left Brussels, he fervently kissed me farewell. Then, apparently brooding about the written instructions he said had been given the guides not to become involved with foreign women, he informed me stiffly it was all my fault. After all, I *let* him kiss me!

By summer's end I was reading books on Soviet affairs. I decided I wanted to be a Moscow correspondent, to see if this mysterious land was as paradoxical as it sounded.

To my joy, the UPI decided to send me there as a permanent member of the bureau, to get a woman's view of the
Russians as well as to carry my share of the more
serious stories—the Khrushchev speeches, the rocket
launchings, the shifts in ideology—in fact, to help report
the historically important picture of a nation emerging
from a deep and ancient shadow.

I had some time to wait for a visa and the departure
of my predecessor from the Moscow UPI office. To keep
busy during the interim, I set about learning as much as
I could from and about "ex-Russian Russians" on the
western side of the "Iron Curtain."

Many Russian émigrés from various "liberation" groups
in West Germany had visited the Brussels Exposition,
where they tried to pass anti-communist brochures to
Soviet tourists and Soviet pavilion workers. In Munich I
visited some émigré acquaintances I had made, to see
what they were up to.

One was a dark, soulful-eyed young intellectual right
out of Dostoyevsky. He had fled to the West while visiting
East Berlin with a group of Soviet tourists because "I just
couldn't stand it any longer." While his fellow tourists
were examining paintings in an East Berlin museum,
Dmitri slipped away and ran to the subway leading to
West Berlin. He chose to take with him only his dearest
possession, a book by the Russian writer Pushkin.

Dmitri took me to meeting after meeting of Russian
émigré groups. Each "club" had a different idea of how
the Russian government should be organized; most groups
already had constitutions drawn up. One meeting I attended called for a semi-Marxist socialist, semi-capitalist
society with a freely elected parliament. "Big business

would be state-owned, but we would allow small private businesses, private farming, and a free press," one ex-Russian Russian explained eagerly to me.

Another group consisted of representatives of peoples conquered by both Imperial and Soviet Russia—Georgians, Armenians, and the like. They desired no part of Russia—not even other émigrés. All they wanted was for their own countries to be freed from Soviet control.

Although there seemed to be no potential Lenins among these presently ineffectual groups, what devotion to the Motherland they revealed! I could think of no other nation whose émigrés seem so fervently concerned about the future of their native land.

In Berlin I acquired a new Russian friend, but a loyal Soviet, named Mikhail. He was visiting in Berlin for a few weeks on a cultural mission. As a representative of the Soviet theatrical world, he came into respectable contact with foreigners, and it was at the home of a mutual German acquaintance that we were introduced.

Mikhail was not a Communist party member like other Russians I had known. He was nearly middle-aged and, although he had an established position as a leader of Soviet culture, the "bad days" of the Stalin era were still fresh in his memory.

Often he said, "I know I shouldn't be afraid any more, the police days probably are over," but he was still frequently as nervous as a rabbit. When we went to the theater in East or West Berlin I had to walk half a block behind him, and sometimes we even sat in separate seats. He constantly suspected we were being followed by Soviet embassy personnel.

Sometimes Mikhail acted as if he thought I might be an

American spy. At other times he envisioned me as a Soviet spy. "American journalists are spies, we are told," he remarked once. Another time we discussed the case of Guy Burgess and Donald Maclean, of the British Foreign Office, who had defected to Moscow.

"You see? Many of us feel it is dangerous to be friends with foreigners, not because they might be western spies, but because they might be Soviet spies and report something about us," he blurted.

Once he switched to picturing me as an innocent endangered by McCarthyism. "The Americans may arrest you," he cried. "You've been seen with Russians! You must protect yourself by making pro-American statements in front of those German correspondents who saw us together. They may be American agents!"

Actually, Kurfuerstendamm, the gay main street of West Berlin, is a haven of spies, counter-spies, and counter-counter-spies. Anything was possible. I was becoming extremely nervous myself.

In December my visa finally came, and I made ready in Frankfurt, West Germany, for my trek into the "wilds" of Russia. When my friends squeezed me into my little white MGA sports car, it was so loaded with western fripperies it looked like Macy's. One cause for my small mountain of boxes and bags was a letter I had received from my boss-to-be, Henry Shapiro. "Welcome to Moscow," he wrote warmly. "And," he added, "please bring half a dozen solid toilet deodorizers, one pair of black kid gloves without stitching size 6¾, and four pairs of white double bed sheets."

How often was I to write similar letters over the next few years!

Following Shapiro's advice, I packed for myself woolen winter underwear in assorted colors, a trench coat (foreign correspondents really should have trench coats, I thought), fur-lined boots, fur-lined gloves, and a fur-lined coat. I also bought a supply of spare parts for my car. I was determined to take my MGA to Moscow even though everybody, including the Soviet embassy in London, kept telling me, "Impossible without permission on your visa!"

Somehow the car also held an Indian brass pot (a bargain from the London flea market), two heavy antique Dutch cookie molds, and other untravelworthy souvenirs of my wanderings around Europe. A friend piled on a blue plastic garbage pail with a white top. He was sure such a "luxury" would not be buyable in Moscow (as it turned out, he was right). At the last minute a reporter from UPI in Frankfurt ran over to wedge in a box of photographic developing paper for the Moscow bureau.

The trip to Berlin was a nightmare. I had to stop at three checkpoints, manned by the East Germans, apparently designed to discourage West Germans from traveling to Berlin and Berliners and East Germans from going the other way. At each stop, loudspeakers blared "invitations" to come to East Germany to live. Tables were stacked with communist propaganda leaflets in the hope of influencing travelers from both directions.

At the first checkpoint on the East-West German border, I applied for a permit to enter East Germany in order to reach Berlin. I was led inside a small office decorated with portraits of Lenin. Thinking the unsmiling man behind the desk was Russian, I announced in my primitive Russian that I was going to the Soviet Union. With a bored expression, he said he was German. He

looked me over and examined my little car outside bulging
with baggage. He kept thumbing through my documents
and staring at me in bewilderment until a German soldier
peering over his shoulder pointed to the word "Journalist"
on my passport. That seemed to explain everything.

At three different windows I had to wait in line to pay
Deutsche marks for permits. I was depressed by my first
glimpse of eastern bureaucracy—the drab rooms, the ever-
present portraits of Marx and Lenin, the grim clerks, the
lines of weary Germans waiting for scraps of paper that
would allow them to continue on the highway.

The formalities took so long that by the time I completed the last one at the second checkpoint it was dark.
I churned off down the *Autobahn* into one of those
paralyzing fogs that often blanket Germany at night. The
highway glistened with patches of February ice. One
incautious touch on the brakes, I knew, and my little car
would shoot off the asphalt and crumble in a ditch.

I was told I was not to stop on the highway for any
reason. If I did, I might become just another American
detained by East Germans. The cottony fog shrouded the
edge of the road and the forest beyond. Not a service
station, not a light. For miles I nervously hugged the back
of a truck, groping along at 10 miles an hour. I kept
thinking, Please don't skid, little car, I'll never make it to
Moscow. . . .

There was another agonizing delay at the third checkpoint, so that I could have hopped out to kiss the ground
when I spied the sign, "Berlin. Turn right for American
Sector."

After two more days of paper work at the Soviet, East
German, and Polish embassies, at last I held in my hands

a train ticket to Moscow and visas to the other half of East Germany and to Poland.

I was told I could not drive to Russia during the winter. The Polish, East German, and Soviet consulates insisted that I could not even ship my car to Moscow unless I had permission marked on my visa. But the bureaucrats underestimated the persistence of a woman. Why not ship it as a piece of baggage? The East Berlin shipping company clerk paid little attention to the fact that my package was (a) a car and (b) going to Moscow. The gas was drained out and the car shipped by rail.

By this time my baggage had multiplied by six boxes filled with cameras and film needed by UPI in Moscow for the forthcoming tour of British Prime Minister Harold Macmillan. An hour before the stores closed on my last day "outside," another telegram came from Henry Shapiro: "Bring antihistamine pills, green eyeshadow, and six picture hooks."

I was near collapse from excited shopping when my Berlin friends took me to a cocktail party for a Hollywood movie at the glossy Berlin Hilton Hotel. It was to be my last look for a year and a half at the "decadent" West. I ate a hearty meal.

Then we took a taxi to the railway station in East Berlin. We hurried through the Russian sector, where the streets were dark and almost empty. All of a sudden, Germany seemed to dissolve, and there was Russia bursting upon me: Russia, in the form of the "Blue Express," its name painted on the side in Russian letters; Russia, in the form of short, stocky Russian porters and Soviet army officers in fur caps and ankle-length coats returning to Moscow. And the smell! That thick Russian scent that is

so peculiar to all parts of Russia—from their sweet cigarettes, I thought, or heavy perfume, or perhaps the shiny
varnish on the wood—pervaded everything.

A Russian woman at the railway station sewed gray
burlap around the boxes to be checked through in the
baggage car. Then she painted on the address in Russian.
I still had enough small boxes and suitcases to fill half
my compartment. As I climbed aboard, a man from UPI
in Berlin rushed up with a last-minute box containing
photographic developing paper, Scotch tape, and en-
velopes for the Warsaw bureau!

Russian trains have separate compartments. My luxurious little home was decorated with blue plush drapes,
blue figured wallpaper, an Oriental rug, white lace curtains, a table, a bronze lamp with an olive-green lamp
shade, and four berths—one containing a handsome
Polish man.

Passengers, no matter what sex, share compartments.
Dressing and undressing in the dark seemed the only
solution. I finally got used to seeing my roommate trot
off to the washroom down the hall in his green and white
striped pajamas.

The first day and a half there was no dining car on the
train. I ate from a sack of provisions given me by my
Berlin friends. The porter brought me towels and a bar
of red soap; but in addition to fixing my meals I had to
empty the ash trays, carry out the trash, and make my
own bed.

The first night I felt as if I were the subject of an Alfred
Hitchcock movie thriller. Three times I was awakened
by frightening pounding at the door; first the East Germans, twice the Poles appeared, requesting passports,

counting money, poking into luggage, and disappearing into the night. The East Germans argued I did not have the right currency documents. I turned my handbag inside out, a staggering job for any female, until at last, as the train was pulling out, the officials threw up their hands and hurried away.

At Warsaw a girl from the UPI bureau climbed aboard to rid me of the box of supplies. But she gave me in return four gifts and four letters to take to the Shapiros in Moscow. Then I felt like the postman as well as Macy's.

Word got around that there was an American female traveling alone to Moscow in mid-winter. That evening every passenger, it seemed, trooped past my door to stare at me and my American magazines.

At night we reached the Russian border at Brest. I was not traveling on a tourist visa; but a man from Intourist, the Soviet agency that looks after tourists, came directly to my compartment. I wondered how he knew I was coming. "I suppose it is possible you may sit in the Intourist office at the station," the glum-looking functionary said in the roundabout, maddening way Russian officials often express themselves in English.

There was a long wait while the train was switched to the wide-gauge Russian tracks. I escaped from the Intourist office to examine Russia for the first time myself.

The newsstand was a shock. There were newspapers and magazines in heaps—but only from communist countries. I headed for the restaurant and met with the Russian custom from which there is no escape: you cannot enter a restaurant or theater with your coat on. The aged keeper of the *garderobe,* or cloakroom, put up his hand and refused a tip. I was truly in the land of socialism.

The dining room had very high ceilings with yellow plush drapes and a huge brass chandelier—I did not know then I was to see hundreds like it in monotonous array in the Soviet Union. Many soldiers were eating at the tables. The waitresses wore nylon stockings, which struck a blow at my notion that Russian hosiery was fantastically expensive.

Before we left Brest that night, the customs man marched into my compartment. I was so nervous I couldn't quiet the churning in my stomach. I honestly answered "no" to the document asking whether I carried hashish or opium. But "foreign literature"? In my suitcase was not only *Inside Russia* but *Doctor Zhivago*—and, even worse, several anti-communist books in Russian, such as *The New Class,* left over from literature given me by the émigrés; I *hate* to throw anything out. I speculated as to whether I would be evicted from the Soviet Union before I reached Moscow. But the customs official, the gentlest in the world, made a swift check and that was that.

In the morning I pulled back the blue drapes for my first eager glimpse of the land. Russia looked a bit like Montana, I thought at first; but I quickly changed my mind. This part of Russia was so flat—the endless snow-covered fields, fir trees mixed with birch, no lofty mountains. I watched the horse-drawn sleds, the horses wearing their traditional wooden collars; peasants in boots and fur hats; women in quilted jackets repairing the railroad tracks. Clickety clack, clickety clack, we raced across the Great Russian steppe. Snow in dirty patches, a thawing stream. An unpainted, grayish log house with delicate blue carved shutters like a gingerbread fairy-tale cottage. A train loaded with logs. Children waving, looking like roly-poly dolls in their heavy coats. Four boys fishing through the ice of a river, their horse standing by. More unpainted houses, outhouses in back, rutty roads, no sidewalks but television aerials. Clickety clack. A cemetery, and crosses! Crosses hung with bright-colored wreaths, graves enclosed with neat little blue picket fences. Piles of wood buried in back yards under snow. Jet planes leaving white furrows in the blue overhead.

The people, I wrote in the diary my Berlin friends gave me, looked "very short and fat."

At last the dining car was attached to the train and I ordered a square meal. The beef stroganoff did not taste like the beef stroganoff I remembered from Romanoff's restaurant in Beverly Hills. Another shattered illusion!

The waitress pointedly expected a tip. I complied. Was this socialism, after all?

A Russian couple sat at my table. My Russian was so bad I could not make out most of what they said. So we spoke about simple subjects, such as the ancient abacus the waitress used to add up the check. I wondered where the cash registers were in this great mechanized country.

I understood plainly, though, when my table mates asked in Russian, "Why do Americans want war?" and I realized than that I had crossed deep into alien territory, into the thick of what we know as the cold war.

2

No. 13
People's Street

"Why, they're people," I said as the UPI office car slipped over the snowy ruts.

For me the Russian people had been an unknown quantity. Now there they were, brown, unsmiling, heavy figures, in their *shubi* (heavy winter coats) and fur hats, hurrying along the slushy, crowded streets, looking so Slavic and, well, not western.

"Yes, and you don't see any horns," Henry Shapiro drily observed. Henry has been listening to comments such as mine and probably answering them the same way for the twenty-seven years he has served as UPI bureau chief in Moscow.

I was in for more surprises that February 19, 1959. I had no sooner stepped inside the UPI office than the door opened and in whirled Howard Milks, then bureau manager for our heated rival, the Associated Press. The AP was quartered on the fifth floor of the same building. "Welcome to Moscow!" he said jovially, pumped my hand, and rushed out again. This was like Gimbels welcoming Macy's. In Moscow, as I learned later, any arrival of a new correspondent from the outside world is a stirring event to the small, inbred foreign press corps.

To travel from the UPI office to my apartment required one step. They were one and the same thing.

Correspondents, Henry explained to me, are not given regular office space. He said this isn't available for foreigners in the crowded city. Besides, it's easier to keep track of correspondents if they live and work in the same place. This arrangement has at least one advantage for the correspondents, too: a staff member living right in the office can be on hand to handle important stories that might break during the night.

At this writing (1961), foreign correspondents still work and live in the same premises. There's no such thing as apartment ads or apartment hunting in Moscow. The government houses scribes, diplomats, and their families in *diplomatichestkia doma* (diplomatic houses), known by some members of the foreign colony as "diplomatic ghettos." Correspondents make offices out of some of the rooms and live in the others. In 1959 when I arrived many journalists were living and working in hotel rooms. We could not because we would wake up transient customers with the teletypes from Tass, the Soviet news agency.

My new home was at 13 Narodnaya Ulitsa (People's Street), in the Proletarsky Rayone (Proletarian District). Other diplomatic houses are situated on equally socialistic-sounding streets, such as Prospekt Mira (Peace Street). Our building is a nine-story apartment house filled mostly with Russians. But we have never been able to chat with our Soviet neighbors in the elevator. The foreigners' separate wing is completely cut off from the Russian-occupied portion of the building, and we use the back door. Our section is filled with diplomats from Israel, Britain, France, Holland, and Thailand. When I first arrived, our back "yard" had dark brick walls and a shabby entrance with a door that banged loudly. Near by was a wooden shack which housed large garbage cans.

A British embassy diplomat in our building caustically referred to our door as "the garden entrance." In the spring, as I saw later, the courtyard turned into one mucky mud hole. A year later, as a measure of slow Soviet progress, our building finally was painted yellow with white trim. The shack was torn down and the courtyard paved.

A Russian policeman stands in or near a sentry box in our courtyard twenty-four hours a day. In one side of the little house is a little peephole where the officer on duty can keep an eye out for who comes in or goes out. His telephone rings frequently as headquarters—or so foreigners deduce—calls to check who is home and who is not. Our sentry personified my first brush with Russians' ingrained suspicion of foreigners, as much a part of the country's tradition as *blini* (pancakes) and onion-shaped domes.

The policeman's job is to keep out unauthorized Russians who have no business with foreigners in the building. This discourages many Russians you might want to invite home. But he also is supposed to keep out thieves, and to protect our cars from vandals. In the summer the policemen help me lower the top on my sports car. (One who didn't get the hang of it broke the top one day in his eagerness to be helpful. The repair bill was enormous.)

My first day in Moscow I felt quite foolish when the policeman grandly saluted me as if I were an ambassador, but even that I got used to.

I got used to other things, too, such as having photographers developing pictures in my sink while I was trying to bake a cake or defrost the refrigerator. I also got accustomed to the Tass teletypes down the hall from my bedroom, which are housed in a wooden box to cut down the racket. The boxes have to be kept partly open or the clacking machines will become too hot and catch on fire. When this happened once in the AP bureau upstairs, Stanley Johnson, a correspondent, nearly burned in his bed.

After introducing me to the machines and the two-room office, Henry Shapiro led me down the hall to my quarters. I was so happy to have an apartment instead of a hotel room I didn't mind that the office was in it—or that it was like a "railroad flat," with many doors leading off a long corridor. First comes a darkroom for developing and printing photographs. Next, my kitchen, a large room with two Russian cabinets for dishes, a broom closet, table, old American refrigerator, and Russian stove. The last is a gray, four-burner gas affair, with an oven but no broiler, like many European stoves.

My new home turned out to be a cold-water flat. Over the kitchen sink stands a Finnish electric hot-water heater. For hot water, I plug in the cord and wait ten minutes. The bathtub down the hall has an infernal gas contraption, also separate. The bathroom sink has no hot-water tap, period.

The toilet, as in all Russian and many European living quarters, is in a separate room. (This system was apparently "discovered" only in recent years by avant-garde architects in America.) However, the lavatory has a serious drawback: it has no window. In fact, I have yet to see a window in a Russian toilet. When I first entered the one in my apartment I understood why deodorizers had been included on my shopping list.

My bedroom and living room are spacious, with high ceilings, and were furnished by one of my predecessors with modern pieces shipped from West Berlin.

The windows in all the rooms seemed gigantic at first. They open completely, like French doors. Russians handle their winters seriously. The windows, as in every Russian apartment I've seen, are double. In both the inside and outside windows are small apertures that can be opened for air without opening the entire window. In Montana we put "storm windows" over the ordinary windows each winter.

My Moscow windows are sealed shut each winter by strips of paper glued over the cracks and hinges. This is a Russian custom as old as the icons. The sealing job is done when the first snow flies. Farther north, as I later learned on a trip to Murmansk above the Arctic Circle, the Russians put cotton batting underneath the paper strips for insulation.

The radiators in my apartment are set, uncovered, under each window. I was surprised to see that the hot-water pipes *and* the electric wiring were installed on the *outside* of the walls and neatly painted the same color.

The building is postwar, but some of the wooden floor parquet boards are loose around the pipe holes in the living room. Around many doorjambs I saw holes that served as "garden entrances" for mice and cockroaches. The white tiles on the kitchen and bathroom walls, I found, dropped off like dying petals.

Although the Russians made beautiful sputniks, I could see that their buildings do not yet get off the ground. But it was home, comfortable, and in Moscow considered luxurious, and I was happy to crawl over my mounds of luggage to curl up in bed that first night with the banging teletype down the hall to keep me company.

I had no sooner drowsed off from exhaustion than I awoke, my stomach tense from fear. I could distinctly hear footsteps squeaking six steps down, then retreating in the other direction. I traced the sound to my open kitchen window. To keep warm, the policeman on guard duty was pacing back and forth over the packed snow that squeaked under his heavy black boots. His footsteps sounded from the blackness and then his figure emerged in the glistening light of the Russian moon, startling in the black, bulky, fur-lined leather coat that hung almost to his ankles.

I crept shivering back to bed. But there was no sleep for me that night: the Central Telegraph Office called with telegrams from UPI in London. I wrote them down with freezing fingers.

Two cats shattered the night with their yowls of love-making, a homey and comforting sound in this alien land. So they do have cats in Russia, I thought.

Some Russians passed under my window on their way home, crooning a tipsy tune, one merrymaker playing an accordion. They did not fit in, either, with my mental picture of a militant, rigidly disciplined people. The songs were punctuated by an occasional clatter from the kitchen —possibly a mouse or another white tile biting the dust.

Such was my first night in Moscow.

Now, nearly three years later, I feel as if I haven't had a good night's sleep since!

The next day I went out to explore People's Street. At the corner I found a food store, labeled simply "Produce

Store No. 18." Its sign hung flat and unlit above the door, like the signs on most Russian shops in the old districts. Girls in white uniforms were selling cheese, butter, milk, meat, sour cream, candy, and sausage. There was a line for sausage but not many customers for meat. A shoe shop was in business next door and a clothing shop around the corner.

I watched my Russian neighbors picking their way through the slush: housewives in princess-style coats and hats like the western styles of the thirties; children swathed in rabbit-fur coats, peaked caps, and scarfs tied under their collars and around their waists so that they resembled overstuffed cocoons; men in square-shouldered coats and fur caps, most wearing brown, black, maroon, or dark blue, occasionally a bright red cap or green scarf.

Although the clothing was not the latest Paris fashion or fit, I noticed virtually all the people were dressed neatly: scarfs folded just so, not casually slung around the neck as in the United States; hats sitting firmly, legs in sensible heavy stockings, coats properly buttoned.

The streets around No. 13 boasted only a few neon signs. I noticed wire mesh hanging sling-style around the lower part of two block-like apartment houses. What could that be for? Why, to catch the brick tiles that fall off the new buildings, of course, explained one of the Russian maids who worked in our building.

For the first six months, almost every day in Moscow was a happy adventure for me. I could hardly wait to tumble out of bed and get outside to make fresh discoveries.

To search for a taxi one of my first days I walked up the crowded hill from No. 13 to Taganskaya Ploshchad (Little

Trivet Square). Like many citizens, I plodded in the gutter to avoid the surge of determined-looking figures hurrying downhill. On a side street at last I saw some buildings that looked more "Russian" than the newer apartment houses. A tiny gold-domed church had a gleaming gold icon encased in a window. The church was "in operation," a passer-by told me. I found several old log cabin-type houses with intricately carved shutters. To many foreigners they are the most charming bits of architecture in Moscow and are certainly much less drab than the new factory-like apartment buildings. Most such houses have a water pump on the street and an outhouse in back, and some don't sit straight on their foundations, as in a child's painting. Thus to Russians these houses aren't lovely. Later I was told they all are slated for demolition to make way for the new Sovietized city.

In other areas in my neighborhood I found unpainted brown shacks. Yet downtown I saw the new Soviet-style buildings marching up Gorky Street, the "Broadway" of Moscow, which is wide enough for eight or ten cars to move abreast. Elderly women swept snow from the sidewalks with curved twig brooms, as if in another century. But next to them blue snow-clearing machines that would be the envy of New York scraped, brushed, and swept the streets clean. Some even sprinkled sand. Smaller machines scraped snow from the sidewalks.

What a city of paradoxes, I thought.

"The longer you stay, the more confused you'll be," one correspondent told me. "Your first impressions are the best. After a while your mind just runs in circles."

Many American tourists say, "Moscow looks better than I thought it would," or, "It looks better than we've read," the kind of statement the Soviet newspapers pick up with glee. Why do foreigners have such misconceptions and lack of knowledge about the Soviet Union? Henry Shapiro reminded me that for years the Russians themselves made it difficult, if not impossible, to report on everyday life in the Soviet Union. Only a minuscule corps of journalists was allowed in the country, and they could report only the bare political facts. If and when they had time to write about the people, many stories, even some from *Pravda,* the organ of the Communist party, were not cleared by the censors. Articles about shopping in the stores or about church weddings, for instance, were seldom passed; it was taboo to write about prices and religion.

To me Moscow looked worse than I'd expected. My mental image was culled from Khrushchev speeches about the march forward to communism, from western political books, and from the propaganda dispensed at the Soviet pavilion at the Brussels Exposition. These sources described a machine-like state, all newness and polish. I had a vague picture of people practically lock-stepping to work, possibly in uniform (like the Chinese, who wear standard outfits even to visit or study in Moscow), like the workers depicted on Soviet posters, marching with hammer and sickle, their determined eyes fixed on the horizon.

On my first trips around Moscow I gaped at the Russians milling all over the streets in such astonishingly large numbers. I had expected them to resemble newsreel shots I'd seen of Defense Minister Rodion Malinovsky—fierce and bushy-browed. But the average Russian on the street appeared to be a rather amiable fellow. I kept thinking,

They're Russians, not machines; in fact, they're downright disorganized-looking.

Like many tourists, I somehow expected to find the army running Moscow. But ordinary policemen in navy-blue uniforms direct traffic. Later I traced my confusion to the fact that foreign correspondents often incorrectly translate the Russian word for policeman, *militsioner,* as "militia-man."

At first I looked anxiously for the secret policeman following me. But I never could be sure I had seen one, although they certainly do exist. When I first arrived in Moscow, persons from various embassies filled me full of stories about hidden microphones. There was the tale of the Russian workmen who laughed when they uncovered a microphone while replastering a hall at the British embassy. There was the American who found microphones under the floor boards of his apartment, even in the bedroom.

Moscow diplomats work under the assumption that they are followed much of the time. Correspondents used to be, quite obviously, but at this writing only the fluent Russian-speaking scribe is likely to be tailed continuously, and this often lasts only until his habit patterns are established. The rest of us apparently are checked periodically. We assume everyone's telephone is tapped, and conversations periodically listened to or tape-recorded for future checking.

"If the volume on your phone drops and it's hard to hear, they've turned on the recording machine," a Russian acquaintance who worked in a western embassy told me.

Diplomatic houses are thought to be "bugged," more so than correspondents' quarters.

Henry Shapiro advised me not to brood about it. His philosophy was, "I stopped looking over my shoulder years ago." As he pointed out, we have nothing to hide. So let them listen to our telephone conversations. We don't even hang curtains on our office windows, so that all can see we are not transmitting plans for the theft of the "Vostok" spaceship.

It was easy after I'd been in Moscow several months to spot the secret-police cars trailing diplomatic autos. But I never did detect a sleuth after me—although later I discovered I *had* been trailed.

Henry Shapiro is dean of the western Moscow press corps, one of the most famous foreign correspondents and, I heard before arriving, a tough reporter. I was the first correspondent not fluent in the Russian language who was sent to work for Henry. Therefore I felt I had to work twice as hard to keep up. Henry has a Russian-born wife, Ludmilla, an attractive blonde with large eyes, whom he married in the days when foreigners could live freely among Russians.

When I arrived in 1959, the Soviet authorities had just decided to allow each news agency three foreign correspondents. Our other correspondent was Robert J. Korengold, or "Bud," who arrived three months after I did. Like me, he was an innocent to the land of the Soviets, and as stunned and baffled at first as I was. (During Stalin's day, each news agency was allowed one correspondent; after his death, two.)

We are allowed to hire as many Russians as we want, and we have a staff of six. Two are photographers. Victor, our chauffeur, pilots the office car. His main job is to take cabled stories to the Central Telegraph Office. As the UPI office is not in the center of the city, he also drives us around on business. Then he spends hours at the customs offices getting food and supplies we order from abroad. He runs errands, delivers local mail (which is what you do if you want it to get there in less than two days), and gets our visas renewed and airplane tickets bought.

Victor comes from a line of peasants, and represents progress in Russia. He went to school and carries a book to read during spare moments. Yet he retains a few mannerisms from the old days: he shaves his head and calls Henry "Master." Victor cheerfully helped me with my Russian lessons as we drove around, and had a fascinating store of peasant wit and proverbs.

Arthur, our senior translator, was born in the Soviet Union and was taken to the United States at the age of twelve. He attended the City College of New York during the Depression. In the thirties, like some others in America, the family moved back to what they figured to be the promised land. Arthur worked as a reporter on the English-language newspaper, the Moscow *News*; but one day Stalin got it into his head that anybody who had lived in America was suspect, and the paper was shut down.

Despite such heartaches, Arthur is a loyal Soviet citizen. He staunchly defends his country and sometimes twits us about America. Right from the beginning Henry advised us not to indulge in political arguments with the staff. But Bud and I were too fresh from America not to get indignant at times. Once when translating from *Pravda* Arthur made a joke about "American imperialism."

Bud asked, "And what about Estonia, Lithuania, and Latvia?"

"Now, now, let's stick to the work," said Henry in his usual fatherly way.

Arthur sometimes talked as though New York must look the way he left it in depression days. He was interested in the latest gadgets from the U.S. One day I borrowed some ice cubes from the pink refrigerator upstairs in the AP apartment. Arthur said with surprise, "Oh, they have colored ice trays in America now!" I patiently explained that "they" have had entirely colored refrigerators for many years.

We were the first westerners whom Slava, our younger translator, had known. Bud and I thus regarded him as "virgin" territory and delighted in getting his reaction to bits of Americana. He smacked his lips with delight over his first drink of that "symbol" of the U.S. made notorious in the Soviet press, Coca-Cola. One night I whipped up a cake from American instant mix. "This is what you would call a prefabricated cake," said Slava.

Like many Moscow citizens, Slava and his young wife live with his parents in one apartment. Once he announced that what he wanted most out of the 1960's was a new car and an apartment.

Slava was quite surprised on his first day in our office to see us working at bedlam pace on a big story in order to beat the other news agencies. "So this is capitalistic competition. I am not used to this," he said in amazement.

Our third translator is Lev, whom we acquired only recently. When he began working for UPI we were startled to hear him reel off colloquialisms in his stilted English, such as, "Well, I see you're heading for the barn," or "Too many cooks spoil the soup." Girls were "babes," anything was "stuff." It turned out he had some Ukrainian friends who used to live in Canada. We knew without asking that those Ukrainians hadn't heard New World slang since the thirties. Now and then we try to teach Lev a more modern phrase such as, "and all that jazz."

After I had met the office staff and unpacked my baggage, I telephoned Mikhail, the Russian friend I had met in Berlin. He lived in Leningrad, an overnight train ride from Moscow. He had given me his office telephone number, rather than that of his apartment where he lived with his in-laws and a son (his wife had died of starvation during the war). He had said since he spoke English there would be nothing odd about an English-speaking person telephoning him.

"Ah, yes," he said in a businesslike tone when I telephoned long distance. "I'm coming to Moscow Saturday. Let's meet for dinner at the corner by the Metropole Hotel."

I stepped out of the taxi at 7:30 near the hotel, and stood watching Russians bound for the stores that stay open until 8:00. It was sharply cold. I edged close to the building for warmth as well as to escape the pressing crowds. "People in Russia won't stare at you," Mikhail had insisted in Berlin. But they did, especially at my black pumps with pointed toes, then a rarity in the Soviet Union. I felt very conspicuous. I remembered the times when Mikhail was sure we were being followed by Soviet, American, German, or what-have-you agents in Berlin. I remembered his maddening suspicion that everybody, including me, might be a spy or counterspy.

That was Berlin. Here we were in Moscow, which

seemed a hundred times more dangerous: Russians could see me, a foreigner, meeting a Russian. For one frightened moment I wanted to walk quickly away. . . .

"There you are," and his hand was on my arm, leading me toward Gorky Street.

"I told you to buy a warm *shuba,* and you have the same light wool coat you had in Berlin," he scolded.

"My fur-lined coat is being shipped," I explained. "And you said nobody would stare and they did and oh, am I glad to see you. . . ."

We ate dinner in a private booth in a restaurant, the curtains drawn, in accordance with his passion for secrecy.

"I told you when you came to Russia I'd buy you a decent meal. I've lots of rubles here. Remember when we economized on my small expense account in Berlin?" he said.

In the middle of this caviar, vodka, and reunion talk, I remembered Henry Shapiro's rule: always let the office know where you are.

"I must phone the office!" I said and hurried off.

When I returned to our table, Mikhail looked at me carefully. He said nothing.

After dinner, we stood awkwardly on the sidewalk. I was wondering where couples go in Moscow if they want to be alone. My apartment with a translator inside and a policeman outside? His hotel with room clerks on every floor? He took me to a taxi and I went home.

Although I was disturbed by the abruptness with which the evening had ended, I unpacked a scarf to give him as a gift and made plans to see him soon. The scarf lay in my drawer unused. I was not to see Mikhail for a year.

When a week went by and he did not call, I became

worried. I telephoned his hotel. He had returned to Leningrad.

But on February 21 Prime Minister Macmillan arrived in Russia, and we were plunged into work. I was too busy to think much of Mikhail, too excited to be covering the beginning of a thaw in the Soviet Union's icy relations with the West. The Prime Minister's visit marked the trend toward a liberalization of Soviet policy toward the West. Russia's doors, long jammed shut to foreigners, gradually opened again, and it was a hectic but memorable time for Moscow correspondents.

3

The Censor Who Never Was

Not long after I set up housekeeping in Moscow, we correspondents were electrified to find a group of Yale University students serenading Russians on Red Square. Foreigners singing in front of the Kremlin! The infiltration of westerners into Russia really was barreling along.

"Yale students serenaded a stone's throw from the tomb of Lenin and Stalin tonight," wrote Bud Korengold in his cable for UPI.

A censor sat on this story for an hour. Finally it was returned with the words, "a stone's throw," firmly crossed out. As our UPI chief, Henry Shapiro, expostulated, "Who ever would throw stones at Lenin and Stalin?"

Working under censorship was one of the strangest of the many strange aspects of Moscow life for me.

Before the snow melted that first winter, I was confirmed in my belief that being a Moscow correspondent is a prize journalistic assignment. Pounding out stories on Warsaw Pact meetings and dogs and men whirring around the earth is more glamorous to me than all the interviews I've had with stars like Elvis Presley and Debbie Reynolds put together.

I quickly learned it's also one of the toughest reporting jobs. We found ourselves working seven days a week, and often twelve to eighteen hours a day, to cover one of the world's hottest news centers. Living conditions can be a headache, the red tape in getting stories monumental, and being restricted to a 40-kilometer (25-mile) area around Moscow (unless one asks for permission to go elsewhere) can be frustrating; but writing with the censors' eye over your shoulder was the most unusual condition of all.

Except for a brief postwar interval, until March 1961 no copy could be sent from the Soviet Union by mail, cable, or telephone by non-communist correspondents without first being passed by Soviet censors.

From 1945 to 1961, the censors operated at the Central Telegraph Office, where international telephone calls and telegrams are arranged. Therefore the correspondents worked most of the time at the telegraph. Our cables could be handed to a cable desk only at this main office. Three copies were needed, one for the censors' file, one to cable, and one for us to check any "corrections."

Our telephone calls for the purpose of dictating copy had to be placed there. We could make personal calls from our apartments, although that had been permitted only since Stalin's death in 1953.

The telegraph was (and still is, although direct censorship has ended) our office-away-from-the-office. The Russians provide eight cubicles, each one big enough to hold a small typewriter table and a chair. World agencies occupy five cubicles: UPI and AP of the United States, Agence France Press of France, Deutsche Presse Agentur of West Germany, and Reuters of Britain. Cubicles are shared by the Baltimore *Sun*, *Le Monde* of Paris, the New York *Times*, CBS and NBC, West German Radio, the New York *Herald Tribune*, *Corriere dela Sera* of Milan, and other leading newspapers and radio networks of the world.

The cubicles do not house everybody, as by 1961 we were forty-one non-communist correspondents, including sixteen Americans (compared with four foreign scribes in 1950). The others bring their typewriters to the telegraph waiting rooms. When the tables are filled, they type standing up at the telegram counter. The back waiting room is called the English-Japanese room, as it is usually occupied by newsmen from those countries.

Foreign communist correspondents—including one from the U.S., one from England, two from France, and two from Italy, plus those from satellite countries—telephoned their copy from the comfort of their apartments during censorship days if they wished. The censors were only for the "bourgeois" press.

The telegraph office has a checkroom, rest rooms, and two hard divans where all of us spent many an aching night waiting for copy to emerge from "the oven," as we called the censor, or for a telephone line.

In the main room at the CTO are sixteen booths for international calls, for "civilian" as well as journalistic use. These are seldom filled. In this city of six million, you'll see only ten or twenty citizens during one day placing calls. They often are Mongolians telephoning home to Ulan Bator or Russians calling relatives stationed in Warsaw or Bucharest.

We seldom fill the booths either. At this writing, Moscow has apparently only three lines to London, one often taken by the British embassy or by Tass sending telephotos. Reuters, AP, and UPI file their important copy to London, meaning there is a mad dash to order lines at the telegraph when a big story breaks.

The telegraph also has four closet-size broadcast booths for radio correspondents, with misspelled signs in English: "The Micpophone is Turned On."

My first day at the Central Telegraph I thought, Here I am, believe it or not, eating caviar sandwiches at the Central Telegraph Office in Moscow with the famous Henry Shapiro. Henry introduced me to the friendly girls who handle the telephone lines behind a desk opposite the telephone booths. The girls accepted our copy for cables and telephone dictation, then stepped behind a door covered with a green curtain into a reportedly large room where the censors worked in secret so we couldn't argue with them.

During the Macmillan visit I saw little of the censors because censorship was lifted for foreign correspondents for the duration of the Prime Minister's stay (February 21 to March 3). The Russians were making an effort to establish friendlier ties with England.

After the Prime Minister left, we were off to the Kremlin for my first Khrushchev press conference, a technique he had just picked up from the then President Eisenhower. The session in Sverdlov Hall was concluded by a wild, screeching race of press cars back to the Central Telegraph Office. I started to run to the telephone. "No, no!" cried Shapiro. "You must write the story first for the censor!" The race was just to place telephone calls. But it was futile because no copy was returned immediately. It was the next morning—ho, hum, or was it afternoon?— before the censors passed the story.

For journalists censorship is regrettable in any country. It also meant wasted time and extra work for us. But along with the difficulties, the censors could be a daily source of chuckles. For instance, I quickly learned, they were very sensitive about Khrushchev copy. Once a French correspondent, Edouard Babrovsky of *Le Figaro,* wrote that in that sterling Soviet "adventure" film, *N. S. Khrushchev in America,* the Premier looked like Marlon Brando. The Frenchman waited an hour for his copy. Finally a girl emerged from the censors' chambers with the query, "Who is Marlon Brando?"

"He is a very famous and talented and handsome American film actor," the correspondent assured her.

After another twenty minutes, the girl came out again and beckoned to Babrovsky. "Does he play serious roles or comedy roles?" she demanded.

"Oh, very serious roles," sighed the tired, hungry scribe.

At last, a half hour later, the copy was returned. All references to Marlon Brando had been deleted. The censor was not taking any chances.

Khrushchev himself was censored. At first all his statements at embassy receptions were passed by the censors. Then in 1958 he made headlines by scoffing that the French didn't know anything about politics. After that reports of his embassy reception interviews were often held up by the censors until the next day, presumably so that Party Central Committee officials could make sure their outspoken First Secretary said nothing to embarrass the government.

At one embassy reception Khrushchev made some interesting comments about China to some assembled ambassadors. But the comments did not happen to reflect the official Soviet attitude of undying, unbreakable, and everlasting friendship with the Chinese People's Republic. Henry Shapiro's cable story arrived at our puzzled London

UPI bureau reading, "Khrushchev said today quote unquote."

The censors were also sensitive about Russian police activities. Any mention of a police attempt to control an unruly Russian mob was taboo. The last night of the American Exhibition at Sokolniky Park, the Russians behaved like overexuberant puppydogs. They did not want to go home. There was much pushing and arguing, and the police had literally to pry them loose from the displays.

I emphasized these facts in my story, and after two hours it still was in "the oven." Finally another correspondent, Max Frankel of the New York *Times,* tipped me off about describing crowds and police. I asked for my story back, rewrote the police out of the lead. The copy was approved as fast as the girl could rush into the censors' office and out again.

The censors usually did not understand jokes. In a story about the 1959 rush of tourists and delegates, I wrote that often it was "easier for them to get a conference with Khrushchev than to find a waiter to pay the bill." This was not too much of an exaggeration. However, the censor banished the line.

Sometimes we all merrily plotted ways to get around the censor. You couldn't plot too far or you'd plot your way out of the country: the Press Department collected clippings of our stories. But there were subtle subterfuges.

For example, the censors could not listen to all of us telephoning all of the time. We could add a line or change a word or even try to sneak out an important bulletin held up by the censors. Sometimes we got by with it. Other times there was that sickening sensation of dead air, indicating that a censor had pulled the switch on you.

Now and then I slipped in a phrase only to have the newsman taking dictation in London yell, "What was that?" My stomach would tighten as I tried to repeat the forbidden words.

Another trick in telegraphmanship was to use phrases that might befuddle the censor. When Soviet Marshal Rokossovsky, then Minister of Defense in Poland, was returned to Moscow an American correspondent wrote, "He was as popular there as Sherman marching through Georgia." The censor, no expert on American Civil War history, passed the copy.

Tom Lambert, of the New York *Herald Tribune,* described the photographs of the 1960 communist "summit meeting" in Moscow as looking like those of "the graduation class at Appalachan." That notorious gangland meeting near New York meant nothing to the censor. The copy was quickly approved. So was the description of the picture by Marvin Kalb of CBS: "Post-office photograph."

Many stories were not just lacerated but completely killed. During the 1960 May Day parade, an armored vehicle rumbled across Red Square, slipped a tread, and kept rumbling right through a wall into the Moskva River. Correspondents stood on the bank watching the mobile anti-aircraft gun being fished out of the muddy water. By the next morning, the ragged hole in the wall had been completely patched up—with *old* brick, a lovely Russian touch. You would never know any mishap had occurred. To our amusement, our stories about this accident were killed. As far as the Russians were concerned, it just never happened.

Also completely annihilated by the censors were stories about Russian hoodlums burning a synagogue near Moscow in 1959, and one about an important official's suicide during the exposure of widespread corruption in agriculture at the January 1961 Party Central Committee meeting.

If a story was important enough, some correspondents used cloak-and-dagger methods to get it out without risking loss of visa. When an Austrian airliner crashed near Moscow in October 1960, correspondents had only to say "Austrian" on the telephone to their foreign offices and the line would be cut. Finally Bud Korengold called the London UPI bureau and after some chit-chat casually mentioned, "Say, call Franz Cyrus and ask him to check his equivalent of BEA to see if there's any news there of interest to us."

The censor listening didn't know it, but Cyrus was UPI bureau manager in Vienna. His equivalent of British European Airways was Austrian Airlines. Cyrus broke the story shortly in Vienna—hours before the censors started to pass the correspondents' copy in Moscow.

Shortly after the U-2 incident, an army band from Frankfurt, West Germany, was scheduled to fly to Moscow to play at an American embassy Armed Forces Day party. I heard that the band was unable to get visas—the first U-2 incident casualty. The censors held up my story, probably for checking.

I remembered that a friend, Ernie Wetherall, of the American army newspaper *Stars and Stripes* in Frankfurt, had written to me he was going to fly with the band to Moscow. "Ask Ernie Wetherall of *Stars and Stripes* why he isn't coming to see me," I told our London office.

UPI in Frankfurt soon had the story on the wires. Ah, it gave us a feeling of triumph to outfox the censors' obstacle course.

Of course, the censors had their tricks of the trade, too. They would turn the volume on the telephone down low so that a correspondent had to shout loudly and slowly—a guarantee that he would stick to the script. Or as a warning a censor would turn off a scribe's phone but not the other end so that he could hear his office but his office couldn't hear him.

Sometimes the censor's penciled slashes on copy could be a clue as to what was going on behind those medieval, crenellated walls around the Kremlin. When a Khrushchev protégé, Alexei Kirichenko, a Presidium member, was reported demoted, I wrote a story describing Kirichenko as a "trusted lieutenant" of Khrushchev. The censor sent back the copy with the word "trusted" neatly crossed out. With a collective "hooray," the correspondents beat out stories that Kirichenko had toppled from power. He was fair game that day.

More often, however, the censors were no test of truth. Their job was to kill anything that conflicted with the picture the Russians wanted to present to the world. They didn't prevent correspondents from making fools of themselves or writing errors.

The most extraordinary part of the whole system was that the Russians blandly maintained there was no censorship. Khrushchev himself said in Paris that foreign correspondents were prevented only from writing "lies." The Russian word for our censor was "Glavlit," meaning Main Literary Office.

A Soviet magazine, *New Times*, attacked a Swedish

correspondent in Moscow, Ingmar Lindmarker, for sending "lies" to his newspaper in Stockholm. "Is *New Times*
accusing the Soviet censors of not doing their job correctly? Doesn't *New Times* know we have a censor and
therefore cannot send 'lies'? Why? Why?" I asked Henry
Shapiro in bewilderment.

With a smile he gave his favorite reply, "How long
have you been in this country? You should know better
than to ask why."

During World War II the censors (who the Russians
say never existed) sat in plain sight at a table in the
Press Department of the Foreign Ministry. Newsmen
were free to argue over their cuts. Henry Shapiro once
wrote that so-and-so had been elevated "to the secretary-
ship of the Party Central Committee," only to have that
line censored. Why? Why? "As is well known [a favorite
Russian phrase], the Central Committee has no navy," the
censor calmly told him.

Another correspondent referred to Soviet author Ilya
Ehrenberg as a Francophile because he speaks French
and collects French paintings. "How dare you call our
fine writer a friend of that dictator Franco!" cried the
censor.

But in Moscow in my day the censors were forever unseen. One New Year's Eve some of us dropped in at the
telegraph with a bottle of champagne for the censor on
duty. The reception desk girl emerged from his lair with
a smile and a firm refusal.

Another time Vero Roberti, then in Moscow for *Corriere dela Sera* of Milan, hatched an elaborate trap. He
presented two scarce tickets to the ballet to the Glavlit
reception girl as a gift for his censor. Then Roberti set-

tled himself in the row behind to see who would claim the Bolshoi Theater seats. They remained empty.

There had to be censors for various languages, of course. One day the Glavlit reception girl told the three Italian correspondents they could not file any stories that day: the Italian-language censor was sick. The Italians happily took the day off and went swimming.

All this nonsense came to an end on March 22, 1961. On thirty minutes' notice, foreign correspondents were summoned to the Foreign Ministry to be told direct Soviet censorship had been abolished (but we still can lose visas for writing stories the Soviets regard as incorrect). It was considered a sign of confidence of the Bolshevik regime. It was also a sign that after forty-four years they deemed censorship ineffective. Stories which had been suppressed, such as Khrushchev's famous anti-Stalin speech in 1956, eventually got out anyway.

Glavlit had a typically Russian demise.

To the very end, the Russians stuck to their stand that there never had been any censorship. That word was not mentioned by the head of the Press Department, Mikhail Kharlamov, who conducted the press conference. He merely announced that correspondents could telephone their copy directly from their offices and apartments. For cables we now hand in one copy as in any other country.

The stories in which we first reported the forthcoming end of the censorship that never was were held up ten days by the censor! Only with the official announcement did Glavlit, as its censorial swansong, release our copy.

Now we work more at offices and less at the Central Telegraph Office. John Chancellor of NBC even broadcast on a telephone line direct to New York from inside the American embassy when it was besieged by Russians demonstrating against the attempted invasion of Cuba in April 1961.

The end of Glavlit saves us hours of time every week and much wear and tear on the disposition. And it has brought other improvements in the lives of members of the foreign press corps. We correspondents have been told we will be able to install "telex" machines so that for the first time Moscow journalists can transmit their own stories directly to the outside world. The days of the press corps huddle at the Telegraph Office may soon be gone.

Beginning with the sensational story of Yuri Gagarin's trip into space, Soviet authorities sometimes let photographers ship out TV film and undeveloped negatives legally so that they don't have to slip them on the sly into the pockets of departing tourists. We have heard that news agencies may be allowed to import more staff members to lighten the work load. Moscow may not become like Paris for correspondents, but at least like Warsaw.

Some correspondents will miss the "club" at the Telegraph Office. With or without Glavlit, we have our lighter moments. Shortly after my arrival in Moscow, the press group pounded into the CTO from a conference given by a British trade delegation on an important change in Soviet life: the Russians had decided to import British consumers' goods, such as shoes.

I managed to get my copy back first from the censor. I snared a telephone line to London. But my triumph was brief. An hour later Vincent Buist, then Reuters bureau chief, said, "The funniest thing—when I called my office in London they asked who was the girl who called from Moscow and dictated the story. . . ."

The telegraph girls had got their wires crossed. I had dictated my story to a competitor, Reuters, in London. Everybody had a good laugh. Except me.

In Russia they have yet to build what westerners call a quick-lunch bar. There are no corner soda fountains. So during long hours at the Central Telegraph, correspondents' wives brought down coffee and sandwiches, and sometimes beer. It gave the telegraph a picnic atmosphere.

The elderly ladies who tended the cloakroom were supposed to keep out Russians who had no business in the international section, but often some slipped by. A pretty Russian girl sauntered in looking for a foreign "date." A little boy stuck his head into my cubicle and whispered, "Have you chewing gum? Have you pencils [meaning ballpoint pens]? I am studying English. . . ."

Once a middle-aged, balding Russian appeared at the telegraph every day for a week. He said his sister in Long Beach, California, had written she would telephone him. For days he waited in vain for the call. Finally one day he grabbed my arm when I came in, and said, "I talked to my sister, first time in twenty years! We have been afraid even to write each other. Soon maybe she can visit me or I can visit her."

One Halloween night, Preston Grover of the AP in a burst of nostalgia bought a big pumpkin at the public market. He and two Italian correspondents scooped out the insides and carved on a face, patterned after the visage of China's Mao Tse-tung. Then we stuck in a candle and put the jack o' lantern in the telegraph window. The

Russians did not appreciate our touch of home: next day the pumpkin had vanished.

So did some attempts at funny décor by Max Frankel, of the New York *Times*. When some Soviet rockets were launched, correspondents labored in their cubicles over the rates of speed and other scientific problems we knew little about. Max hung signs over each cubicle designating each as a department of our own Academy of Sciences. The next day the signs were gone.

To file cables, censor or no; to get into press conferences; or even to get past the policeman at the front door of any government office, a correspondent must have a press card issued by the Foreign Ministry. I worked on a temorary press card for one month after I began work in the U.S.S.R. The day the Press Department summoned me to the Foreign Ministry for my permanent card, good for a year at least, was a day of relief for me. Some writers are given only temporary three- or six-month cards. At the entrance to the ministry, a fascinating example of "wedding cake" architecture of the Stalin era, the policeman checked my name on a list to make sure I had an appointment. Only then did he let me in. After the usual cloakroom formalities, I was told to wait in the lobby. A girl soon emerged from the elevator and accompanied me to the ninth floor: no visitors are allowed to wander around alone.

I was told to wait by the elevator. After several minutes the girl returned, saying, "You are late and have missed your appointment."

"I didn't know it would take ten minutes to get upstairs," I said apologetically.

The Russians decided to let this American female cool

her heels for a while. I telephoned repeatedly for another appointment. Finally I was summoned again.

This time the guide again came to the lobby and accompanied me to the ninth floor. She said nothing. I will never forget walking down that long dark hallway, the woman silent in front of me, her large hips moving in her too-long skirt, the bun of her hair set squarely on the back of her erect head.

I was ushered into a huge room, decorated like most Soviet offices with pictures of Lenin and/or Stalin and Marx, with tall, gracefully draped windows and dark, oversized furniture.

A Press Department official, straight-faced and speaking softly, questioned me thoroughly about my background. At the conclusion of the interview he reminded me smoothly, "Please remember the stories you write can help improve relations between our two countries."

This was my first close touch with the government, the officials, the Party. It was the first time I felt the chilling power of those who control the Soviet Union.

Now that I had my press card in its blue leather case, I launched into the normal routine of a Moscow correspondent. I could call the Committee for Cultural Relations with Foreign Countries to request interviews for feature stories. Requests for political interviews go through the Press Department. Once I was chastised for trying to line up an interview on my own.

Political interviews are seldom granted resident foreign correspondents. A visiting publisher has a much better chance of getting to see Khrushchev or Mikoyan. Feature requests are usually granted with pleasure, but take two to thirty days to arrange. Some are refused, such as a request to live with a farm family for a day.

"Hard" news, or regular news, is the most difficult to obtain. You can't drop in at the Academy of Sciences or the Foreign Ministry to check a story as you can in most other countries, even Poland. Khrushchev's comings and goings are almost impossible to find out. Tass will report, "Khrushchev left Tashkent today," but the story never says when or how or where he went.

If you call the Press Department, the usual reply is, "When we are able to give you the information, we will call you." They may call a week later and say, "You may be at the airport in two hours for the arrival from Vienna of Premier Khrushchev." It is useless to reply that the arrival was announced by the Austrians in Vienna the day before.

We read in the New York newspapers the news about Khrushchev's entourage for his first trip to America. It was announced by the Americans in Washington. When Prime Minister Macmillan visited Moscow, we heard about his meetings with Khrushchev at briefings with a British Foreign Office spokesman. The Russians told us nothing.

After the end of direct censorship, many members of the Press Department staff made a greater effort to be helpful in personal matters. But on news queries, they usually presented the same blank wall. On a request from our New York office, I telephoned the Press Department to inquire whether reports at U.N. headquarters were true that the Premier of the Soviet Union would attend the U.N. discussion on Cuba. After a few hours, a functionary telephoned to say, "As the people in New York seem to know so much about it, why don't you ask them?"

We glean news mainly from official outlets. Our Tass teletypes and Moscow radio and television are carefully watched by our three translators. They wade through eleven—yes, eleven—Moscow daily morning newspapers, two evening newspapers, ten tri- and bi-weekly sheets, and mailboxfuls of out-of-town newspapers and magazines. Foreign journalists are also often invited to press conferences.

The Press Department and the Cultural Committee, sometimes, stage "junkets," trips for the press around the country, so that they can write about something else besides Moscow. Junkets can be fun as well as educational. When foreign correspondents were taken to Murmansk in the Soviet Arctic, we pestered our guides for a look at the reindeer bred on collective farms several miles from the city. The animals provide meat and hides for Laplanders, a minority people in that area.

The Russians were perplexed because we preferred to see reindeer rather than visit a factory. Finally the animals, looking like miniature moose, were trotted out for us on the frozen Kola River. We climbed aboard the wooden sleighs, each pulled by four animals. Then off for a breathless gallop! The reindeer pounded over the ice at 30 miles an hour. There were no jolly Santa Clauses in red suits to guide them, but Laplanders wearing ancient-style tunics of reindeer hide and fur leggings and brandishing long wooden poles. The smokestacks of the new Sovietized city of Murmansk were only a few miles over the hill. But from my sleigh they seemed to be centuries away.

There was one quite serious moment for the British and

American correspondents on that junket to the Far North, too. Late one afternoon we stood at the hilltop graves of three American and twenty British casualties of World War II. They had been killed in the Allied effort to bring supplies by ship across the Arctic Ocean to Murmansk. Below us, shadowy in the falling snow, lay the Soviet port. Puddles of mud sloshed around the mounds, and a raw wind whistled over the little cemetery, separated from the Soviet war dead by a little blue picket fence. We laid two funeral wreaths at the entrance to the graves of our countrymen, buried so far from home.

On junkets journalists are usually invited to factories, collective farms, mayors' offices, dams, and so forth. At each visit the Soviet hosts traditionally lay out oranges, apples, soft drinks, and cakes, and at mealtime vodka, wines, meats, and salads. Invariably after the "press conference" come the toasts.

Vodka can be the greatest hazard to a foreign correspondent in the Soviet Union. Not the secret police, nor censorship, nor the housing problem confronts a visitor with such perils. One correspondent suggested that vodka is the secret weapon with which the Communists are wearing down the bourgeoisie.

Foreign journalists in Moscow still recall "the 1959 Mine Disaster" that occurred during a junket to the Ukraine. The writers were taken deep into a mine. They emerged hot, exhausted, and hungry and ninety minutes late for a banquet given by the mine operators. By the time each correspondent's country was toasted, the scribes were beyond help.

Next on the program was a tour of a mine-safety institute. The institute director tried to deliver his lecture to the foreigners. But they appeared to be asleep. So he canceled the tour and escorted them instead to: another banquet—with vodka.

The correspondents made a pact among themselves not to become trapped into toasts. But one American made the error of standing up to get a pencil out of his pocket with which to make notes. His Russian hosts thought he was proposing a toast. They leaped, smiling, to their feet. Toasts! The Russians remained in intelligible condition; but for the foreigners it was a calamity.

The first junket I went on to Leningrad was particularly interesting to me because sitting among the officials making speeches was none other than my Russian friend Mikhail.

I had missed Mikhail, even though I was too tired and busy to have many social thoughts. He spoke on a theatrical subject, but I could hardly concentrate on taking notes.

After the press conference, I wandered over to the speakers' table. Mikhail smiled. Then he turned and strode from the room.

I thought he had decided not to see me in the Soviet Union. I stood in confusion while correspondents chatted with the speakers. Some fifteen minutes later, I glanced out the window and saw him just leaving the building. Suddenly I remembered the game we had played by pre-arrangement in Berlin. If he wanted to see me there, he would walk out of a room and I would follow a few minutes later.

Grabbing my coat, I hurried outside and down the street. He was nowhere to be seen.

Having missed our tour bus, I walked three blocks to a taxi stand. After fifteen minutes I managed to snare a work-worn Pobeda. As the car bounced along I examined every red brick on the street. I stared across the Neva River at a factory with the ever-present red communist banner. I felt very lonely and far from home. I put my hand to my face so that the cab driver couldn't see I was beginning to cry.

4

Keeping a Marxist House

The best-selling book among foreigners in Moscow is a 5 × 3 inch tome entitled, *Catalogue—Ostermann-Petersen Bros., Ltd., Copenhagen.*

Russians claim that "soon" foreigners will no longer have to import food, clothing, toilet articles, and household goods to Moscow in order to live in the style to which they are accustomed. Until this day arrives, however, housekeeping in the Soviet capital will be done mainly by mail order.

After I was settled in my work routine, I tackled the daily adventure of keeping house in a Moscow apartment. The other permanent correspondents are men, almost all with wives at home to cook their meals, wrestle with the plumbing, and stand in line at the market. But while I waited for a telephone line to London or for a Tass communiqué, I perused the O-P catalogues, my "homework."

The Soviet government liberally allows us to import virtually duty-free a certain amount of food, from English marmalade to Italian sphaghetti: 180 kilograms of fresh fruits and vegetables, 200 kilograms of canned goods, and 120 bottles of liquors, beer, and wine every six months (a kilogram equals 2.2 pounds).

Some Americans stationed in foreign countries are dismayed if they can't have their home brand of toothpaste or beer. The sight of American housewives in Frankfurt buying stale American cupcakes when great pastry is for sale in a German bakery down the street doesn't make sense to me. But even I admit that it's difficult to live in Moscow on the Russian economy.

In the first place, many items we import are nonexistent in Moscow, such as fresh frozen broccoli, cake mixes, and French and German wines and whiskey. The Russians import only a few food items, mainly from communist countries, such as tinned pears from Bulgaria or beans from Rumania.

Most of the foods purchased from Copenhagen and Helsinki and other nearby western capitals are of better quality. For example, Russian sugar is coarse. Russian and eastern European canned vegetables and fruits do not taste as good as the Danish variety.

Imported foods generally are less expensive, even after you add the cost of shipping and packing. A one-pound can of Danish butter, for example, costs the equivalent of 82 cents. The same amount of Russian butter bought in Moscow costs the equivalent of $1.25 (all prices listed at the rate of one ruble equals 90 cents).

Furthermore, choice foods are scarce in Moscow. Frozen green peas and strawberries, of medium quality, are available in Moscow—one out of ten times you go to the food shop. And that lucky time you may have to stand twenty minutes in a queue.

Even some Russian items are more easily purchased abroad. Russian crabmeat is 65 cents a can in Copenhagen. Russians tell me they have not seen any in Moscow "for years." When they did, it cost $1.11 a can. (One Russian told me the Soviet government does not sell crabmeat to

its own people because it is radioactive from atomic tests!)
We buy Russian vodka for 81 cents in Copenhagen (a half
liter). The same bottle costs $3 in Moscow.

Liquor is tax free in Copenhagen when purchased for
export. A bottle of good Scotch is $1.24 for us. The finest
of French and German wines sell for between $1 and $2.
The wine and liquor prices in the O-P catalogue are so
fascinating that for my first order I got carried away and
wound up with one of Moscow's finest wine cellars—but
little food.

Making out an order from the catalogue is a couple of
evenings' work. Which items have too stiff a duty? Once
a correspondent's wife ordered some plastic flowerpot
holders, price 10 cents. The duty was close to $50. I didn't
discover it's unwise to import cosmetics and paper goods
such as paper towels and paper napkins until my first shipment arrived. I had to pay the stiff duty or send the entire
shipment, food and all, back to Copenhagen.

The orderer is faced with other problems. Which is the
best year for French Bordeaux wines? (Telephone a
French correspondent.) When the crates arrive how do
you figure out the directions on the Danish dried soup and
the canned Dutch chickens? (Call friends at the Danish
and Dutch embassies.) Thanks to these imported delicacies, foreigners in Moscow sometimes eat like kings.

Orders for the winter's supply must be put in before the
snow flies. Otherwise, as I found out, the canned peas
arrive frozen.

Fresh fruits and vegetables are in very small supply in
Moscow during the winter. I paid the equivalent of $3.40
for a medium-sized cauliflower and $3 for two pounds of
strawberries. Our office invested in a deep freeze which

we filled with fresh meat and frozen fruits and vegetables ordered by telephone from Helsinki and shipped by train to Moscow in one day.

To supplement such orders, a "little corner American grocery store" operates in the heart of Moscow. There, some Americans can stock up on everything from Ritz crackers to Jello pudding—just a few feet off a main boulevard where Russians walk by, ignorant of this private cache.

The haven for homesick American housekeepers is the commissary of the American embassy, a tiny three-room PX. Prices on many items are three times higher than in America, due to transportation rates, rationing, the new "hard ruble" rate, and so forth. Thus the store is used more or less for emergency shopping.

Only embassy personnel are supposed to buy the store's fresh meats and fruits and vegetables brought in by embassy courier plane or train. But correspondents can buy canned goods, liquor, dry foods such as sugar, household cleansers, paper goods, cigarettes, and candy. A few shelves are devoted to drug supplies including shaving lotion, razor blades, and sometimes ladies' hair lacquer. Ink, ballpoint pens, thread, zippers, playing cards, and cigarette lighters are usually for sale. Thus, to a great extent, American embassy personnel may live as they did at home.

Some of the foreign wives break out of their apartments for forays into the Russian markets and food stores. Those who don't, miss the adventure of shopping as Russians do. They miss some good things to eat, too.

In the summer it is pleasant to walk from our apartment-office across a bridge and nearly a mile to the nearest outdoor market. Opposite the entrance a big sign hails the "workers of socialist labor." Inside, peasants from collective farms sell their privately grown produce in a very capitalistic way, setting the prices according to supply and demand. In outdoor stalls elderly peasant women in kerchiefs sell heaps of sweet purple plums and grapes, tomatoes, and great mounds of soft green lettuce leaves torn from the stalks. It's fun to watch the bustle at the market. Everyone crowds and shoves and stuffs purchases into string shopping bags or brief cases or the pouchlike shiny brown handbags many Russian women carry.

Every October 1, prices on fresh fruits and vegetables soar. During the winter the only vegetables commonly seen are potatoes and cabbage. Cucumbers grown in hothouses can be had for a czar's ransom—if you can find them. Many Muscovites eat apples and tangerines flown up from relatives in the South. Now and then you see winter lettuce—limp and squashed, probably because it was jammed into the suitcase of a speculator who grew some in Georgia or Armenia and then flew in a load to sell in snowy Moscow. (Such capitalists are the object of many complaints and exposés in the Soviet press.)

Generally prices average, per kilogram (2.2 pounds): beets, 16 cents; carrots, 22 cents; cabbage, 25 cents; onions, 44 cents; salted cucumbers, 44 cents; sauerkraut, 15 cents; potatoes, 11 cents; apples, 99 cents; oranges, $1.54; tangerines, $1.32.

Beef per kilogram ranges from $1.40 to $2 for steaks. Once Gum, the biggest Moscow department store, which delivers food to foreigners, sent me sixteen $3 \times 2 \times 2$ inch steaks for the equivalent of $3.80. Russian steaks have to be dosed with garlic or onion salt or sauces to make them tasty. Some days the open-air market or stores have pork, veal, or mutton; some days they don't. Many an embassy cook has had to open canned ham when she couldn't find good meat at the market that day for a scheduled luncheon.

The peasants send most of their best meat, fruits, and vegetables to the "free" market, where the prices are pegged higher than in the state-owned stores. Restaurants are not allowed to buy from the "free" market, so they go without fresh vegetables most of the winter.

The Russians have some good things to eat. The sour cream, the equivalent of 33 cents a half pint, tastes marvelous. Cucumbers are so good you can eat the skin. Russians still make some varieties of ice cream with cream. A scoop of the best kind of ice cream costs 22 cents.

Russian caviar, that symbol of capitalism, is wonderful —that is, if you like caviar. A one-kilogram can costs $20. Russians imitate foreign cheeses and some foreigners can't tell the difference. A Gouda type is called "Gollandsky" after Holland, and I also found native Russian Rocquefort.

Grocery stores called "dietary shops" sell what I think is better chopped liver, or *pashtet,* than I bought in the delicatessens on Fairfax Avenue in Los Angeles. Mushrooms, a Russian passion and practically the national symbol, are not only beautiful to look at but big and delicious.

Russian ravioli, called *pelmeny,* can be purchased frozen and are used in soup. Two stuffed cabbages in a can from Bulgaria are a popular buy at 46 cents.

Some items are discouraging to foreign shoppers. Chickens come even from fancy food stores with the insides intact and head and feet still dangling. When Mike

Romanoff, the Beverly Hills restaurateur, visited Moscow, he observed tactfully that the slender Soviet chickens "have been running a lot."

Bread is the country's dietary mainstay. Russians can't imagine how anyone can get through a meal without several large pieces. Russian bread is heavy compared to western breads. It comes in assorted colors—white, gray, black, and brown plus at least twenty-five varieties of buns with poppy, anise, or thyme seeds. Russian white bread costs 13½ cents for a 200-gram loaf.

Eggs sell for from 10 to 15 cents each. The milk brought daily to my apartment door by a girl in a blue uniform is thin. In winter the milk is powdered.

Russian pastry tends to be heavy and very sweet. A large chocolate bar costs $1.20 and foreigners remark it's coarser than candy from western or eastern Europe. (In fairness I must add after a sampling of European food that American chocolate bars, pastry, and bread are no prizewinners, either.)

Shopping for household goods in Moscow, I found, is simpler by and large than in other cities. Most stores carry the same products and the prices are standard. There's no risk of missing a bargain down the street—at least not on everyday items that are in plentiful supply. Most of the large shops are on or near Gorky Street, once a dirt road lined with wooden houses, now a wide boulevard flanked with office buildings and stores.

Moscow is so crowded that shoppers fill the downtown sidewalks and spill over into the streets. Although shopping can be an adventure in the Soviet capital, it can also be an ordeal. It may take ten minutes to elbow your way to the counter through the throng, another ten to be waited on. Then you must pay your bill at the cashier's window before you can collect your purchase from the clerk.

Gum, in Red Square, sells goods in individual stalls as in the old markets, only here the stalls are topped by a glass roof like a gigantic hothouse or Victorian railway station. Children play around a fountain in the center of the store, and girls in white uniforms sell ice cream to hurrying shoppers.

Walking up Gorky Street, a shopper passes food and book stores and then a big electric appliance shop. Russians say you can buy electric razors there for $12 and up, *if* they're in stock. Samovars are just souvenirs for tourists, now. Russians, instead, buy electric teapots or shiny tea-kettles. Electric mixers with attachments sell for $105.

Side streets and arcades are interesting browsing grounds. Plastic items began to appear plentifully in 1959. Lattice-designed plastic plates sell for 31 cents apiece, plastic vegetable graters for 60 cents, plastic boxes at all prices. Plastic baby's bibs and even tablecloths have shown up in the stores.

A common sight in Moscow stores or on the streets is a sudden queue of Russians who have spotted a choice item. Once in 1961 I followed a line of patiently waiting citizens that wound down four flights of stairs in a department store. At the end of the queue clerks were selling colored thin foam-rubber cushions. Some Russians claimed these were the first to appear in Moscow.

I have traced other queues, to discover Russians will line up for inexpensive petal-shaped glass ash trays; fleece-lined leather gloves from East Germany; and tangerines, pineapples, and oranges in the winter. Czech phonograph records, Cuban rum, or a shipment of nylon nightgowns from East Germany may also start a queue. For New Year's in 1961 a razor that ran on a battery was introduced one day at $16. The supply vanished in one day. Russians who spy a good buy tell their friends, and the stampede is on.

Speculators take quick advantage of those shortages. In the early morning they buy scarce articles in Gum— and then sell them to customers on the street behind the store. In the Gum television department hang photographs of speculators caught selling their places on the waiting list for TV sets.

Shopping for housewares in Gum has eased even since I've been in Moscow. After the war, pots and pans were almost as scarce as diamonds. When I arrived in 1959 the shop windows were stacked with pans made of plain non-shiny aluminum and costing the equivalent of $1.25 for a quart size and up. In 1961 shiny aluminum pans with mustard-colored tops and black plastic handles appeared in the shops for $2.50. From the glad looks on shoppers' faces, I judged this to be a milestone of sorts.

Russian floor wax provides a brilliant shine and a strong odor. Toilet paper is a newfangled custom that has only begun to replace the local equivalent of the Sears Roebuck catalogue. The first Russian apartment I visited had torn strips of *Pravda* in the lavatory. The Central Telegraph Office fittingly uses old Tass copy. In 1961, heavy pink toilet paper and the slick kind in separate sheets went on sale in some Moscow paper-goods stores. In Gum it was carried periodically in the stationery department.

My problem was to find what I wanted on the one day a month I could spare from the correspondents' merry-go-round. Solid brown linoleum at $9 a meter usually is available. But I spent an afternoon searching four shops and found none. A foreign friend had better luck and found linoleum in a gayer brown and white pattern. Another day I pressed through the crowds at Gum to buy a skirt zipper. The only color available was bright purple. I never could find artist's heavy cardboard mounting board.

Many foreigners import scouring powders, floor mops, soap, and vacuum cleaners, believing them better and easier to obtain than the local variety. But getting my maid, Tonya, a wonderful girl with a timeless Russian face and sturdy body, to use these modern gadgets is another matter.

Tonya, like Victor, our chauffeur at UPI, is from a peasant family. A peasant thinks he or she knows what is best, and what is best is the way grandmother did things. After knowing Tonya and Victor and their stubborn peasant ways, I wonder how Mr. Khrushchev can induce the peasants to farm the way the Party desires.

Tonya cannot be wooed from some Russian housekeeping methods as old as St. Basil's Cathedral. Why, anybody knows the only way to clean a rug is with a broom. And the broom has to be made of large twigs curved at the bottom so that her poor back is bent as she sweeps away. I have often dragged out my vacuum cleaner. Tonya nods, uses it if I'm watching, and then immediately abandons this mechanical nonsense.

Floors were washed with soda, windows with gasoline, and dishes with hot water but no soap, until I suggested some rules. To dampen clothes for ironing, Tonya fills a cup with water and then blows with gusto to spray the water on the clothes. Spit on the hands is dandy for removing cats' hairs from furniture and clothes. She scrubs the floor on her hands and knees, scorning the long-handled mop.

Dry cleaning takes at least two weeks in Moscow and your suit jackets come back with the buttons off and an aura of gasoline fumes. So I introduced Tonya to cold-water soap with which to wash my sweaters. But nonetheless she washed my Italian mohair treasures in hot water, leaving them fit for a four-year-old.

"You can't get anything clean in cold water," explained Tonya with her usual smile, bursting with vigor and friendliness.

Despite various mishaps, I love Tonya like a sister. She brings gifts of eggs and flowers from the country and cares for me when I'm sick. She is a good, honest, happy person, the wife of an electrician and mother of two children. She can pick up my furniture with one hand. With her sturdy arms she symbolizes "Mother Russia."

Tonya makes *borsch* (beet) or *shchee* (cabbage) soup and *blini* (pancakes) now and then for me. For $1.90 she buys cabbage, hunks of soup beef, onions, and turnips for a huge pot of *shchee*.

She also takes care of my laundry. At first she took my sheets to a neighborhood laundry. For some mysterious reason each time they came back a lovely shade of gray. Now another maid in our building washes two sheets and a pillow slip each week for me for $2.

Like most Russians, Tonya is passionately devoted to bread. She thinks a person who doesn't eat half a loaf a day isn't healthy. When I was bedded with back pains one winter, Tonya announced that the root of the trouble was I did not eat enough bread. Each summer my cat begins to shed hunks of her winter fur, as cats always do. But Tonya scolds, "That's because she doesn't eat bread!"

I have had a never-ending procession of household adventures. One Monday morning I heard a slow, rumbling noise. It was not unlike the portentous reverberation one hears while awaiting an eruption of Old Faithful in Yellowstone National Park.

The thunder changed to a loud gurgling, emanating from the lavatory. I fearfully opened the door and watched in fascination while the gurgling blossomed into a geyser —of soapsuds gushing out of the toilet! At times sparkling foam spewed forth magnificently toward the ceiling, at times the suds were tamed to a spout. This phenomenon occurred every Monday, and I challenge any other householder to match that statement.

It had one distinct advantage. Those Mondays were the one time the lavatory floor was washed with soap. On the other hand, the display could be disconcerting, particularly if somebody was closeted in the lavatory at "Old Faithful time."

The only way out was to write UPDK, the government office which handles problems for foreigners. If we want to buy an airplane ticket, make a hotel reservation in another city, get a car repaired, hire a maid, rent an apartment, or have a door made, we must write a letter in Russian on the office letterhead and have our chauffeur deliver it to UPDK.

UPDK serves two purposes which fit the Russian tradition. It often gives us better and quicker services and goods than Russians are able to find, a measure of Russian hospitality toward foreigners. It also segregates foreigners and tends to keep us from dealing with Russians.

Our letters to UPDK about "Old Faithful" finally stemmed the flow of soapsuds. They probably were caused by foreign detergents that Russian maids were using, as the gushing occurred on laundry day.

I soon discovered I had numerous roommates with numerous feet. Again I fired off a letter to UPDK. A Russian exterminator, a pleasant woman in a white uniform and cap, arrived with a satchel. The thought that Russians managed to fit exterminators into their seven-year plan was amazing. She sprinkled lye around the edges of all my rooms. The décor looked a little powdery, but the big black cockroaches vanished.

Next came mice. This was not difficult to predict, considering the holes where doors didn't meet floors and where tiles had fluttered off the walls. UPDK sent another white-uniformed girl. She exterminated the mice by funneling red poison seed into the holes. Then she stuffed the holes with newspaper. This lasted until the mice ate the paper.

One day I was working in the office when Arthur, one of our translators, remarked that there was a bedbug on my desk. I had never seen a bedbug before. It looked like a wood tick from Missoula, Montana.

I raced to my bedroom. Bedbugs were marching through the hole in the ceiling into which the pipes stuck. I could hear hammering and scraping noises from the Russian apartment next door.

"They are making repairs, so the bedbugs moved in here," said Tonya.

After a week of frantic appeals to UPDK, another young girl arrived in a white uniform. She confirmed that the *klopi* had taken up quarters with me because the repair noises disturbed them. Nobody seemed to think it unusual that the bedbugs had been living next door up till then undisturbed.

The exterminator tied a paintbrush to one of my mop handles. She painted the wall, bedsprings, and picture holes with kerosene. She sprinkled powder along the base of the walls which were crawling with transparent baby bedbugs.

Several other foreigners in our building reported having bedbugs, too. In fact, the problem seemed so widespread that an exchange of bedbug experiences became frequent party small talk.

Many Russians talked authoritatively on the subject. One suggested to me that the bedbug invasion was due to the tearing down of so many wooden buildings for "urban renewal." Bedbugs lie dormant for years on wood, he said. I once showed a Russian friend two old icons I had bought. He immediately whipped out his cigarette lighter and burned the crevices in the old wooden backings of the religious paintings. "Dormant bedbugs may be in there," he explained. "You must always burn cracks in icons."

When the first tourists I knew from America showed up in Moscow and inquired, "How will you fix up this apartment?" I decided I'd better decorate the place.

To hire a painter meant more letters to UPDK and a wait. I decided to join the Russian do-it-yourself movement.

Up on Tagansky Square was a big hardware store where you could buy wallpaper, paint, pots and pans, dishes. After wriggling my way to the paint counter, I saw several open "sample" cans of paint. A sign on the wall announced which colors were in supply that day.

Beige wall paint was not available so I bought white
with the idea of mixing in some artists' brown "color in
oil." After two weeks of combing artists' supply houses, I
found a tube.

Victor, our chauffeur, painted the walls. He scorned a
borrowed Danish paint roller and instead bought a
Russian brush which took longer and left marks. At last
Victor, his shaved head speckled with white paint, happily
showed me the finished walls. They looked like the "water"
taffeta party dress I had in high school.

"There was not enough paint so I mixed it with water,"
he explained proudly.

I had bought enamel paint for the bathroom and kitchen
in olive green and teal blue, the favorite peasant colors.
The young girl in a blue smock who waited on me had
asked if I wanted *"olipha"*—something that looked like
linseed oil. When I got home and opened the paint cans,
I saw why.

Russian paint is almost solid, so that it took me hours
to thin it, by mixing and mixing *"olipha"* and paint in
numerous separate cans. The resultant paint took more
than a week to dry; and for a good ten days, every time
I walked into my kitchen or bathroom my clothes acquired dabs of green and blue.

To spark up the apartment, I painted the outside of the
old-fashioned bathtub and sink and the living-room and
bedroom doors bright colors. I made the lavatory even
jazzier. In its original state it reminded me of a gas
chamber I had seen at Dachau, where tiles covered two
thirds of the walls. The ones in my bathroom were neither
decorative nor useful, so over them I glued Russian wallpaper that looked like an Oriental rug from Tashkent.

Russians traditionally hang their rugs on the wall instead of putting them on the floor, and my wallpaper created that effect. I could not find any wallpaper paste in Moscow, so I mixed flour and water, a painstaking job.

Unfortunately one 20-cent roll of wallpaper was not enough. I had to return to the hardware store for another. But when I opened it at home, the roll fell apart in the middle; the entire roll was defective. I salvaged enough to finish the job, but the new paper wasn't the same color! I could see that in Moscow it is wise to buy all your wallpaper from the same dye lot made the same day.

"Who ever heard of decorating a lavatory?" said our translator, Arthur, shaking his head in wonderment. "An American craze."

The correspondents from the AP upstairs dropped in to inspect my handiwork. They announced it would never last; wallpaper wouldn't stick to tile. That night I leaped out of bed at the sound of rustling wallpaper, thinking I would find it lying on the floor—but the noise was only the paste drying. I am proud to say the wallpaper still is on the wall now, two years later.

I have to add one P.s. to this account of my attempt to decorate a Moscow apartment. Although the Russians may be way ahead of America in the machine-tool industry, they haven't yet made much good oil wall paint. Even now, whenever anybody leans against my new beige walls, he walks away beige. In fact, most men in Moscow have paint dust on their suits.

After I had been living in Moscow for two years, the foreign colony benefited from the Russians' gigantic crash building program for alleviating the housing shortage.

One of Mr. Khrushchev's highly publicized new prefabricated buildings was set aside as a "diplomatic house."

Most of the apartments in the new building on Kutuzovsky Prospekt consisted of two small rooms. Some had three small rooms. It never was clear exactly why foreigners were allotted quarters suitable for bachelors. As one apartment was too small by foreign standards, UPDK gave most of the married foreigners two apartments each. Thus while there were not nearly enough dwellings for overcrowded Russians in Moscow, foreigners were busy connecting their two adjoining apartments by ripping down brand-new walls that had taken precious hours to build. And now they wallow in the luxury of two bathrooms and two kitchens apiece!

The end of censorship and more apartments available improved correspondents' lives. Many living in hotels at last were able to turn in their hotplates for the blessed comfort of private homes. Children stopped complaining so much, wives who'd been washing dishes in hotel bathtubs smiled more. Now we understood the evident joy of Russians we saw moving to new abodes—a daily phenomenon—the entire family packed into a truck along with their big heavy furniture, potted rubber plants, and often a family dog. What a difference a private place to live makes!

Speaking of privacy, there's a chance now that my quarters might improve, too. If the Ministry of Communications decides to allow teletypes into the new Kutuzovsky building, our office-apartment can be installed in two separate, but connecting, apartments, and no longer will I have six Russian roommates and teletypes next to my bedroom.

A word about Soviet souvenirs. Examples of various national handicrafts are on sale in every gift shop and department store and even in hotel lobbies. Some tourists complain they can't get used to the Slavic style and comparatively high prices. The least expensive souvenirs are wooden dishes and spoons painted gold, black, and red, from 20 cents up. Lacquered black cigarette boxes painted with fairy-tale scenes range from $10 to $200. Silver and enamel vodka "shot glasses" cost $16. Ceramic painted figures in primitive peasant style are $2.50, much higher than similar art in Mexico. A carved wooden plate is $90.

Antique-collecting tourists head first for the "commission shops," where antiques that Soviet citizens bring in are sold (the state takes a percentage). The legend that Russians aren't interested in old items is disproved by the crowds around the showcases in these establishments, gawking at paintings, dishes, jewelry, art objects. Just before the introduction of the new "heavy" ruble, many Russians were afraid of being short-changed. Consequently they turned their savings into "hard goods" and cleaned Leningrad and Moscow commission shops out of silver, jewelry, and other valuables. Moscow abounds with legends of czars' treasures found in commission shops, but embassy wives and tourists seem to have snared most of the prizes by now. Some embassy wives visit the commission shops twice a day. Correspondents' and diplomats' wives recently have gone in for collecting painted china and marble eggs. Like every business, including ice-cream stands, the commission shops are state-owned.

Prices on antiques are fixed by the state, of course, so I have the comfortable feeling I'm not being cheated. Some of the salesgirls appear expert. If a clerk says that a hand-painted cup is sixteenth-century French, it probably is. She will also point out any defects such as chips or cracks.

Since there is a great emphasis on books in the Soviet state, a book store is one of the better souvenir haunts. Even if a tourist can't read Russian fairy tales in Russian, the intricate lettering and colorful drawings in such books make them treasures to take home. Old, prerevolutionary books are numerous and cost much less than they do in western rare-book shops. I've never been able to find any old Russian maps.

5

Some Observations on Russian Men

"I can't meet you until eight o'clock. I have to go to a Communist party meeting first."

That opening line for my first real "date" with a Russian staggered me, since I was fresh from a country where even if I had known a party member I wouldn't have broadcast it. It soon sinks in that in Moscow a Communist is an honored member of society, or at least the influential part of society.

He is the Regime. Therefore he is more or less trusted these days. For that reason a Communist is the safest date in Moscow for an *inostranka* (foreign woman), both from her viewpoint and his. She can't be accused of trying to subvert the citizenry; he can't be accused, at least during this more liberal Khrushchev era, of being lured by the wily ways of the decadent westerner.

I would much rather have spent evenings in Leningrad with my friend Mikhail, the non-party Russian I had met in Berlin. But as the months hurried by I never heard from him. I tried to call him a few times from hotel lobby telephones in case our telephone was tapped. But I feared my furtive actions might look suspicious to Mikhail. Henry Shapiro warned, "Be aboveboard in meeting Russian friends."

Mikhail seldom was in his office. When he was, he

always said in an artificially bright voice, "Well, I'm going to Kiev today," or gave some other excuse.

I gave up and decided to find Russian friends elsewhere.

Fortunately I arrived in Moscow on the coat tails of British Prime Minister Macmillan. Before his visit, many Russians still were cautious about having foreign friends. But as the rosy glow of *mir i druzhba* (peace and friendship) permeated the city during and after the Prime Minister's stay, the ice softened and Russians became friendlier. Most Russians with no reason to contact foreigners remained isolated, but many party members began to step out into the formerly forbidden area of the foreigners' world.

I was introduced to one member of this advance guard while I was dashing through the Ukraine Hotel with the Macmillan party. His name was Ivan, and he was a translator. Several months later Ivan telephoned my office to invite me to the first Russian ice show to be unveiled in the Soviet Union. He asked me to meet him downtown in front of the Bolshoi Theater on Sverdlov Square. Considering the policeman standing outside my front door, I decided this arrangement was natural enough.

Ivan had a car. Later I heard it probably belonged to his office: a company car, so to speak. Off we went to the gigantic Lenin Sports Palace near Moscow University. I don't know which was more engrossing, the audience or the show. It was the first time I had seen 15,000 Russians all together. And the ice show was astonishing for Moscow. Cheesecake! Onto the rink glided twenty young curvaceous beauties, prancing to lively jazz music. They wore brief penguin outfits that left their whole legs bare, and their behinds were decorated with provocative little tails. The girls were plumper than western ice skaters or chorines, but not bad.

"This is very new to us," said my Russian companion, grinning.

The next time Ivan and I met in front of the Bolshoi he brought along two fellow Soviet translators. Alexander was suave and an expert on many subjects. Nikolai was a handsome fellow with a dry sense of humor, a sort of Russian Jack Lemmon. He was forever teasing me.

After that we four had a warm, gay, if curious relationship. Once Ivan asked me to meet him for lunch. When I arrived, Nikolai was there, too. Nikolai later told me Ivan told him that I insisted he be there. Sometimes I would go out with Alexander alone, or Nikolai alone. But more often three or four of us would be together. I called them "the Rover boys."

All three were likable, bright young men in their thirties, stalwart representatives of the "new class" that communism has bred, an ambitious post-revolutionary generation that is taking over the country. They were attractive, well dressed and wore ties, then a rarity in Moscow. They were not what I would call intellectuals, but affable friendly men who enjoyed life. When I was with them I felt as if I were a member of the Moscow "in" group, but they certainly were not sophisticated in the western sense.

The first time we four were together we went dinner-dancing. I had dreams of investigating wee bistros and mingling with "the People" on some dark side street while gypsy violins wailed "Dark Eyes." But Ivan's car deposited us at one of the ornate marble and potted palm tourist hotels, the Sovietskaya.

The dining room there is the size of a gymnasium. We had the traditional and best dinner—caviar and vodka, cucumber salad, beef stroganoff, and ice cream. Between courses we danced to a Soviet-style jazz band. Occasionally a plump girl in a long blue bias-cut crepe dress, *circa* 1936, sang Soviet popular tunes. She threw in an occasional American number such as "Some Enchanted Evening."

My friends were fair dancers. When the faster tunes came along some pseudo-jitterbuggers, including Alexander, took to the floor. I thought Stalin must have been turning in his tomb.

After dinner, we moved into the next room—a bar!— where the stools are so tall that I imagine only high-altitude basketball players can manage them gracefully. The bartender made drinks—what he called "cocktails"— out of sweet liqueurs. Only Soviet vodka, cognac, and wines are sold in the Soviet Union, with rare exceptions. Cuban rum and French cognac appeared in some stores in 1961 for a few hours before the shipment was snapped up.

In the dining room and bar most of the customers were young couples—the men wearing their hair a little too long and their trousers too wide to look like westerners. I thought some of the girls would have been beautiful if they did not have fuzzy permanented hair and unimaginative dresses. By Paris standards most of them could have benefited from lipstick and girdles. The scene reminded me of Saturday-night dances in a Montana town twenty years ago, only transported to this world capital and with a background of elegant marble and chandeliers.

The next time I had a "date" with two other Russians, photographers this time, I announced I wanted to go to a little side-street restaurant where I could see "the People."

This amused them, and they decided to bring along a Russian girl. At this time the bulldozers were plowing through the mud in Sokolniky Park to make way for the American Exhibition, and Russian-American friendship was sprouting all over the place. In a scene familiar in any western city, one of my escorts popped into a gray corner telephone booth to call a girl to meet us at the restaurant.

Off we went to the restaurant built on an old riverboat anchored on the Moskva River. A block away was a medieval church with brilliant green domes and pink carvings. It was a warm evening and many Russian couples strolled along the streets.

Up the gangplank we walked, only to be greeted by the usual sign, "No Places." An elderly man in uniform guarded the door against the usual crush of exuberant Russians dying to get in—but, as often happens, he saw I was a foreigner. Since nothing is too good for a guest, he swept us in with a grand gesture.

Upstairs we found a little table. Next to us a large group of Russians was celebrating a wedding. In the next room was a real gypsy orchestra with singers and dancers, the only "floor show" I have ever seen in Moscow. The Soviet press regularly castigates gypsies as wastrels and idlers, but they seemed to be very popular at the riverboat restaurant that night.

Watching the gypsies was a crowd of Russians, and watching the Russians was me. Through the layers of sweet-smelling cigarette smoke I caught glimpses of shy female eyes, ruddy cheeks, straight blond hair wisping over men's foreheads, pink crepe dresses, jewels dangling from pierced ears.

We drank much vodka. Soon through the smoky haze

glided our fourth, the first Russian girl I'd met. I later decided she was not typical. Nina had long blond hair drawn
into a bun at the back of her head. She wore mascara,
blue eyeshadow, and layers of crimson lipstick. She giggled infectiously, and her laugh was piercingly high. She
spoke English and was a model at Gum.

Nina announced she had ditched her date to join us. A
racy female, I decided, thinking of the prim lectures on
morality one sees in the Soviet press.

After several vodkas and dinner, it was decided by Nina
and the photographers that they were going to my apartment to drink my Scotch whiskey. Almost as an after-
thought they invited me along.

One fellow asked when our Russian translator left the
UPI office for the night. They never had been inside the
iron gate and fence surrounding our back-yard entrance.
Always before when they had driven me home on other
"dates" they had stopped at the corner to let me out.

"But the policeman might take your license number,"
I said.

"We are Soviet journalists, we have legitimate business
in your office," said my friend, shrugging, and downing
another vodka.

Off we roared, like a sputnik, down the Naberezhnaya,
or river boulevard, to my apartment house. We careened
through the iron gate to a screeching stop right under the
nose of our Soviet policeman.

I clambered first out of the car. We all spoke English
loudly except Nina. She giggled.

"He thought we were foreigners," one of the Russians
said after we were safely inside.

I poured out four Scotch-and-waters in highball glasses

and dragged out my phonograph and records. After fifteen minutes I noticed nobody had touched the drinks.

"Well, Alina [as they called me—Russian female names have an *a* on the end], you know we do not drink water in Russia . . ." began one photographer.

Russians drink whiskey or any other liquor as they do vodka—straight, as if the American army were marching through Leningrad, and in one grandiose swallow. I filled old-fashioned-size glasses half full of whiskey for them. That was gone in one gulp. After we'd played some of my American jazz records, the entire bottle was empty.

Nina pulled off her gray suit jacket, unloosed her hair to her waist, and did some sort of neck-winding Oriental dance. I taught one of the men to jitterbug. When they left at 6.00 A.M. another bottle was half empty.

When I had lunch a few days later with one of the photographers, he said, "Alina, don't mention to anybody we were at your house. It's better for us and better for you to say nothing."

To illustrate in what a small social circle we correspondents had acquired elbow room, a month or two later my UPI colleague Bud Korengold had his first date with a Russian girl. It was arranged by some of his Russian friends, for meeting Russian girls presents more of a problem for a foreign man than finding male companions does for me.

"She was blonde, spoke English—" began Korengold the next day. She sounded familiar.

"And she giggled," I said.

Sure enough, it was the same Nina.

My various Russian friends came several times to my apartment. Once I cooked an Italian dinner for Nikolai, of "the Rover boys." He patriotically turned up his nose at *lasagne*. So I introduced him to the American word game "Scrabble." Although his English is fluent, the game was agonizingly difficult for him. He soon became bored and returned to cognac.

My friends often teased me about the fact I might some day write a book about my adventures in the Soviet Union. "I will start the first page, 'I have some Russian friends who like to drink whiskey,'" I said, which sent them into tremors of fake (or real?) anxiety.

I always look forward to dinner, arguments, and jokes with these friends. The foreigners in Moscow are a compatible group; but in an ingrown small world in which everybody knows what everybody else is doing, I want to feel not segregated but part of the whole. However, as yet I have not surmounted the barrier that hangs between me and my Russian friends; I can seldom reach out and make contact. It's an achingly lonely feeling at times.

Once Nikolai at my begging said he would try to take me to a real Russian New Year's Eve party at a Russian apartment. I excitedly hurried home from an American correspondent's New Year's party to wait for Nikolai to pick me up at 11:30. Sitting alone in the office, I listened to the "bong . . . bong . . . bong . . ." of the Kremlin's Spassky Tower clock usher in the New Year on Moscow Radio. He never arrived.

"I asked the other guests if I could bring a foreigner," he explained a few days later. "They were hesitant. Then when I said you are an American correspondent, they nearly collapsed at the very thought of it! Oh, the party was great, it lasted two days," he prattled on.

But I, unlistening, thought sadly, What am I doing in

this country where people push you away as if you're a spy and do not accept you?

It was clear that I had been relegated to one compartment of his life, never to bridge the gap between his outward manner and his actual being, never really to share his inner thoughts and feelings.

Two years after I had first met "the Rover boys," I happened to wind up in the same hotel dining room with two of them one night. I arrived with some British friends and stopped off at the Russians' table. They were sitting with two lovely young women—who turned out to be their wives.

To my surprised question, Ivan explained that both he and Nikolai had been married about six months before. Since then, I suddenly realized, most of our rendezvous had been lunches instead of dinners. They never once had explained why.

"I thought we were friends!" I sputtered indignantly, while the non-English-speaking wives chattered to each other. "Why didn't you tell me? I would have congratulated you and invited you and your wives to dinner. . . ."

I didn't really care whether they were married. I wasn't interested in having serious entanglements with Russians. But once again I felt the isolation of the foreigner in Russia, and realized how little one might know of even those Russians he considers friends.

One Soviet wife tried to explain the situation to me. "Sophisticated Russians aren't afraid to see foreigners any more," she said. "A few years ago, yes; not now. But they don't relax or act themselves around foreigners. I thought of giving a party and inviting foreigners and Russians, but even if the foreigners are Communists—Poles or Czechs—

my friends still do not behave the same as they do when we're just Russians together. It's been drummed into Russian heads for too many centuries about not mixing with outsiders."

During the *mir i druzhba* period in the Soviet Union, it wasn't difficult to spend evenings with Russians other than "the Rover boys." Usually the occasion was a group party at my apartment, accompanied by much eating, singing, drinking, and dancing.

All those dates were with what I call official types. There's another category of Russians which is easy to meet these days—your quite unofficial fellows who seek out foreigners. These range from outright *stilyagi*, or playboys, to dissident students, speculators, or just flirtatious well-heeled young men who want to talk to westerners.

When you start off for Russia, westerners usually say, "But you'll never get to talk to real Russians." These younger Russians are so friendly your only problem is how to escape them!

When I arrived in Moscow the National Hotel restaurant was filled with young Russians hoping to practice their English on the visiting British press corps. One night after working late at the Central Telegraph Office, two British correspondents and I walked two blocks to eat dinner at the National. Five young men at the next table soon joined ours. One, Vladislav, showed me a little book in which he had written down English phrases picked up from tourists, such as "so's your old man" and "hot dog."

The maître d' twice ordered the boys not to sit at our table. This often happens in Moscow restaurants. It may be that the maître d' thinks Russians bother foreigners, or perhaps he doesn't think Russians ought to get to know foreigners. At any rate, our new friends kept returning persistently to our table. They ordered a sumptuous meal for us.

Vladislav was well dressed. He said he was the son of "a high government official." The others appeared shabby, unshaven, wore no neckties. But at the end of the meal, each pulled out a roll of rubles the size of grapefruit.

Vladislav educated me in the slang of this new fast young set. It was amusing to discover that "the new Soviet man" can also be a playboy who speaks slang just like his counterparts in the "decadent" West. His vocabulary (in Russian, of course) included:

> trash—police
> to fill up—drink
> rupees—money
> an oak—a ruble
> ancestors—parents
> scum—a stupid person
> produce a spray—do something stupid
> oatey—very dull
> smoke it up—do something interesting
> kok—cocktail lounge
> Broadway—Gorky Street, the main street of Moscow
> post-meningitis—a girl's Italian-style hairdo

After that evening, young Vladislav called me every day for several months. He wanted jazz records, he wanted to take me dancing. Henry Shapiro advised me against seeing him. One correspondent in Moscow who associated with these restaurant "johnnies" has never been able since to get a visa to re-enter Russia. The Soviet authorities regard these boys as semi-dissidents and parasites.

I also decided on my own that association with Vladislav would be dangerous when I discovered that some of these boys knew Dmitri, my Dostoyevsky-like Russian friend who "moved" to Munich via East Berlin. I deduced that his friends in Moscow might be watched by the security police.

Months later, Vladislav telephoned to say he was leaving for Siberia to work on Mr. Khrushchev's pet project of settling the "virgin lands." I told him I was glad somebody had finally got him to work. A month later he was back, an idler and a playboy once again. "We can no longer go dancing at the National; we are forbidden to enter there," he told me. "Now we go to the Budapest and Warsaw Hotels."

I checked the National restaurant and sure enough, the young *stilyagi* crowd had vanished. Probably because foreign tourists stayed there, they were funneled instead to the Budapest and Warsaw where few foreign tourists are quartered. Vladislav still is there every night, I suppose, spending his family's money on caviar and vodka.

After more than two years of research into different types of Russian men, I have some general observations to make.

They are at times mysterious. I don't know whether it's because of their easygoing nature, or the ever-present barrier between Russians and foreigners, but on two occasions two different Russian men stood me up without telephoning their regrets. Then, after I had expressed my anger, came the emotional apologies, gifts of candy, and even an icon.

Russian men get drunk better than anybody. At this they most certainly surpass men of other countries and even overfulfill their production quota. One sees many inebriates on the street. They are amiable, talkative, and singing drinkers! They defy gravity. Men amble down Gorky Street at 2:00 A.M. or 11:00 A.M. at what appears to be a 90-degree angle without falling over.

Parties with Russians have exhausted me. Russians traditionally don't sip a cocktail or *apéritif* before eating. Everybody sits down to the food and drink at the table, and the toasts begin—one after another. And each time my companions insist it be "bottoms up," or "to the end" as they say in Russian. Otherwise there are taunting cries about how Americans can't keep up with Russians.

After one try, I finally admitted defeat. I conceded that Russians are superior to Americans in this field and I never tried to surpass them.

One Russian acquaintance decided to try to "Americanize" her Russian friends with an American-style, two-hour cocktail party. After she told me her plot for a five to seven soirée, I furnished her with martinis and hors d'oeuvres from my kitchen.

The next day she telephoned to wail, "They scorned the hors d'oeuvres. They raided my refrigerator, drank and ate everything in the house including tomorrow's dinner, and wound up drunk on the floor at 2:00 A.M.! They want Russian-style parties!"

Russian men are violently sensitive and proud of their country. Once I had a long argument with a Russian friend about communism over lunch at the Budapest Hotel. To balance my criticism, I added that in one way I understood the Party's fight against the grip the Orthodox Church had held over ancient Russia. In the czar's day, I went on, the church was corrupt, meddled in government affairs, and owned land while the peasant went hungry. "It was pagan—superstitious, why, like the Church of

Mexico many years ago which built huge cathedrals with gold-leaf-covered walls while the Indians went hungry," I went on, thinking to soothe his ruffled feelings.

"What do you mean, comparing the Russian church to the primitive Mexican church!" he exploded.

Then as I began to laugh, he realized his Russian sensitivity had got him into an impossible corner. He, a devout Communist, was defending the church his party was fighting tooth and nail.

"I almost wanted to protect the Russian church," he said stiffly.

Before I went to America in 1960 to cover what turned out to be Premier Khrushchev's shoe-pounding act at the United Nations, I had a farewell dinner with another Russian friend. I remarked that I planned to go shopping in New York because I needed some articles from abroad.

"Communists do not need anything from abroad," he said reverently. Then after a minute he added, "But Communists' girl friends do. Please bring one of those stiff petticoats, red, waist size 28."

Another Russian complained to me about an American newspaperman who had called the Soviet Exhibition in New York "naïve." (The critic was right; Russia certainly is not sophisticated.)

Russians laugh and joke like people in any other country; but around foreigners, at least, their sense of humor becomes mixed up with their sensitivity. I thought I would please one Russian date by showing him a *New Yorker* cartoon that paid tribute to Soviet science. It pictured two Moscow housewives chatting on a street while their babies scribbled advanced mathematical problems on the sidewalk.

My Russian friend studied the cartoon for several seconds. Then he shook his head and said seriously, "But it's not true, you know."

That ended that.

Russian men are direct. They seem more akin to certain kinds of rough Americans than to hand-kissing, flattering Europeans. At times Russians are downright wolves. Once I was the only woman at a party with five Soviet men. It wasn't long—about three vodkas—before one I barely knew pulled me to his lap and roundly kissed me.

Alexei Adzhubei, Khrushchev's energetic son-in-law and outspoken editor of *Izvestia,* is a lively extrovert who likes to flirt with females at receptions. Once at the House of Journalists, Adzhubei after a few vodkas began to twit me about the decadent West. Then he reached over and slowly and deliberately proceeded to wipe off my eye make-up and lipstick with his thumb. If I'd been in another country, I'd have slapped his face, but this is Russia, and the face in this case belonged to Khrushchev's son-in-law. I was so hurt and astonished that I just stood there like an awkward idiot. The Russians around us looked embarrassed. Finally I shakily pulled out my lipstick and put some back on, and turned away.

The fact that a Russian man is married does not keep him from romantic pursuits any more than in other countries. A Russian could hardly "set up" a mistress in a private apartment because—where would he find the apartment? But among members of the "new class," many of whom have a private apartment per family, there is reportedly some extramarital activity.

In fact, despite pious pronouncements in the Soviet press about the equality of women, Russian men often go to parties without their wives, Oriental style. One Russian complained to me that he and his wife had been battling for three days because "she does not want me to go out nights with my friends." He explained, "I want to be emancipated, like an American husband."

"American!" I gasped. "If an American husband goes to a party without his wife, that's the end of him. The wife is more or less the boss in America."

He appeared stunned. "I thought it was otherwise in America," he said. "But Russian wives are not like American wives. Russian wives do not want to go out to drinking parties with their husbands. My wife wants me to stay home with her." (One Russian wife I know disputes this.)

The tradition has been for officials' wives not to appear at public functions, but because western women occupy such an important place in the social and business life of their husbands, Russians have begun to bring their wives to receptions in Moscow. As I watched Mme. Khrushchev at diplomatic functions, and departing for America with her husband, I thought it must seem very strange to her— as well as to him—to be sharing his public life.

Russian men can be fun. They are fiercely emotional. They like to argue politics and recite poetry. They like to eat and drink and stay out late, and listening to a Russian sing the haunting "Song of the Steppes" while beating on the table with his fingers is a memorable experience.

I have to admit I have not seen many handsome Russians. The good-looking men I see in Moscow are from Armenia, Georgia, the Ukraine, or the Baltic states. And they'd all look more attractive if they'd only buy western clothing and cut their hair shorter, *and comb it!*

6

In My
Merry MGA

Want to meet Russians and talk to them by the thousands? Bring an automobile to Russia.

Russians are crazy about cars the way Americans are about visiting royalty and the French are about bicycle races. Next to Lenin's tomb, the biggest attraction in Moscow happens to be my automobile.

In the first place, the little, racy, white MGA was the first sports car to take up residence in Russia, and is still the only one at this writing—not counting one red MG-TD, a couple of Triumphs, and an Austin-Healy that have taken spins across Red Square with their tourist owners.

Besides, I am a woman driver, a species that Russia is not blessed or cursed with yet, except for some women professional taxi and tractor drivers.

If admission could have been charged, I'd be rich from the sidewalk spectators who have laughed at, ogled, patted, stared into and under, and even jokingly tried to lift my little machine.

It has been here nearly three years. But I still can't edge through crowded shopping streets without an audience of Soviet citizens tying up traffic as they crowd around the car.

At first when it was parked downtown in front of a shop or hotel, I usually obliged by giving a sidewalk lecture

91

about the vehicle when I returned to the mob surrounding it. Any foreign car brings a crowd in Moscow. In the summertime the line-up of tourists' cars in front of the Metropole Hotel has a steady audience of from 50 to 75 lookers. My car, being of unusual shape and color, draws a better house and more queries than, say, a visiting Peugeot sedan or Buick convertible: "How fast can it go?" "What country is it from?" "Is it a racing car?" "How much horsepower and how many cylinders?" and so forth.

As an encore, I would lift the hood. This never failed to bring even more spectators. In fact, one American embassy official joked that my car should be part of a U.S.-U.S.S.R. cultural exchange program in which the Russians sent an equal curiosity to the States. Even though, of course, an MGA is a British car.

At first I thought being the center of attention was great fun. Nobody had looked twice at me or my MGA in America. I was curious to talk to Russians, and this was the quickest method.

"Are you German? How can you be American? You have light hair and all Americans are dark," a friendly housewife said to me as she fingered my sweater.

"I knew you were American. Americans are all blonde," another Russian woman remarked with just as much conviction.

Or, when I climbed out of the car once with another correspondent, a Russian man said in surprise, "You, Americans? Why, we thought you were Czech or Polish because you're like us. You look like ordinary nice people."

I was worried that my car might arouse angry resentment in a country where the waiting list to buy a car is from two to five years (sometimes depending on bribery).

But not one Russian ever wrote "Yankee go home" on the hood or cast dark glances at the shiny grille. Every tire kicker and dashboard inspector had the same reaction: "A wonderful little machine and we enjoy looking at it."

Once before my Russian friend Mikhail started avoiding me, he laughed ironically and said, "It's a good thing you brought your car. Now the security police always will know where you are."

But one of my pious Communist party friends from Brussels, Anatoly, reproved me sharply. "Oh, you should not have brought your car," he said. "You let the people see things they cannot have yet."

Another Russian friend said, "If the Russian people had known what the outside world was like these past forty years, they would have never been able to work, or stand for what they had. That's why western four-engine passenger planes were not allowed into Russia until we had our own!"

After that I felt embarrassed about the car, as if others must think I was merely flaunting my possession. Besides, as I found out, the headaches of being a foreign motorist in the Soviet Union are grandiose.

Despite tales to the contrary, getting a car into the Soviet Union is the least of the problems. Mine arrived wrapped as a piece of baggage on the train from Berlin three months after I did. The Russians at the freight office unwrapped the car and that was that. No tax to pay, not even many papers to fill out.

From then on, it wasn't so easy.

At last through the usual string of letters to UPDK, I got an appointment to apply for a Moscow license plate. I was the first correspondent to bring in a private, non-chauffeur-driven car since the cold war began. For two hours I drove around with a police officer or parked while he checked brakes, clutch, engine serial numbers, and so on.

But with my new black license plate with white letters, "ZN [apparently for "*zhournalist*"] 00-87," I still was not ready to set forth.

Where are the service stations? There are a handful in all of Moscow. The streets are not clogged with as many automobiles as those of other countries, although the number appears to have doubled during my stay in Moscow. I was told by other correspondents that foreigners can buy gas at only two service stations. Our chauffeur said we can't drive up and hand the attendant money as Russians do. We have to write a letter to UPDK! This indomitable bureau sends us coupons that entitle us to so much gasoline. "Why?" I asked Henry Shapiro. "They are not short of gasoline, are they?"

"How long have you been in this country?" came Henry's favorite reply.

Ordinary gasoline is cheap here, about 25 cents a gallon. It's fine for Soviet trucks but gives my delicate sports car indigestion. A high-compression motor knocks and sputters on low-octane gas.

One day an American correspondent told me he had found a new service station where he had bought high-octane (98) gasoline. It cost more, about 40 cents a gallon, but his car didn't knock. And no UPDK coupons are necessary—one of those unexplained Russian mysteries.

"Why haven't we been using that gas?" I asked Victor, the office chauffeur.

"We chauffeurs know that the fumes from it make your head ache and they are bad for your lungs," he said.

That sounded to me like my maid Tonya's saying that the cat's hair falls out because the creature doesn't eat bread. I began buying that high-octane gasoline.

Moscow "service stations" really are gasoline pumps period. A woman unlocks the pump. She hands me the hose. I put the gas into the car myself. Having the windshield washed, tires filled with air, or oil checked or visiting the comfort station will have to be postponed until the next seven-year plan.

Repairs also are do-it-yourself. Repair garages are rare, repairs take a long time, and you have to write more letters to UPDK. Russian chauffeurs do most minor repairs on foreigners' cars. Major repairs are made at several embassies by Russian mechanics.

Oil changes every 1,000 miles are a chore done at embassies. Russian oil is not of as good quality as western oil, so we import ours. I convinced the British embassy, with female logic, that they should service my car because, after all, it's British-made.

Servicing is only part of the battle. Next Henry Shapiro advised me to get a Russian driver's license. I had an International Driver's License, printed in English, French, German, Chinese, and Russian, which I had purchased at a New York automobile club. The license says that the U.S.S.R. signed the agreement recognizing it. Henry was doubtful the Moscow police would honor it, but off I drove.

A person might get by indefinitely with such a license, or no license at all, if he is not stopped by the police. But this is well-nigh impossible. The motorist does not have a fair fighting chance. A hundred policemen, or so it seems sometimes, are pitted against each motorist. This land is one gigantic WPA. The Police Department hires thousands of young fellows to stand on corners in their dark blue uniforms and fur hats. They wait for people like me to drive along and violate one of their 150 city driving rules.

I found that quite simple. One rule orders you to keep the car washed. A policeman will blow his whistle if your machine does not reflect the new Soviet look. The police scold foreigners who drive dusty autos. I was stopped twice by cops and reprimanded because one fender was scratched.

Russian traffic cops, however, usually are courteous and lenient. They are gentle as doves compared to American cops.

· Traffic rules require a genius I.Q. to negotiate. How and where to go is determined by small street signs hung above eye level, although police in 1961 began having standard European traffic signs in some areas of Moscow. Ninety nine per cent of them are unlit at night. None the less, you are expected to realize there is one at every corner and to follow directions. Traffic signals often are manipulated by hand by a policeman sitting at the corner in a little glass tubular house.

When I set out on my first solo jaunt through Moscow, I was as nervous as if I were the first woman astronaut taking off into outer space. I had been waved good-bye to by our Russian employees, who were convinced I could not possibly know how to drive and would never re-enter the earth's atmosphere.

It had been drummed into my head that any traffic

violation is serious. I had heard that if you dent somebody's fender you can lose your permission to drive for a
year, and that injuring a pedestrian can get you ten years
in jail, or, if you are a foreigner, immediate expulsion
from the country.

As I edged into traffic I was surrounded by noisy,
bouncing trucks whose tire tops were level with the roof
of my little car. Trucks account for much of the street
traffic. No lanes except the center line are marked on the
new, wide boulevards. Everybody sways from side to
side, four and five abreast. Drivers seldom signal when
turning or stopping. They rarely bother to look when moving from one side of the road to another.

Pedestrians are the worst hazard. Russians are not
disciplined pedestrians, under communism. I have noticed
that most Germans stand quietly on street corners and
seldom put one foot off the curb until the traffic light
changes. But Russians usually look neither at the light nor
the traffic and walk across the streets every which way
while buses and taxis zoom among them. Many pedestrians
are in from the country where they seldom see cars. Even
city folk blithely read books or talk to one another as they
cross the street. Russian drivers swoop down upon them
without slowing. How pedestrians keep from being
slaughtered is miraculous.

A British correspondent on his way to cover the story
of Boris Pasternak's death hit an army officer. The officer's
leg was broken; all witnesses, including the doctors at
the hospital, testified that he had been drunk. The
journalist suffered through a three-month investigation
and two-day trial. The court verdict: $120 damages. The

Briton's visa was renewed, to the surprise of some who had predicted his expulsion.

I quickly discovered that if a driver violates one of the strict rules it is hard to ignore the policeman's whistle. He has a wonderfully mysterious Russian system for catching up with you without using a motorcycle.

One evening I was looking for a theater. As I turned off Gorky Street I heard a whistle blow. I was not sure it was meant for me, so I didn't stop. Three blocks later, the stop light was red. It stayed red while the policeman in the little glass house put away his telephone, climbed out, and marched toward me. Obviously the policeman three blocks back had telephoned ahead for the next officer to stop me because I had made an illegal right turn.

My driver's license was home in another handbag. I was paralyzed with fright, particularly when a crowd of at least a hundred people immediately assembled.

No matter what the policeman said, I announced in English, "I don't speak Russian." Another foreigner had advised that tactic. Finally a man in plain clothes, possibly one of the security agents who circulate on Moscow streets, pushed his way through the crowd and told the policeman to let me go. I drove on in triumph, figuring I had outfoxed the Soviet cops.

The next time I was stopped, I had been following a streetcar around a little square. Cars can't always go where streetcars go. The policeman waved aside my International Driver's License. He demanded my Moscow license. When I could produce none, he wrote something in a little book and took all my auto documents. I had apparently not talked my way out of that fix.

I simply must get a driver's license, I told myself.

A week later the Foreign Ministry called. I was ordered to report to the Police Department at 9:00 A.M. to "discuss" a traffic violation. I could see that the system was a far cry from simply issuing a traffic ticket on the spot for a violation. The motorist's documents are turned in to the police; and in a correspondent's case, the police notify the Press Department—the last ones I would like to know about my traffic errors, as they control which journalists keep their visas. After the police interrogation, Henry Shapiro warned, the police either fine you and hand back your documents—or keep them, thereby preventing you from ever driving again.

Since my official Russian was rusty, Arthur, one of our translators, was pried loose from the newspapers to accompany me to police headquarters on Prospekt Mira (Peace Street). I did not feel peaceful.

We walked through a modest entrance and waited in a hallway. After an hour, we were led up some stairs to the office of none other than the police chief himself.

He and an assistant were poring over some documents in a folder, presumably my case.

I sat, my stomach tumbling over, while Arthur, who also was a little nervous, began the speech we had prepared: "Miss Mosby was following a streetcar. She did not see the sign that indicated automobiles must go counterclockwise around Taganskaya Square. . . ."

"Taganskaya? Taganskaya?" exclaimed the chief, thumbing through the papers in the folder. "This report says she was stopped for making an unauthorized turn off Gorky Street and refusing to show her documents to the policeman. So! You have committed a second violation!"

I made mental arrangements for storing the car or selling it.

"And you have no Moscow driver's license," he continued. "International licenses are only for tourists." He thumbed through the documents again. Then he inquired gently, "Apparently you are an inexperienced driver?" My female pride bristled. "I have driven since I was fifteen, all over the United States and most of western Europe, and I've never had an accident or even a violation," I replied indignantly.

"Ahhhh," said the chief, looking at my documents. "You are American. Yes, we hear in western countries citizens, even women, begin to drive at an early age." He took off his spectacles, pushed aside the folder, leaned across the desk, and loudly cleared his throat.

I swallowed hard and looked in anguish at Arthur. He said nothing. I sat waiting to be told I could drive no more in Moscow.

"Tell me," said the chief, "are our traffic signs as good as those in America?"

I most happily delivered a ten-minute dissertation on traffic signs. He smiled and asked questions. When we parted everybody shook hands all around. Everybody thanked everybody else, the police chief apologized for disturbing me, I promised to get a driver's license, somebody said, *"Mir i druzhba,"* and it was a lovely morning.

After I was stopped for a few more traffic violations, I decided to take the plunge. First I bought a book of Russian traffic rules and tried to memorize all 150. After weeks of study I wrote a letter to UPDK (who else?) to ask for a driver's test.

"UPDK telephoned to say you must first have a medical

examination by four doctors," Slava, one of our translators, told me.

"So, okay. How do I do that?" I asked.

Slava took a deep breath. "Write a letter to UPDK," he said.

We did. I was examined by four doctors at the modest two-story "polyclinic," or hospital, reserved for foreigners according to the equal-but-separate segregation rule.

I paid the equivalent of four dollars for examinations of my eyes, ears, nose, throat, heart, lungs, and reflexes, a service free to Russians. The doctors were white-uniformed middle-aged women who wore white caps over their hair. Between examinations I waited in a room with dust covers on the furniture, a big potted palm in the corner, and a few Soviet magazines tossed on a table.

Then I was told to go to the State Bank for Foreign Trade, where foreigners can do business, and buy a money order for the equivalent of $1.50, the driver's test fee. I also had to procure four passport photos. Finally I made an appointment for the driver's test. But when I arrived at the police station, I discovered I had forgotten the passport photos. The examination was canceled. I had to write a letter to UPDK to arrange a new one. My money order was also canceled, and I had to return to the bank for another.

At last all was in order and again I appeared for the oral part of the test, in Russian. Across the "negotiators' table" I faced two glum-looking Russians. They pulled out a board and toy cars, traffic signals, policeman, and pedestrians and arranged them into traffic problems which I was supposed to solve.

"If the traffic light facing you is red but the intersection westbound is closed to traffic, can you proceed north-ward?" demanded one interrogator.

I looked at the toy cars and said, "No."

"Wrong!" he said.

"If your car stalls and you call a tow truck, how long must your tow chain be?" shot the other questioner.

"I don't know," I conceded.

"If the policeman is directing northbound traffic to the west, what is a southbound streetcar supposed to do?" grilled one of the Russians.

"How do I know? I'm not interested in knowing how to drive a streetcar," I said crossly.

"If the light turns green for northbound traffic, can you turn west to stop at this corner if a streetcar is approaching?" "How many feet must you stop from a pedestrian crossing?" "At an intersection, which has the right of way, a truck, a bus, or a car?"

"Wrong!" "Wrong again!" they cried triumphantly after each reply. I did not answer one question correctly. I felt helpless, trapped, furious, embarrassed, and stupid.

"You have not passed the test. If you wish to try again, write for an appointment," my tormentors concluded. "And you must get a Moscow driver's license or stop driving."

My only consolation was that later I tried all the questions on Victor, our office chauffeur. He didn't know one answer, either. The test for Russians must be easier.

The driver's test for foreigners also includes driving around the city, and occasionally the applicant is asked to take the motor apart. I still can't remember where the carburetor is—but then there's little danger I'll be exposed to that test. I haven't passed the oral examination yet.

I fared no better under the Moscow traffic system when I had a slight accident. I was on the right side of the street when a truck and trailer, whose driver was not used to little cars on his right, made a quick right turn and sideswiped my fender.

The usual crowd gathered to stare at my dented car. The policeman who arrived was surrounded by witnesses who agreed it was not my fault. When I had to hand over my documents, everybody read over the policeman's shoulder. "*Amerikanka! Korrespondentka!*" they murmured to each other.

Thinking stingily of the repair bill, I said I wanted his employers to pay for the damage. To my dismay, I watched my documents disappear into the policeman's pocket. Now that nice police chief would discover I still did not have a driver's license.

The Press Department telephoned again a week later, sighing that I seemed to be in trouble again. The police chief wanted to "discuss the accident." Somehow I felt that this time he would not be in the mood for a friendly round-table seminar on traffic signals. I never showed up for the appointment.

The police kept telephoning our office. But I never worked up the courage to see them.

Finally six months later they gave up. They turned over my documents to the Press Department to be handed to me along with a report on the accident. The truck driver, it said, was responsible for the truck, but he was not responsible for the trailer which sideswiped me. Therefore, I would have to pay for the damage.

I sat quietly reading the letter, savoring each word. It was marvelous.

After numerous letters to UPDK and after policemen stopped me twice for defacing the community with my dented car, the fender at last was fixed for nine dollars. The touch-up paint the Russian garage used on my white car was gray, I might add.

I finally hired a man to take care of the car's ills and needs. He was a chauffeur for one of the British military attachés who lived in our office-apartment building. Edward, a Latvian, was the handsomest man I've seen in Russia.

Edward lovingly tended my MGA because he was a racing driver on the side. I was amazed to hear the Russians had decided to allow such a luxurious (and dangerous) sport in this strict, officially puritanical country. Edward directed me to a "rally" where several homemade numbered racing cars of the Formula I variety were speeding on a track. Many of the cars had been assembled by workers at various factories. They were modest, but given a little time the Russians may excel at this sport, too.

Unfortunately Edward's hobby influenced his work. He pretended he was on the fourth lap at Le Mans just once too often in a British embassy car. UPDK banished him to driving Moscow taxis, and I made a mental note to look closely at the driver before climbing into a cab.

I decided I could not cope with the gasoline pumps and wash my car in 15-below-zero weather. Besides, I was tired of being stared at and having my souvenir grille emblems, windshield wipers, doorknobs, and side mirrors wrenched off by admiring Russians. I parked the car sideways in our UPI garage and took the subway and taxis for nearly a year.

When I first drove the car, I was deep in my let's-be-friends-with-Russians stage. About the time I gave up the car, I had darkened into an indignant, argumentative, anti-Soviet stage. I passed into an okay-let's-compete-peacefully stage. But after a Moscow cab driver asked me, "Do you have any cars better than our Moskvitch?" I decided to get my car on the streets again.

For a story, I had visited the Moskvitch factory and test-driven a model three times around Stalin's statue on the plant grounds. At $2,500, it could not hold up its head around a $1,100 Volkswagen.

Out came my car. What's more, I hung one of those "USA" signs on the back bumper so that the British would not reap all the benefits of this capitalistic propaganda.

Now I've passed into a Toynbee-esque let's-look-at-this-country-historically mood. It's convenient to drive a car, so I ignore the stares and questions.

Besides, recently my car has been upstaged by a competitor of mine and receives less attention. An AP correspondent, Stanley Johnson, flew to London to bring back a Rolls Royce to Moscow. The prospect electrified the foreign colony. He returned with a "measly" Cadillac, but it's still the longest and finniest in town. The crowds outside the Metropole Hotel where the Johnsons live grew so enormous that the hotel management ordered him not to park the car out front.

Stanley has lived in Moscow nearly five years. He ignored the decree. Eventually the hotel officials gave up.

7

The Great Invasion

One warm spring evening in 1959 I was peeking surreptitiously out our UPI office window at a group of Russians in front of our apartment building. A man was playing an accordion while two girls twirled in a lively, uninhibited folk dance. I was afraid if they saw me watching they would move away.

Suddenly music blared, drowning out the accordion. It sounded vaguely familiar—the score of *Oklahoma!* I thought it was some foreigners in our wing playing their phonograph. Then I grabbed for the radio.

"Ya nyeh mogoo skazat nyet!" wailed a soprano; in other words, "I cain't say no!" I was listening to *Oklahoma!* in Russian, the orchestration lifted note for note from an American record and re-recorded in Moscow.

American correspondents all over Moscow rushed to their typewriters to chronicle the noteworthy event. Up till then, the usual Moscow radio fare had included few western songs, and only an occasional American tune such as a Gershwin melody or Negro spirituals. Any mention of America had been in the traditional anti-American vein—including commentaries about slums, unemployment, warmongering, imperialism, etc.

The playing of *Oklahoma!* over Radio Moscow rang up the curtain on the next act of the *"mir i druzhba"* period.

British Prime Minister Macmillan's visit in February and March was Act I. Next came the American Exhibition; swarms of western tourists and delegations including many Americans; western theatrical presentations; and films from the U.S., England, West Germany, France, and other countries of the "capitalist camp."

Moscow's potted rubber plants and fringed lampshades quivered under the assault from the West that summer and fall of 1959. It was pretty bizarre for us, too. One day I was accompanying Billy Graham, the American evangelist, on a tour of a Kremlin church when we ran into a bevy of sloe-eyed fashion models from Christian Dior in Paris. The combination of Billy Graham and Paris models was somewhat unique for the once sealed Kremlin.

As summer began, Red Square was filled with American tourists wearing sport shirts and carrying cameras. Beverly Hills restaurateur Mike Romanoff (born Harry Gurstad in Brooklyn) showed up to visit his "relatives" and see what was left of his former "czardom." Some Oxford students jolted into town on an old double-decker red London bus. A New York racetrack promoter flew in to sign up some Russian horses.

Hollywood TV star Art Linkletter tried to invade Moscow to film a TV show. But he was refused entry while we waited in vain at a welcoming party. Gary Cooper did make it, to say "Yup" in Russian at the première of *Marty*, the first fresh American movie to hit Soviet screens in thirteen years. Before that, Deanna Durbin was the biggest star in Hollywood as far as the average Russian knew. The procession of outsiders reached a milestone of sorts when two English girls arrived in Moscow in 1961 to try to sell girdles and brassieres to the Russians. Not only that, they posed on Red Square for photographers, waving a two-way stretch on the spot where revolutionists once marched.

I thought I had left press agents behind in Hollywood, but with the opening of the American Exhibition they poured into town by the dozens. Day and night they jangled our office telephone with pleas for us to write about everything from the man who designed the pavilions to the bathing suits.

The Great Invasion had us correspondents working day and night, writing stories with one hand and taking pictures with another. I was assigned to cover the American governors who toured Russia. I trailed them from the Minister of Education's office to Khrushchev's sanctuary in the Kremlin.

Other delegations poured in. "Need 300 words daily on Indiana farmers touring Soviet Union," was one cable from our London office. We tracked the farmers down and sent out copy on their opinions of Soviet corn-growing methods, etc.

We tracked down many others, too. At one time American delegations poking into their counterparts' establishments around the Soviet Union included gem cutters, doctors, economists, realtors, fifty-six Floridans (who stunned the populace with their southern accents), computer specialists, crystallographers, aeronautical experts, a wrestling team, antibiotic specialists, and two pretty Minneapolis schoolteachers who won a trip to Moscow in a contest. We had to write about them all.

Politicians began to include Moscow as a stopover. One of the first was the then Vice-President Richard Nixon, who arrived on July 24 with his wife to open the American Exhibition in Sokolniky Park.

When you consider that as recently as 1957 the only western passenger aircraft flying into isolated Moscow was a two-motored Finnish plane from Helsinki, it was quite a heart-warming day for us when Nixon's silver and orange Boeing-707 jet glided majestically onto Vnukovo Airport.

I was assigned to Mrs. Nixon. I convoyed her from a maternity hospital in Moscow to the Hermitage Museum in Leningrad, from a fashion show in Novosibersk in far-off Siberia to a worker's house near Sverdlovsk. Mrs. Nixon appeared to me to be a charming, extremely bright woman who took her job as a politician's wife very seriously. She treated the business of getting publicity as a job to be done. "Are you taking those pictures for fun or for publication?" she inquired briskly when I started snapping her as she shopped in Gum, the Macy's of Moscow. She smiled when I replied, "For publication."

Usually the women reporters assigned to Mrs. Nixon had to pester her for her schedule. But one day in Sverdlovsk we were all either sick or helping the men report her husband's activities. We did not check in with Mrs. Nixon, but she did not wait to be sought after. She rolled up to our hotel in her limousine and sent in her Intourist guide to look for us. If only all celebrities were that easy to deal with!

"I'm going to a children's nursery and I planned this for you girls," she began when I hurried out to her car.

Most of us could not go, but one woman reporter changed her plans in order to accompany Mrs. Nixon.

At first Mrs. Nixon handed out "penny candy" to Russian children. This may be a selling point in other countries or good for getting votes in Idaho, but many Russians are proud, sensitive souls with chips on their shoulders about being thought "backward." Often when she gave a child a piece of candy the reporters could see resentment in the eyes of the mothers. Finally someone from the American embassy apparently dropped a hint, and the candy handouts stopped.

Some American journalists, just as eager to be generous, tossed oranges, candy, and coins to children from their car and hotel windows when we toured the Sverdlovsk area. Again the Russian parents greeted such gestures with what the Soviet press calls "wrathful indignation." The authorities soon ferreted out the gift-giving correspondents, and only frantic string-pulling by Mr. Nixon's press aide, Herb Klein, saved one scribe from being ordered back to Moscow.

After the Nixons whirred off in their Boeing-707, we settled down to covering the American Exhibition, a day and night watch where anything could happen and something frequently did. Many incidents required subtle handling to get by the censors. For example, one story which was ticklish to tell occurred when the Soviet authorities moved in on preview day and pruned the book display of what they considered "anti-Soviet" literature, for instance a copy of the *World Almanac*. Many stories the censors killed completely—such as one revealing how the souvenir-loving Russians virtually stripped the exhibition clean the first few days. Another story that died a-borning in "the oven" related how the Russians refused to let exhibition personnel hand out miniature lipsticks as souvenirs.

The impact of that exhibition was immediate, and it is still having its effects on the Russian people. The 1957 Youth Festival brought the first flood of foreign influence to Moscow; the American Exhibition the second. The Russians are still arguing about the "typical American house," the abstract-art exhibition, the women's fashions, and household gadgetry. Some foreigners think the exhibition was responsible for the sudden improvement in store-window decoration in Moscow.

To me the greatest value of the exhibition lay in the conversations which took place between the American guides and the Russian populace.

One day when I was prowling through the crowded book section, for example, I watched a young girl American guide argue with a young Russian man over some reference in an encyclopedia to the Russian police terror of the thirties. An elderly man with a beard nudged his way into the discussion group and said to the American girl, "Don't back down. You tell him! These young people don't know what the old days were like."

That same summer of 1959 the Russians sent their exhibition to New York. While the American show in Moscow was a shock to Russians, the Soviet invasion of New York seemed to have a similar effect, at least according to two isolated cases I heard about.

Of the 120 language experts and technicians sent across the sea, I happened to be introduced to two, Larissa and Alexei, who sought my advice before going abroad. Their preconceived ideas about New York were as wide of the mark as the typical American image of Moscow: "There isn't any theater in New York, is there? Aren't the theaters all in Washington?" "I've seen photos of New York, and

I've heard about the people's behavior, how nervous they are, running around to get places on time." "I've heard there is a big park." "I want to see all kinds of New Yorkers, middle-class, workers, the rich. Is there a university there?"

They wanted to see Wall Street, made famous in the Soviet press; the museums, the modern-art galleries, the stores. Skyscrapers didn't interest them. "We have multistoried buildings, too," Alexei said proudly.

Larissa asked if she should take vodka or phonograph records to give away as souvenirs. She planned to pack white shoes, a print dress, and a white bag because it would be late summer. I told her white shoes in sooty New York wouldn't be white very long. I suggested she buy a black silk summer dress, lots of white gloves, a black bag, and black shoes. Then I wrote to several friends in New York asking them to please show these two Russians the good side of America they had not read about in their lopsided press.

After the Soviet Exhibition had ended, I received excited letters from my American friends. They were dazed by their encounter with two live Russians. I saw these friends a year later when I was trailing Premier Khrushchev around the United Nations, and the effect still hadn't worn off.

One, a sophisticated New York woman, told me her husband wouldn't invite the Russians to their apartment because he feared it might damage his business reputation. That sounded just like Russians who are afraid to have foreigners in their homes in Moscow!

Another friend, a successful career woman, invited the Russians to dinner and rounded up ten excited friends.

"Don't dress, the Russians probably won't have dressy clothes," she warned her friends.

The usually dressed-to-the-slinky hilt New Yorkers assembled in casual clothes. Then in walked my Soviet acquaintances—looking like prosperous capitalists; Alexei wore a neatly tailored new suit; Larissa, the black silk dress, white gloves, black shoes, and black bag I had suggested. After they left, the guests were so disturbed by the evening that they argued about the Soviet Union until 4:00 A.M. The women, of course, huddled in a corner to hash over the smart black dress that they feared had showed them up.

Larissa and Alexei visited another New York couple, both artists. By this time, apparently, they were getting used to New York. Larissa inspected the two and a half room penthouse where my friends live and remarked, "Oh, just right for two people, I see."

Larissa told her hosts she had found nothing interesting to buy in New York. She and Alexei also got into an intense argument about abstract art with a Japanese artist who was present.

"We never should have invited that abstract artist," said the American hostess to me when I visited New York later. She was still distraught. "I'm afraid your Russian friends think we took advantage of them by inviting the artist to offend them. We did want them to understand we were friendly."

My American friends unanimously feared that neither Larissa nor Alexei had enjoyed their visit. But back in Moscow I met Larissa for tea one day. She sighed with pleasure as she described one New York experience after another. I could not help wondering whether my visits with Soviet families caused a similar uproar.

Act III in the Russian-American love affair was Premier Khrushchev's trip to America in September 1959. Looked at from the Moscow end, it had some aspects of a comic opera. From the din in the press and radio, you'd think N. S. Khrushchev, not Columbus, discovered America. How America was receiving N. S. Khrushchev with love and affection was hammered daily into Russian heads. Why, some Americans in San Francisco even hauled out the Soviet flag. How brave they were to have expressed their feelings after so many years under a fear-ridden regime, caroled one Soviet newspaper, sounding for all the world like an American newspaper article about police-state days in Russia.

The grand finale of the drama was a sterling "adventure" movie entitled *N. S. Khrushchev in America,* starring none other than that popular "star," N. S. Khrushchev. It played in Moscow theaters for almost a year after his trip ended. (This was part of a series of "derring-do" films with such titles as *N. S. Khrushchev in India, A. I. Mikoyan in Mexico, etc.*)

I stood in line for the première along with eager Russians, many of whom queued up to see what this mysterious America looked like that their newspapers told them was such a terrible place but that they should surpass anyway.

They didn't see much of the United States. According to this movie, Americans live only in skyscrapers—virtually the only buildings shown. The camera did handstands, in fact, to avoid filming many details of American life. When Khrushchev's train proceeded from Los Angeles up the coast to San Francisco, the camera carefully concentrated on the ocean to the left and studiously avoided those comfortable beach bungalows and Santa Barbara mansions on the right.

The plot of the film could be summed up as "boy (Khrushchev) loves girl (American people); boy almost loses girl; boy wins girl." The villain was the American police, always cruelly holding the people back from embracing our hero.

The movie unfortunately didn't include a shot of the climactic moment in the story—Nikita Sergeyevitch climbing out of his airplane upon arrival back in Moscow and shouting happily with thumb pointing upward "Ho-kay!"

The mood of "peace and friendship" neared delirium when an American aircraft carrier happened to discover four Soviet soldiers adrift on a barge in the Pacific Ocean. The youths were so hungry they had eaten part of their shoes. A Russian friend called the UPI office to cry in gratitude, "Thank you, Americans, for rescuing our boys." She even wanted to go to the airport when the boys came home. Hundreds of Russians did. This and the demonstrations in 1961 for spaceman Yuri Gagarin were the only spontaneous assemblages of any kind I have seen in Moscow.

One day during the pandemonium over the four rescued soldiers, I was visiting the lavish country home of Lenin near Moscow. The Russian girl guide was in the midst of her usual spiel: here is the white and gold bedroom where the leader of the proletariat slept; here is where he played the piano, etc. Suddenly she fixed an eye on me and said without breaking rhythm, "and we all wish to thank the United States for rescuing our four boys."

I could only give a startled, "You're welcome."

The next day another Russian thanked me. I began to get the impression that the Russians thought if it hadn't been for N. S. Khrushchev's journey to America single-handedly to lessen international tensions, the Americans would have shot the starving soldiers or left them to die of indigestion from eating their shoes.

With Russia's doors now swinging wildly in the wind, hordes of tourists continued to pour in. It used to take two days to get to London by way of that little plane to Helsinki. Now various western airlines began flying in nonstop jets loaded with tourists.

American buses began to operate between Helsinki and Warsaw. Suddenly there were schoolteachers from Ohio and shoe clerks from Arkansas rubbernecking across the great plains of Russia that had seemed so menacing and forbidding. The millennium was reached the day a tourist parked his Volkswagen in front of the National Hotel with a license plate bearing the inscription, "U.S. Forces in Germany."

The Russians seemed fascinated by this army of foreigners. Children plagued tourists on Red Square for coins, ballpoint pens, postcards, and stamps. Some older Muscovites settled into the business of buying dollars and clothing to resell on the black market. Gum was swarming with young "businessmen" on the prowl for tourists.

"You're from America?" one would say to me with a smile in his classroom English. "I have a nice icon for you. And I will give you 30 [or 40 or 50 or 60] rubles for one dollar" (the tourist rate then was 10 rubles to one dollar).

"I am an American correspondent. I am not interested," I would reply.

The smile would fade and the teen-age "businessman" would melt into the mob of pushing shoppers.

Russian reactions to foreign tourists included arguments over shoes with pointed toes, careful inspection of all tourists' automobiles, and criticism of too informal garb (e.g., wrinkled slacks).

The American tourists' reactions varied from wild approval to wild disapproval. It was always strong.

"Why, what we read in our papers about Russia isn't true," announced a New York State radio station owner as he sat in my living room one day. "Why, the food at the Ukraine Hotel is as good as the food at the Waldorf-Astoria Hotel in New York." After I picked myself up off the floor, he continued, "My Intourist guide told me about the Supreme Soviet. Why, they work just like our Congress. They argue about money and everything. Why, people in this country have freedom. They criticize their government and talk as they please."

At the other extreme was an eminent doctor from Beverly Hills who came to Moscow by plane. After three hours, he was so nervous and "horrified" he immediately applied for a visa to leave. A girl with the first American ice show to hit Moscow burst into tears of fright when she stepped off the plane. Other comments ranged from "The food is terrible" to "The hotels are as good as any place." The most tantalizing question was why the elevator at the main tourist hotel, the Ukraine, never stopped at the twelfth floor. (Microphones? tape recorders? One tourist reported the elevator operator told him, "That's where 'they' listen.")

Almost all American tourists agreed that the elevator service at the Ukraine is abominable, Moscow looks drab, the Kremlin is beautiful, and the Russian people are the most hospitable and friendly of any country in the world.

Hardy was the traveler who escaped an argument with his Intourist guide. "Our guide demanded to know why the United States ringed the Soviet Union with bases," said one bewildered man I knew from Los Angeles. "I said I didn't know. Well—why do we?"

Others arrived with different answers. Another couple I knew from Beverly Hills snapped right back to their guide that the bases were built to prevent Communists from acquiring any more countries. They also kept correcting her on points of Russian and Soviet history.

An American journalist visiting Moscow for the first time in five years told me, "The biggest difference is that the people look happier." On the other hand, a British woman on her first trip to Moscow, in 1961, thought the Russians looked *un*happy. "Why don't the people smile more?" she asked her Intourist guide, who replied, "Because they are thinking."

Some tourists became so enamored of "the workers' paradise," as a *stilyag* once sarcastically described it to me, that they wound up staying. We had a parade of five "defectors" in 1959 and 1960. One, a worker at the American Exhibition, changed his mind and later wrote his family in Cleveland that he wanted to come home; but he never appeared at the American embassy to get a visa, and vanished in the vast country.

Another who had a change of heart was a "Marty" in the flesh. A simple guy with problems, he "defected" for personal reasons, as most persons do. He thought the welfare state would love him and protect him from the agonies of life. When he discovered your problems go with you even beyond the Iron Curtain, he had no money left. The American embassy could not care for him because he had renounced his citizenship. Therefore, while waiting for money from home and a visa from the American embassy, he appealed to some American correspondents to help him.

The night we were waiting for the Soviet rocket to land on the moon, he telephoned to say he hadn't eaten in two days. I bought some groceries, sped to his hotel, and rushed back to the Central Telegraph Office. At last he received an American visa and money from home. We were glad to see him off to New York.

During the *"mir i druzhba"* period, traffic began to move in the other direction for the first time in (how many decades)? The Russians let out a steady trickle of citizens, mainly elderly, to rejoin their relatives in America. Each émigré's story would make a good novel, but at the time none of the stories of waiting and heartbreak got by the censors. One woman wept as she told us how she had worked on a road crew in Siberia for eight years; but we cabled only a bare departure story. Besides, too many printed details in her case might spoil the chances of others to leave the Soviet Union to rejoin their families.

Another case involved a Lithuanian woman who had moved to America years before. Soviet agents, she said, trailed her to the U.S. and over a period of many months convinced her to return to her homeland to broadcast anti-American propaganda. It is difficult to understand their eventual success—they must have had some strong grounds for blackmail. At any rate, this simple nervous woman somehow was herded back to Moscow. She told us, weeping, that she escaped her "escorts" in Helsinki, only to have them find her and force her on the train to the Soviet Union.

In Moscow she finally awoke to what she had done. The American embassy gave her a visa to re-enter the U.S., but the Russians would not let her leave. She called our office daily, begging for advice. Finally she told the authorities that she would not broadcast anti-American propaganda any longer and, furthermore, that she planned to tell all to the foreign press. She quickly received a Soviet exit visa and returned to the United States.

When cultural exchanges from western countries began to flood the Soviet Union, I was kept running for weeks to cover the opening of *My Fair Lady* and then the Russian line-up to see *Marty* (U.S.), *Genevieve* (Britain), and *The Hunchback of Notre Dame* (France).

Russians fight like troopers for tickets to any foreign presentation, particularly from America. But they are critical and discerning. The New York Philharmonic orchestra, directed by Leonard Bernstein, and the Boston and Philadelphia orchestras were actually the only entertainments the Americans sent to Russia that won reviews as glowing as those Americans gave performers the Soviets sent to the U.S.

Van Cliburn, originally "discovered" at a Tchaikovsky festival here, was a wild success on his return trip in 1960, during which he was mobbed by crowds of squealing girls. Such idolatry is unmatched in recent years in this country where everybody is supposed to be sensible and prim. The critics noted, however, that the concert pianist was still young and had a lot to learn.

Marty was the only American movie that received excellent newspaper reviews and word-of-mouth acclaim. *Oklahoma!* and *Rhapsody* were ripped to shreds by the critics, who blithely ignored the fact the Soviet authorities themselves had chosen these movies for their people. *My Fair Lady* was reviewed as first rate, but the performances were called uneven and many Russians didn't understand it. It died in Kiev. The American ballet shocked some reactionary traditionalists. The Ed Sullivan show was branded, by critics and audience alike, as corn.

Nonetheless, each event brought a slight glaze of internationalization. To see foreign entertainers on the stage, be it the Old Vic company of London or the Teatro Piccolo di Milano, was an event in itself. As late as 1956 foreign entertainment had been condemned as decadent.

One of the most noticeable changes was the increase in both social and business contacts between Americans and Russians. Some Russians were savagely defensive, some American tourists were hostile; but they seemed intensely curious about each other and somehow drawn together. At the July 4, 1959, party at the American embassy, the wife of a top American diplomat watched some American tourists cooing over the dapper Soviet deputy premier, Anastas Mikoyan. "Americans and Russians are dying to be friends," she commented.

The westernization, or even Americanization, of Moscow proceeded at such a lively clip that I decided to give an American-style cocktail party at Christmas and invite some Russians. "Now if you call the Union of Journalists and request some journalists to attend, they will send some," explained Henry Shapiro. "That's the way it's done."

But times had changed. Why not try inviting them

directly? I mailed some lively little cocktail invitation cards I'd bought in Stockholm instead of engraved invitations such as those always used by the diplomatic corps. I was told that Russian wives never accompany their husbands to official parties, but I invited the wives anyway, since I did not regard my party as official.

The Russians not only showed up, but they all brought their wives. Moreover, they drank everything in sight, and although the invitation had said "6:00 to 8:00" they stayed until 2:00 A.M.

I also decided to wear what I would wear if I were hostessing a cocktail party in America—black silk slacks and a black chiffon blouse, much to the consternation of my conservative boss.

The Russian wives inspected my hostess slacks from waist to ankle—disapproving, I felt. They also looked over the Danish and German furniture and the Swedish wooden birds and Christmas snowflakes that dangled from the ceiling. They drank nothing—until the bartender wandered by with some canned grapefruit juice and Coca-Cola. Fruit juice is scarce in Moscow, and Coca-Cola is the dreaded symbol of capitalism they've been reading about for decades. Both drinks had a lively business in the bar.

After my party, official-type Russians began accepting invitations to other correspondents' parties. Their telephone numbers were wildly circulated around the press corps. Soon the success of a cocktail fling was measured by how many Russians showed up. If it was a three-Russian party it was good; a six-Russian party made you an entertainer of distinction. And if you could get the editor of *Pravda* or *Izvestia*, you were a smash.

Both of these gentlemen—Pavel Satyukov and Alexei

Adzhubei, Khrushchev's son-in-law—showed up at a party at the Aragvy restaurant for visiting New York *Times* executive Clifton Daniel and his wife, Margaret Truman Daniel. The agile Adzhubei is the life of the Party and the party, too. He started a competitive songfest between the Russian and American guests, leading the Russian waiters and Satyukov in some spirited folk tunes. The Americans floundered miserably through "I've Been Workin' on the Railroad."

Later we got even, though. Adzhubei stood to announce jokingly that he now knew what Americans were like: the matches on the table read, "Join the U.S. Army."

Our astute ambassador, Llewellyn Thompson, immediately rose to his feet and said quietly, "But if you turn the matches over, you'll see it says, 'Help Put Out Fires.'" That was the only time we correspondents saw Adzhubei at a loss for a comeback.

Mikhail, my long-lost Russian friend, stayed in Leningrad and refused to come to my party. But after he heard how many Russians showed up, he decided the ice of the cold war must be getting a little slushy. He actually telephoned and invited me to lunch on his way back to Leningrad from a trip to Paris with a cultural delegation.

"Because it was a foreign country, I thought of you," he said. "I found myself looking for you on the street."

"Why didn't you look for me here? I was hurt," I confessed, "because you obviously didn't want to be friends after I came to Moscow. Have you been afraid to see me?"

After a few minutes he said, "There was something in your face, that first time we had dinner; I sensed you were holding something back, there was something I did not know . . ."

"Oh, Mikhail, ye Gods!" I said. I assured him, distinctly and carefully, that I did not work for (a) the CIA, or (b) the KGB.

We had several lunches after that, and walks in the park in Leningrad and Moscow. It was a pleasant, happy friendship—while it lasted.

8

Miss Moscow

New Year's Night of 1961 some of us foreign correspondents celebrating in the National Hotel restaurant were electrified by the sight at the next table.

"Could it be?" "Impossible!" "My God!" were our comments.

We were staring at some young Russian blades entertaining two fashionable creatures who could have been seen in a smart restaurant in London, Rome, or New York. They were wearing short dresses that had more than a nodding acquaintance with Paris. Their Italian bouffant "beehive" hairdos towered to the sky and were draped, heavily lacquered over their foreheads. Their drawn-on eyebrows swooped upward. The rims of their eyelids were black as soot.

We struck up a conversation with our neighbors to find out who the dazzling females were. The girls, we were told, were Russian fashion models from the government designing center, Dom Modeli. They had been abroad with a fashion show, had bought foreign clothes, and had learned how to do their hair and make-up. They are a sign of the changing face of the Soviet girl.

The subtle transformation of the hefty, muscled Bolshevik revolutionist into a pretty thing in curls and lipstick is one of the more provocative minor revolutions I have watched in Russia. The revolution of 1917 brought into being a type of woman more or less unique to this country. They are the elderly women I saw in 10-degrees-below-zero weather neatly sweeping snow off People's Street with their curved twig brooms. They are the perky, short girls in coveralls marching along the street by our office-apartment to their jobs as plasterers on the new apartment buildings. They are the sturdy women digging ditches, driving tractors, and getting their pictures on the front page of *Pravda* for picking ten bushels more corn than the next girl.

They are the girls who astonish tourists and sometimes bring patronizing remarks from westerners. I find their sturdiness and seriousness admirable. To me they have more purpose and character in their work-worn little fingers than all those party girls in Hollywood put together.

In many areas of the Soviet Union I have seen women in men's jobs. On a trip to Petrozavodsk, in lumber country like Montana, I watched lady lumberjacks grappling heavy logs with three-feet-long hooks to keep them on conveyor belts. The girls, some with braids peeking from beneath their headkerchiefs, wore blue coveralls, padded blue jackets, and knee-length black rubber boots. They slung those logs around as though they were matchsticks.

On a tour of a machine-tool factory near Moscow, I saw working women at close hand, to put it mildly. I excused myself to slip through a door marked "Women." There before me stood about thirty of those Soviet female factory workers, in cubicles with no doors. Each worker, heavy skirts slightly pulled up, stood on a platform reached by four little steps. Towering above me, in their bulky padded jackets, black *valenki* (felt peasant boots), and heads wrapped in dark scarfs, they looked for all the world like powerful Amazons. (They also confirmed what I'd heard from a Russian woman that peasant women don't wear bloomers because "if you do, how can you make pee-pee?")

Watching those hefty creatures I remembered what one psychoanalyst who visited Moscow had said: "Women basically like to suffer and make sacrifices more than men. After a revolution, women often take over and become more hard-working than men in the service of the cause. . . ."

Another category of Russian women are the *babushki,* or grandmothers. They are usually charged with raising the children now because mom is busy working. These old women are the bulwark of the Russian Orthodox Church, filling the houses of worship to overflowing on Sundays. Each one dresses virtually like the next, with a heavy beige wool scarf (costing from $40 to $80 but a lifelong possession) wrapped around her head and *valenki*. The Soviet press constantly rails against religion and religious customs left over from Old Russia, but I have watched these women stubbornly buying "holy water" in the churches from huge vats. They take the water home in milk pails or jars, to sip a few swallows each day, throughout the year.

Then there are the middle-aged career types, like the judge I saw at a traffic trial or those women in mannishly severe suits marching to their seats in the Supreme Soviet, their hair drawn back from cosmetic-less faces.

Apparently the younger city generation, under thirty-five, has had enough of the "equality" their mothers fought so hard for. They are trading a little of it for some old-fashioned femininity. They want more powder puffs and petticoats like their western sisters.

The government and Party are cognizant of this trend and have shifted from the revolutionists' idea that women should be like men. The year 1959 should go down in Soviet history as the year that pointed-toe shoes and Italian hairdos infiltrated right through the Iron Curtain.

Beauty shops, for example, have sprouted up all over Moscow and they are jammed, mostly with young girls. Most hairdressing "salons" in the Soviet Union are primitive, unclean, crowded, and old-fashioned by western standards.

First of all, you have to face up to standing as long as two hours in line to be waited on. So far the government's hairdressing trust has not invented the idea of making appointments.

Russian shampoo smells strange to a western nose. It also leaves the hair sticky. Most foreigners bring their own shampoo to the shops.

A Russian hairdresser usually wants to fix each customer's hair the same way: rolled up in metal curlers that went out of style in other countries twenty years ago; gooey wave set based on linseed oil plastered on the hair unless you firmly caution *"nyet."*

Hair dryers in some shops consist of three prongs of metal on a pole emitting one temperature: exceedingly hot. To keep the heat on your head, a towel is draped over the prongs. In most shops the operator does not give the customer a hair net to cover her hair or cotton to keep her ears from frying. After waiting in line to be served in the first place, the customers usually have to queue up again for the dryers.

The décor of a beauty shop is the usual Soviet Russian style. The "drying room" of the Metropole Hotel salon, for example, has a chandelier trimmed with white bugle beads, pale green walls, brown brocade drapes with a ball fringe, and straight chairs for the clientele.

After being baked, the customer returns to the operator for a comb-out. She or he often wants to apply metal clamps to squeeze in waves that can make you look like a marcelled shopgirl of the thirties. The hairdresser uses the same metal comb on everybody. Once a Russian translator showed me where she had been scratched by one of those metal combs: an infection had caused dangerous swellings all over her face and head.

All beauty shops when I arrived in 1959 had machine permanent waves which virtually vanished in western countries in the thirties. The Russian variety is an infernal-looking box of dials dangling long cords that are clamped onto your head. The hairdresser hands you a little sand "hourglass." After the sand runs through the hourglass a certain number of times, you are properly cooked.

But late in 1960, beauty shops began to improve. One of the stimulating aspects of life in Moscow is that you can watch the city and the people change before your eyes. This progress in *parikmakherskayi,* or hairdressing shops, was quite possibly helped along by the American Exhibition's hairdressing display, which was a rousing success, right down to the colored plastic hair rollers and hair lacquer.

The first machineless, chemical permanents arrived in Moscow at the Metropole Hotel in late 1960. They were made in East Germany. The resultant lines of hopeful customers extended down the hallway. The Metropole also recently acquired new hooded hair dryers made in Czechoslovakia.

One of the American hairdressers from the 1959 Exhibition visited a newly opened hairdressing salon on Kuznetsky Most, the street that used to be the elegant shopping center of Moscow in czarist days. He showed the operators how he cut hair with a razor blade and "teased" it to make a so-called Italian or bouffant hair style.

By 1961 this shop had evolved into an establishment approaching those in Warsaw and Prague, if not Paris. At least three operators know how to set hair in the bouffant western styles. The shop has machineless permanents, hair nets, hair spray, and plastic hair rollers acquired from East Germany, Budapest, and helpful foreign customers.

The price is the best part of all: the equivalent of 75 cents for a wash and set. I paid $6.20 for a haircut and permanent at the Kuznetsky Most "salon," as it is called, to borrow a French word. There you also can buy a "face mask" for 80 cents, a facial for 90 cents, and a make-up job for 90 cents. (Most customers tip up to double the bill. To counteract this bourgeois tendency, "communist brigades" have been formed in some Moscow beauty shops. By their mirrors is a sign: "We do not want tips.")

Tucked among the political propaganda in two women's magazines now are articles on clothing, make-up, and hairdos. The advice is most unlike the avant-garde set on Kuznetsky Most. "The most popular hairdo at present is either almost straight with slightly curling ends or very big waves with bangs," one 1961 article says. Another offers a do-it-yourself hair-lacquer recipe: "Spray your hair lightly with a solution of one part rosin to ten parts alcohol and a few drops of perfume."

Soviet women are so interested in how they look that there's an institute for plastic surgery that does nose bobs. One "polyclinic," No. 6 on Kalinin Street, dispenses shots of a "liquid of youth" that is supposed to take years off your face. Customers buy the "elixir," actually a solution of "2 per cent Novocain," as the box says, on prescription at a drug store. The women doctors at the polyclinic told me the results haven't been as good as they had hoped. But the women still flock in for the shots.

Although cosmetics were not in favor after the revolution, it's acceptable now for women to march toward communism wearing make-up. Anything more than a little is still frowned upon, however, both by the press and in private society.

Since the late fifties, cosmetics have been cheap and plentiful in Moscow—a fact which undoubtedly stimulates their more widespread use. You can buy them in perfume shops, at sidewalk stands, and in department stores. Young girls are the main customers.

I tried cleansing cream in tubes for the equivalent of 41 cents with such names as "Lanolin" and "Almond." For 61 cents I bought whitish face powder called "Moscow" in a small box decorated with views of the Kremlin. Lipstick ranges from 50 cents to $1.25. The powder is heavy and the lipstick greasy. The predominant lipstick color is purple.

Lipstick brushes and eyelash combs have not reached Moscow yet. Mascara has, and costs only 40 cents in a cardboard box. I never could find any underarm deodorant. Several Russians I've asked never heard of such a product. Its absence is noticeable in restaurants, subways, and theaters.

Soviet planners have imported some cosmetics from the communist bloc, and in 1961 some lipsticks from England. One skin-cream factory in Latvia copies a western skin cream, Nivea, right down to the same navy-blue and white label. The factory labels the cream "Nivea" in Russian letters. A tin the size of shoe polish costs 61 cents. It is heavier than the western kind, and I don't like the smell as well.

For the girls down on the *kolkhoz* (collective farm), one Soviet women's magazine, *Worker*, offers a homemade face cream: beat one egg yoke, add glass of cream, juice of lemon, *and* an ounce of vodka. It sounds like a Golden Fizz but you put it on your face.

Another cream is made in villages out of cucumber juice. It's supposed to whiten the skin.

Russian toothpaste is tasteless. It makes no claim to whiten, deodorize, or abolish cavities. No cosmetic advertising warns a *Moskvitchka* she won't catch a husband unless she uses "Sputnik" lipstick. Soviet packaging is plain. Western cosmetics could be sold more cheaply, too, if their manufacturers did not spend most of the retail price on advertising and packaging.

But do women *want* make-up cheap and plain? "I have a friend who spoils me, he brought me this from Paris," a well-dressed Russian woman standing next to me at the Gum cosmetic counter told me. She pulled out an Elizabeth Arden lipstick. For her the lovely gold case apparently was half the fun.

The perfume business looks more western. Whoever runs the perfume trust must have overfulfilled his seven-year quota already. Department stores in Moscow devote approximately three times the space to perfumes that the average western store does.

The scents are packaged with tassels, colored paper printed with Russian scenery, and in bottles shaped like the Kremlin towers. Prices of real perfume range from $5.00 a half ounce up, cologne from $2.50 for three ounces and up.

Soviet men are not dragged into danger by wicked perfumes. In this land of strict morality the perfumes are staidly named "Red Moscow," "Evening," and "Stone Flower." To the last sniff, they are heavy and sweet.

Much of a Russian female's beautifying still takes place at the public baths, a holdover from the old days. There she can check in for a complete beauty overhaul—a hairdressing, pedicure, manicure, and steambath. The last is a welcome change from the crowded bathroom queue in multifamily apartments.

I finally mustered the nerve to visit a public bath. In czarist days Pushkin and Chekhov sat in the men's section and sipped champagne. Merchants took their "lady friends" to private "family" bathrooms; but now even husbands and wives go to separate sections.

After paying the equivalent of 71 cents, I entered a room resplendent with gold chandeliers, statues, orange-fringed lampshades, and brocaded walls—faded reminders of prerevolutionary elegance. Russian females of all sizes were undressing on long settees. Knee-length pink cotton bloomers are popular in Moscow, I noticed. Some of the older women wore blue satin brassieres and cinched themselves into pink satin corsets. Many of the young girls wore knitted vests, garter belts, bloomers, and knitted slips.

Most of the figures, at all ages and heights, were wide, wide, and wider.

I undressed with many curious eyes on me. One woman asked me where I bought the bag in which I packed my soap. I explained it was a canvas bag that airlines give to passengers.

The only way to enter the steamroom is to walk the length of the dressing room wearing only a bar of soap and a shower cap.

The steamroom looked like a healthy Dante's Inferno. Through the haze of steam I saw twenty or thirty women sitting on marble benches, feet in one pan of hot water, another pan at their side for scrubbing.

For 41 cents a professional scrubber went over me, every inch, three times, with strips of rough linden bark and squash skin. Many women were washing their waist-length hair.

In an adjoining steamroom, nude female attendants poured water on hot bricks while customers beat themselves with birch branches. "Why are you here? You foreigners have private bathrooms in your apartments," a Russian woman remarked between branch slaps.

In another room is a small warm-water swimming pool the size of a Roman bathtub. It is adorned with a silver-colored statue of a nude little boy.

The prettiest girls I've noticed in Moscow are ballerinas, possibly because the constant exercise keeps them slim and graceful. The Bolshoi ballet school is filled with 250 budding stars who some day will take their place on the Bolshoi Theater stage. The school, in an old building off a courtyard near the theater, is a veritable convent where young Moscow beauties, aged eight to nineteen, study six days a week, dedicating their lives to ballet.

One day I had a rare invitation to watch an advanced class. Of the thirteen teen-age students practicing classical ballet, one was a foreigner. I had no trouble picking her out. The twelve Russian girls, students in the school since they were eight, were supple creatures who danced emotionally and dramatically, carefully watching their bodies in a mirror. Each lithe figure was like a Degas painting. The foreign girl moved inhibitedly and with less fire. "She came to us at fourteen and it's too late to correct the mistakes she learned in her own country," the teacher confided later.

I, too, studied ballet under a Bolshoi school teacher, but not in quite the same way. Many foreign women become so enamored of the ballet that they keep up their figures by studying "fourth position, fifth position" from a Bolshoi ballet master in a special class. Twice a week one winter I donned a "leotard"—really long black winter underwear—and struggled through *"plissé"* and *"tour de jête"* in the class conducted in the ballroom of the American ambassador's house. I found it a strain to get one foot onto the lowest rung of the exercise bar. The patient but occasionally despairing teacher would sigh, "Ah, terrible," and "Ah, worse," while the diplomats' and correspondents' wives tried to bend their backs gracefully.

Mrs. Llewellyn Thompson, the ambassador's wife, also organized a Russian folk-dancing class for those members of the foreign colony who prefer to dream they are in the Moiseyev company.

In the realm of clothes, many Russian women have been

incurably hooked by the high-fashion hashish that slipped in when Khrushchev opened the door.

Until the late fifties the Russians were too busy making machinery to bother much with feminine frills, but in 1959 the bombshell hit. The Soviet government agreed to import a fashion show from Christian Dior in Paris as part of the Franco-Soviet cultural exchange. Style shows twice daily for five days were sold out weeks in advance. Even western women were fascinated by the toothpick-slim dramatic mannequins mincing down the runway in beautiful Dior clothes. It was the first western fashion show in the flesh Russians had seen, let alone one from Paris.

A month later I saw Dior-style clothes on the streets—copies of course. Shawl collars, barrel-shaped coats, three-quarter-length suit sleeves, and loose jackets began to appear. (The figures of the Dior models were not so popular. "Spaghetti legs," snorted one Russian woman to me.)

Fashion shows may seem out of keeping with Marxism, but one from England in 1961 was another sell-out success, and nowadays Gum runs its own show twice daily on the top floor of the sprawling store. Here, in a long room with those ever-present chandeliers and heavy drapes, attractive models, rounder than the Paris variety but wearing make-up and short hair, parade on a runway. A five-piece orchestra plays semi-jazz background music. The audience, mainly women, sits sketching furiously in wooden chairs.

The younger, style-conscious Russian women look better each year. Most of the styles shown in Gum would not be acceptable in a western fashion show today because they are outdated, but the Russians are catching up. For instance, I saw a wool dress with a bell skirt at one Gum fashion show that could have passed in any western country. Many outfits still sport the shawl collars introduced in 1959 but no longer popular in the West. A housedress with a detachable peplum was featured at one show I attended (although peplums are not becoming to Soviet hips). Evening gowns are rarely shown, but late in 1960 store windows began to stop pedestrian traffic with short cocktail dresses in colored taffeta with high, discreet necklines, and in 1961 short skirts to the knees finally became Orthodox Marxist for the younger set. (Sometimes the store windows display the closest thing to a Soviet tuxedo—a dark suit, $140, with a dark bow tie—an object of wonder when you consider that some Soviet men still do not wear neckties.)

Members of the new "sophisticated" set in Moscow have their clothes made at dressmakers' or sew outfits themselves at home. Some dressmakers have their own styles or will copy from sketches such as those Russian women scribble at the fashion shows. The wife of an American diplomat paid $60 and furnished the fabric to have a Moscow dressmaker copy her favorite Paris dress; the workmanship was average, she reported. Wool fabrics cost from $5 to $45 a yard.

The younger women also storm the stores for more modern, choice items, often foreign-made. I spotted some fairly fashionable shoes: they were Czech. A blue satin two-way stretch girdle for $15 in one shop window was East German. Even white ruffly falsies are on sale now at $3! (That item isn't needed much in Soviet Russia.)

The average Russian woman, who wears mostly store-bought clothes, is still rather uninterestingly dressed, by western standards, however. So-called ready-to-wear Soviet clothes are not ready for my closet. First of all, they are expensive. Russians pay $25 to $40 for a silk crepe dress; cotton dresses are $7 or $8. Those prices are not bad. But a wool dress is at least $60. A suit that looks to me worth $40 costs $80. An average-looking coat is $160. Plastic "leather" handbags are $7. Raincoats with a printed lining and matching hood cost $25 to $30; I have seen a similar style in New York for $10.

Secondly, Russian ready-to-wear is very out of style—again according to western trends. Uninspired prints, maroon and blue crepe dresses, hip-length mannish fitted suits still fill many Soviet shop windows.

In the third place the ready-to-wear business in Russia makes little effort to provide variety, and even Russians are beginning to complain. But why should clothing factories make different styles, planners reason. Most over-coats for men and women are navy blue or brown, so that the Moscow streets in winter are a mixture of somber colors. The favorite line for women is a princess-style fitted coat with a silver fox fur collar. According to western fashion experts, they couldn't have thought of a better style to make heavy women look heavier. (My dreams of buying Russian furs quickly fizzled. I am told the good Russian furs are exported. Nothing much is on sale except black fox skins at $80 and up, small mink stoles at $800 and up, a two-skin fox capelet at $196, a Kolinsky fur coat from China, styled much more fashionably than the Russian coats, at $1,000; a Russian rabbit coat at $140.)

The average woman over thirty wears a felt hat on the back of her head and shoes with thick heels and round toes or, in winter, ankle-high shoes with a heavy sole. Brown cotton stockings *plus* ankle socks are worn in cold weather. Nylons cost about $2, and are plentiful, even in bright colors, although the colored ones are not popular.

The American Exhibition's fashion show and models in pointed shoes added to the Russians' ideas of what goes on in the outside world fashionwise. Soon after the exhibition, Gum blossomed out with a window full of beautiful pointed shoes, the first I saw in a Soviet store. Crowds still cluster around that window now, two years later (they don't change the window displays often in this country!). The pink and blue and gold brocade shoes are as lovely as their Parisian counterparts. When I rushed to buy some, the salesgirl said the shoes cost from $40 to $70 a pair and are made only to order. I never noticed any on any Russian feet, but I assume some were made. However, in late 1960, red pointed-toe shoes from London with curving "Louis" heels were sold out in a matter of hours at $18 to $25 a pair (the price in England: between $8 and $11)—one effect of the Anglo-Soviet trade pact signed on May 24.

As in any country, plenty of reactionary men are opposed to the "new look" the young girls are acquiring. "Our Soviet women never will go in for those unhealthy pointed shoes. You see, our women's feet aren't pointed like yours. They can't wear those shoes," one middle-aged Russian husband said to me.

He appeared surprised when I yanked off my shoe and showed him my feet didn't come to a sharp point, either.

Another not young Russian man snorted as we watched a make-up demonstration at the American Exhibition, "We don't like our girls with that paint on their faces. Who wants to see a girl in the afternoon looking different from the way she did in the morning?"

The objections of men haven't mattered much in most countries. I'll still stake my last kopeck that Russian women are happily becoming slaves to hairdos and hemlines.

The other day a Russian couple I know was among several invited to a black-tie dinner and dancing party in the foreign colony. The Soviet wife came dressed in a beautiful beige bouffant tulle ball gown, which must have been either purchased abroad or made by a Moscow dress-maker. The next day I asked her what she thought of the gala affair. "You American women really weren't dressed properly," she said with a tilt of her pert Russian snub nose. "You all wore cocktail dresses, not ball gowns. And furthermore," she added, "the taped dance music was not very good. We have better music on our tape recorder at home."

These people are learning fast.

9

The New Soviet Dog

Premier Khrushchev had just returned from France. The Russians were plying American acquaintances with questions about the scheduled summit conference and President Eisenhower's planned visit to the Soviet Union.

But the terse cable that arrived at our office in April 1960 from UPI in New York had little to do with the gradually warming Soviet-western relations that were shaping world history:

> 02111 shapiro chicago client says returning tourists report seeing no dogs moscow stop asks story explain stop billfox

I was surprised to discover dogs and cats in Moscow after I arrived, too. Communist China had a well-publicized "sanitary" campaign to eliminate dogs and sparrows. My mental image of Russia had been of a militant, emotionless society that had purged its pups and pusses.

There are pets in Moscow, although not as many as in western cities. In this semi-Oriental land, animals were not regarded with much gentleness even thirty years ago. But the liberalizing forces at work in the Soviet Union have wrought a kinder attitude toward animals, too.

In the last few years Russians have become as daffy

about city pigeons as the English are about wild birds. Many households have dogs and cats. Most children have either goldfish, guinea pigs, or fancy white pigeons. Swans now paddle around ponds in Moscow parks. A Russian woman told me, "Thirty years ago little boys would have stoned those swans to death."

An American correspondent I reported this to guffawed sarcastically, "So they killed off peasants in forced collectivization; they colonized central Asia and are set on the world's becoming communist—but at least they don't stone the swans any more!"

Anyway, the Soviet government now has a calculated policy to regard animals and birds with kindness.

Many tourists think Muscovites have no pets because pets are barred from many privileges. You often see as many dogs as humans on a London bus or a Brussels streetcar. There's hardly a Paris grocery store without a cat washing his face while perched atop the vegetables. Pets in Moscow are not allowed as guests in restaurants, stores, or buses. Thus they are seldom seen downtown where tourists abound. But when you investigate back streets you'll see cats decorating apartment windows and dogs walking their owners.

Moscow has street cats, although not as many as one sees in Rome, Paris, and other cities. I've never observed any in Moscow that appeared to be starving. The *liftorshiki* and *dvorniki,* the grandmothers who care for the elevator and yard of our apartment house, daily leave out food for a clan of homeless cats that resides in a basement storeroom. The house manager once declared the "cat room" unhealthy and boarded up the open basement window to keep them out; but our sympathetic policeman-guard helped the *dvorniki* pry back the boards.

Recently an American correspondent saw a Russian man on the street holding a Siamese cat in his arms. He was surrounded by a crowd of Russians, many of whom wanted to buy it. Such cats apparently are rare in the Soviet Union.

Otherwise the only alleged "thoroughbred" I could track down is the Russian Siberian. Russians claim the Siberian is a definite breed. It looks like what in the United States is called a long-haired domestic (alley) cat. However, Siberian cats have a distinct personality, a flavor of wildness from the rough plains. They "talk" a lot, retrieve toys like a dog, and race furiously up and down chairs, people, and curtains.

When a Muscovite decides to acquire man's best friend, he goes the whole way. In a manner that seems impractical to outsiders, he buys the biggest dog he can find. A large pet hardly fits the crowded small apartments. A Pekingese would be more appropriate. But the most popular breeds are German shepherds, boxers, Airedales, and Irish setters. I have seen several dachshunds, two unclipped large French poodles, and a Scotty on the streets.

"Big dogs guard our apartments against thieves," a Russian explained to me.

The Soviet economy does not allow many consumer goods for people, let alone four-footed citizens. Thus, shops featuring mink-trimmed sweaters for poodles do not exist. However, one day I saw a dachshund in a little green sweater his mistress had knitted for him. The only dog accessories you can buy are muzzles, leashes, and collars in hunting-fishing equipment stores.

Food shops have never heard of canned dog food. A Moscow dog or cat gets meat scraps and bones sold at outdoor markets, or leftovers from the family table. Dog pedicures and clips aren't regarded as necessary to a dog's life, either. Most French poodles in the city either go unclipped or are cut by their owners.

In addition to being unwelcome in shops and buses, dogs must follow other strict laws laid down by the Soviet regime. A dog must be leashed when he's outside. Rest rooms are limited to curbs; parks are out of bounds. If a dog lives in a communal apartment, he must keep to his family's rooms and out of everybody else's. Big dogs must be muzzled out of doors, and all dogs must have rabies shots.

Moscow has three dog clubs that stage ten dog shows a year. You can buy puppies there for $20 and up. One American embassy wife bought a black French poodle for $25 (but the white star on his chest would disqualify him as a thoroughbred in western dog shows).

The Soviet school system includes a canine school where for $7.50 for ten lessons a pooch can learn how to be well behaved in Soviet society.

Some Russians say the pigeon craze was ushered into Russia as part of the "doves for peace" campaign. Or perhaps the sensitive Russians wanted their cities to look like other western metropolises. Now while most other cities from Paris to Pittsburgh are trying to discipline or eliminate their pigeons, the Soviet government actually encourages them!

The pigeon population, estimated in the press at 80,000, must observe the rules of controlled "communist morality," just like dogs and humans. For example, Moscow is dotted with "sidewalk cafés" for pigeons. These are areas on public squares, or corners of wide sidewalks, marked off with neat pigeon-high blue picket fences. Signs read, "Watch out for pigeons" or "Pigeon feeding place." Not only did city officials build these areas, but the government actually feeds the pigeons. Although Lenin decreed, "He who doesn't work, doesn't eat," women in white uniforms daily take seed and water to the nonworking birds at the pigeon restaurants.

This plan, intentionally or otherwise, seems to discipline the birds to remain in or around those fenced-in areas and not to seek handouts from people elsewhere.

Some pigeon feeding places are right in the streets. Moscow traffic rules include one ordering motorists to drive carefully around such spots so as not to assassinate the diners.

Many apartment houses also have marked-off areas where you can toss food for the feathered neighbors. The pigeon restaurant for our apartment house is underneath my kitchen window. I don't dare lean out for fear of being pelted by a shower of bread crumbs from above. Russians in our building also leave twigs in the courtyard for the birds to take away for nests.

Pigeons benefit from the Soviet Union's seven-year plan calling for 15 million new apartments. Birdhouses have been built around Moscow. True to communist tradition, they are communal apartment houses, each little building accommodating twenty bird families—and identical pigeon apartments and blue-fenced sidewalk cafés for birds can be seen in the other big cities of the U.S.S.R.

Many Moscow youngsters breed fancy white pouter pigeons in wooden cages on the balconies of their apart-

ments. These and other pets are bought and sold in a
lively spot of free enterprise on a square about a mile
from our office. This is Moscow's "Bird Market," still thriv-
ing in an old section of the city.

At the entrance one day I found black German shepherd
puppies wriggling in a basket. Boys held out white pigeons
in little wooden cages. Children shoved and crowded to get
around a big box alive with gray, black, and white rabbits.
Teen-age boys examined tropical fish in glass jars held by
other teen-age boys. In covered stalls, caged canaries sang
their lungs out in hopes of finding a new home.

That day the hagglers at the Bird Market offered no
kittens—my reason for being there—so I went home
empty-handed. During my first winter in Moscow little fat
brown mice moved into my warm kitchen. Henry Shapiro
decided a cat would be cheaper than calling in the exterminator every week. So he issued an *ukaze*, or order,
that the office-apartment could acquire a cat.

The Shapiros' Tartar maid, Rya, knew some Tartars who
had Siberian cats in their basement. The mother cat had
kittens regularly in the coalbin next to the furnace. Rya
brought me one imp with long charcoal-gray fur. I named
her Natasha, after the heroine of *War and Peace*. My
maid, Tonya, immediately gave her a diminutive, as
Russians do: Natashka.

Henry's wife, Ludmilla, and Rya gave Natashka a bath.
After the soapsuds and the coal dust were rinsed off,
Natashka turned out to be white, orange, and black.
Natashka had the manners of one born in a coalbin; but
after a few days she got used to her sandbox in the bathroom and quickly demanded the elegant life, as cats will
do.

There is no cat food as such in Moscow. I told Tonya to buy beef liver, kidneys, melts, or heart, which are cheap cat dinners in America. But these items are either as expensive as steak or hard to find. Tonya brought home instead a whole fish. Apparently as in the manner of her peasant home, she slapped the critter—head, tail, bones, and all—on the floor of the kitchen for the cat to eat.

"Food is not put on the floor. Cats should not eat fish bones, and the food must be cut into bite-size pieces," I said.

Next day Tonya brought beefsteak cut up in the market for beef stroganoff. "I told the butcher this was for a foreign lady whose cat wants little pieces," said Tonya with a hearty laugh.

I suspect this incident was the week's joke in our neighborhood.

Despite my pleas for cheaper fare, Tonya still brings stroganoff meat. What else but the best for a foreigner's cat? Natashka has grown quite insufferable, scorning thin Russian milk and insisting on sleeping under my blankets.

She earns her keep, however, by nabbing a mouse occasionally. During the night when I hear a crash and scurry in the kitchen, I quickly shut my bedroom door. I have learned from experience that, like all cats, Natashka brings the mouse and deposits it on my pillow in the middle of the night—usually still alive—as a present.

Before long I discovered Natashka brought worms from the coalbin. She was vomiting them like spaghetti. Tonya told me to take her to a cat and dog hospital. Yes, there are such establishments in Moscow. We found twenty-four listed in the 1958 business telephone directory.

Off we went, winding for miles through an old part of

Moscow that tourists seldom see, past sagging log houses, a crematorium in a building that looked like a palace, a factory, a new apartment building, finally through a gate to a large yellow and white stucco building. Russians stared and smiled at our big office car, an American Chevrolet, gliding through the streets with Victor, our chauffeur, in front and Natashka riding in style in the back window.

The hospital was like a people's polyclinic only on a more modest scale. One woman doctor, one woman nurse, and four assistants cared for the patients, including that day a tiger and two guinea pigs.

The arrival of their first foreign customer brought me quick service and the usual hospitable tour through the place. The doctor said there were no pet hospitals in Russia before the revolution. Now each district of Moscow has one.

The nurses showed me the sick tiger (from the Moscow circus) and twenty dogs, mostly boxers and German shepherds, in big cages. In the waiting room sat a little girl with a black and white short-haired tomcat. He was carefully swaddled in a blanket just like a Russian baby so that he could not move his arms or feet. Two boys held a big boxer and a woman caressed a white Spitz.

In the examination room under a picture of Lenin were cabinets holding penicillin and other modern drugs. Natashka was weighed by my stepping on the scales first with her, then without her. Her case history also was taken.

The UPI calico cat was deposited in a clean, small cage in a separate building for cats. Her ward mates were a collection of eight Siberians and alley cats.

It was two weeks before Natashka came home, covered with oil which constituted the worming treatment. She had to be de-wormed three times and almost died, the doctor said.

A few months later we had a new problem. Natashka began rolling seductively on the floor. Tonya offered the traditional peasant solution: "Put some oil underneath her tail and let her out to enjoy love."

Having her spayed at the hospital sounded like a safer idea, as the office could not hold a family of cats. When we first called for an appointment, the hospital was quarantined for some unexplained reason. Finally when we thought we could not bear Natashka's cries any longer, Arthur, our translator, left me a note: "I called the cat hospital. The surgeon says Natashka can be accepted Thursday. But you must have a surgical gown made for her, to be put on four legs, across her stomach, and tied on top, since she must be prevented from licking her wounds."

In America cats are taken home as a rule the day following the operation with a simple bandage wrapped tightly around their abdomens. No cat can dig her way out of that. A week later the cat returns to the hospital to have the stitches removed. It is a most uncomplicated matter.

Tonya made Natashka a little white surgical gown, a copy of the kind people wear. I was told by the doctor to call back in a week to inquire as to Natashka's condition. When I did, I was told to call back in another week. Then came another delay. I sensed they were afraid to tell me Natashka had had difficulties. Finally the doctor said she had slipped out of that surgical gown and ripped open her wound.

Four weeks later, Natashka finally came home. The wound still wasn't healed and was covered with purple medicine. She had to hobble around the house in her surgical gown for another week, looking like a space dog ready to take off in a rocket.

Two other correspondents encountered similar difficulty having their cats spayed. The doctor told one his cat broke her stitches because "she is too fat." The fat had to be cut out. The animal arrived home too weak to stand, covered with excrement, and with an infected hole in her side. Then, after all that trouble, the cat came into heat anyway and eloped with a tomcat down the street. The operation was not a success.

However, Moscow residents explain that spaying cats is an operation only recently begun in Soviet pet hospitals. The technique has not yet been mastered.

The same Russians claim to have made great advances in cancer and heart research; they have eye medicines unavailable in the West; they have stamped out many diseases through vaccination. Natashka's adventures in the hospital indicate that Soviet medicine, like some other aspects of Soviet life, can be uneven. Nonetheless, just the fact that a once semi-Oriental city now has twenty-four pet hospitals is notable progress in itself.

Natashka (and my pocketbook) benefit from the free medical service available in the Soviet Union. There was no charge for her initial examination. After that she was charged the equivalent of 41 cents a day for room and board and 61 cents for worm medicine.

In addition to pets, other animals are occasionally seen around Moscow. Some horses, with the traditional wooden collar around their necks, pull carts through the streets. Although the Party officially frowns on gambling, the Hippodrome track for harness racing caters to a group of stubborn touts. One cold Sunday I braved a blizzard to cheer the ponies at races held traditionally in the dead of winter with the customers sitting outdoors.

In Sukhumi, Georgia, I visited a monkey farm where monkeys are used for medical research on everything from cancer to nervous breakdowns. The famous Soviet space dogs that survived their trips, including Belka, Strelka, Chornushka, and Zvezduchka, were introduced to foreign correspondents at press conferences.

In fact, the favorite research animal in Russia since the days of Pavlov and his tinkling bell is the dog. When I covered Hollywood for United Press, I interviewed many four-footed actors from Trigger the horse to Lassie the dog. But no film-town interview was as strange as the day I strolled around Moscow with a two-headed dog.

Pirat, the dog who owned one of the heads, was an experimental German shepherd at the First Medical Institute, an ordinary stone building on a side street. A transplanting surgeon, Dr. Vladimir Demikhov, grafted the head and two front legs of a puppy onto Pirat's neck, joining the major blood vessels.

The puppy's head lived thirty days. I went for a walk with the dog, or rather the one and a third dogs, twenty days after the operation. Children in school uniforms clustered around us to stare as their grandfathers must have ogled at horseless carriages.

At first Pirat resisted the walk because he had to be led by his ears. Where would you put the collar? Otherwise he didn't seem to care whether two heads are better than one.

"The big dog feels some kind of inconvenience but he doesn't know what it is," explained Demikhov. "Sometimes the puppy will playfully bite the ear of the big dog and Pirat will shake his head. But Pirat never has tried to scratch or kick off the extra head."

I felt slightly ill. When interviewing two-headed dogs, it's better not to have lunch first. Finally I recovered from the shock and petted big Pirat. The puppy head became drowsy in the sunshine and dozed off, indicating that the two heads slept and woke independently.

The doctor explained that the maintenance of normal behavior in both dogs was the reason why he thought the operation could be as sensational as a sputnik medically. Other head graftings had been tried but normal activity was not retained.

While we stood in a yard behind the institute, the doctor put a pan of water under the puppy's nose. It drank, probably because its mouth felt dry. The water ran immediately out of the puppy's esophagus, the end of which stuck out of the big dog's shaved neck. The puppy did not need to eat or drink because he was nourished by the big dog's body on two rabbits a day, porridge, and bread.

Dr. Demikhov said he has had unsuccessful experiments with at least 150 dogs who died, an admission that would bring down the wrath of American anti-vivisectionists. His staff "dog-naps" lean strays in the country or suburbs for experimentation.

I have visited Demikhov's Frankenstein-like laboratory

several times. Once he spoke about operations in which he planned to transplant a second heart into a human being and graft a leg onto the body of a girl who had lost her own. At this writing the operations have never gone past the announcement stage.

10

The Private Life
of a Muscovite

One sunny Sunday two correspondents and I decided to eat dinner in a restaurant at the suburban river port of Khimki.

As we drove up, we saw people hurrying to board a big pleasure boat which left at 8:00 P.M., returning at 11:00 P.M., time for dinner aboard. We joined the crowd streaming up the gangplank. Some of the men were playing accordions or guitars, the women softly crooning Russian folk songs. It was one of those moments that made me smile and love the country.

As the big white boat churned down the calm river, we hightailed it to the dining room; but instead of finding the expected queue, we entered an almost empty dining room. After eating we walked around the boat to discover why. Four couples danced to a staid Soviet "jazz" orchestra on deck. Through some of the open windows we could see other couples eating, singing, and drinking in private cabins. Most of the windows were discreetly shuttered and the curtains drawn.

"It's a floating motel!" said one of my companions.

We sauntered back to the dining room for a Turkish coffee. It was a warm evening, so I slipped off the jacket of my striped linen suit. My blouse underneath was black, low-cut, and sleeveless.

The teenagers at the next table looked at me and began to giggle and whisper. Within two minutes the maître d' walked over and stiffly ordered me to put on my jacket.

There might be love-making going on in the cabins, but, by the beard of Lenin, no woman was going to have a bare look in *his* restaurant!

The sum and substance of sex among the Socialists may be illustrated by that evening on the Khimki boat. In the first place, it points up an apparent Soviet attitude: sex and morals are Victorian, too, along with the fringed lampshades and lace curtains. This appears to be a combination of traditional Russian reticence toward sex with a thick frosting of strict Communist morality. But beneath the Victorian primness about low-cut blouses, the Russians go about pursuing each other in their own quiet, unaffected way.

Exactly what goes on in the love lives of Russians is difficult to discern exactly because no figures are available. The U.S.S.R. Union of Writers has yet to come out with a Soviet Kinsey report. There are no published statistics on abortions, illegitimate births, or prostitution. The only available "statistic" is one on divorce. The Soviets boast that their divorce rate is lower than that of the U.S., but this is not regarded as useful because total figures on marriages and divorces are not published. Because of the difficulty in obtaining a divorce and the apartment shortage, there also are many "unregistered" or common-law marriages in the Soviet Union.

In 1960 a prominent sociologist I knew from California toured a Moscow hospital for unwed mothers.

"What are the reasons why these girls have babies?" the sociologist asked the hospital director.

"Because they don't want to be married," was the reply.

As in any society, teenagers probably are both lusty and chaste. Moscow University used to have coeducational housing for its students, but when foreign students appeared on the scene and Russian girls began to go out with Africans, Egyptians, Frenchmen, and others, segregation by sex was instituted in the dormitories. Now no girl is even allowed on the men's floor of a dormitory at Moscow University. I was denied admittance to interview an American student there.

One hears conflicting reports. A 25-year-old Komsomol (member of the Young Communist League) assured me that young men marry around twenty-four or twenty-five and seldom have premarital relations. "The Party stresses an active program of sports to take the minds of young people off, er, well, sex," he said, blushing. "This is one reason for the sports palaces and the Young Pioneer Clubs [the communist "Boy Scout" branch] where ballet, hobbies, and sports are taught."

On the other hand, the only Soviet book I heard of on the subject, *Problems of Sex Education,* by a Dr. Atarov (no first name listed), said there was some premarital sexual activity among young people. But, said Dr. Atarov, such relations are "often very genuine" and "very frequently end in marriage."

Author Atarov decreed that under communism sex should be "natural but regulated . . . not occurring without love, affection, and comradeship." He says the equal status of men and women, which the Soviet propagandists claim the Communist party virtually invented, has resulted in "decent" relations between Soviet men and women.

However, the book admits that beneath this Russian-communist code of morals lurks many a strayer. The author labels them, "the Vamp," "the Seducer," and "the Promiscuous Rat" (meaning married men who have affairs on the side).

Foreigners who have lived long in Moscow comment, "Russians are prim on the surface, but underneath they're not." One Russian friend told me, "We have a much healthier attitude toward sex and regard it as a natural thing. In western countries you treat it as something shameful and dirty."

I asked another friend, Nikolai, whether Russians are passionate people as Latins are reputed to be. "Do not be misled by our sedate appearance," he advised. "You have a saying in English: still waters run deep."

"Girls are easy to get," I heard a Russian intellectual say.

Abortions were acquired easily in "abortatoriums" after the revolution. They were banned in 1936 but legalized again in 1956. They are performed by reputable doctors in hospitals, for any woman who requests one. The attitude toward abortions is not loose. Women's magazines occasionally feature articles discouraging women from having such operations.

One Russian woman I know with two children told me she had had an abortion. She said she and her husband could not afford another child. She whispered the news to me, and said I was the only person she had confided in. She sounded shy about the operation. But other Russians assure me it carries no social stigma.

The official attitude toward unwed mothers in the Soviet Union appears more gentle than that in many western countries. They are called "single mothers." In an article in the *Literaturnaya Gazetta,* a schoolteacher in Leningrad revealed that 20 per cent of the students in her class were illegitimate. My Russian friend Ivan told me that at his place of work there is a single mother of forty and "none of us thinks anything of it."

Both these cases result from the heavy casualties suffered by Russia in World War II. After the war many women could not find husbands but had the children they wanted anyway, without being exposed to the intense social disapproval encountered in some countries.

The Soviet press has called for abolishing the question, "Father's name?" from birth certificates so that such children will not suffer the brand of illegitimacy.

However, many young Russians, for whom husbands are in plentiful supply, appear to be shocked by the idea of single women having babies.

"There is just as much concern over it as in any other country," a relatively sophisticated young wife told me.

"It depends upon the circumstances," a young communist man said. "If a girl is just having a fling, she is regarded as foolish. If there are serious reasons, the woman is not thought to be bad."

Contraceptives for men are easy to buy at an *aptyeka,* or drug store, at 5 cents. One Soviet medical magazine complained they were of poor quality. It also objected to the shortage and poor quality of women's contraceptives.

Many Communists maintain the Soviet Union has no prostitutes. "We have plenty of work for women," my party friend, Anatoly, said, looking me right in the eye. He is either naïve or passing along one of those "unrealities" sensitive Russians are so capable of repeating. Many women have motives other than unemployment for plying such a trade. Moscow does not have as many girls for hire as other cities, but I have seen them hanging around the Central Telegraph Office, the lobby of the Metropole Hotel, and the square in front of the Bolshoi Theater. They usually search for foreigners. Some want dollars. Others are hopeful of marrying a foreigner who can take them off to glamorous faraway places.

There seem to be free "party girls," too, as in other countries. One attached herself to an American television cameraman who flew to Moscow for the Powers spy trial. When he left without her, she was heartbroken but then she tried to be friendly with another correspondent.

One night one of these girls stopped an American correspondent as he was getting into his car in front of a hotel. "Take me to Paris with you. I will be your lover," she begged.

This could be a police trap. The journalist answered curtly, "If you want a visa, go to your Foreign Ministry and ask for one."

"Oh, you . . . you . . . Communist!" cried the girl and stalked off.

The press occasionally prints stories of immorality. One involved a "Don Ivan" who had a little black book listing 521 girls he successfully made love to. He was unsuccessful with the 522nd, and was convicted on a rape charge.

A Russian woman chauvinistically told me that historically homosexuality was known among Caucasians and central Asians, the subjects of Imperial Russia, but not much mention was made of it among the Russians themselves.

Since the revolution it has been noted rarely, according to veteran residents. But in 1961 groups of homosexuals were seen in Moscow, possibly because they felt more daring under the new liberalized regime. One day an American correspondent saw two young homosexuals walking down Arbat Street. One stopped to put on some lipstick. A Russian woman walking by glared at him in open disapproval. Homosexuals also have been observed hanging around the Bolshoi Theater waiting to approach male dancers as they leave the stage door.

As regards dress, Soviet Russians appear very prim. Some have been horrified by foreign women's attire other than my low-cut blouse (which, come to think of it, by western standards was quite unrevealing). The wife of one American correspondent wore black wool jersey slacks and a sweater during piano lessons she took at her apartment. This is suitable home attire in western cities; but the teacher, a shocked middle-aged Russian, complained to UPDK, "I refuse to give that woman any more piano lessons if she continues to wear her winter woolen ski underwear!"

If your slip shows you are regarded as downright indecent. Once when mine was visible below the hem of my suit I was told so in shocked tones by two Russian women who stopped me on the street. (Russians have a trait, which does not always endear them to privacy-loving westerners, of meddling in strangers' business.) Other foreigners have been reprimanded on subways for crossing their legs, a habit also regarded as uncultured.

Two Russian teen-age girls marched up to some actresses in Moscow with the Old Vic company of London and scolded them for wearing ski pants inside the Pushkin Museum.

"Thank you, but it's none of your business," replied a

Russian-speaking British correspondent who was photographing the actresses on their tour.

One of the Soviet subdebs pulled herself up to her full five feet and retorted, "It is, too! We are patriots!"

In this topsy-turvy country, Russians paradoxically emerge nearly nude on the beach. On my first visit to Sochi I was shocked to see every pebble on the Black Sea beach crowded with acres of bikinis. Some women, no matter how wide, swam just in their brassieres and panties. Others changed from their underwear to bikinis right on the beach. Men wore a tiny bikini, period. To them this is proper sports attire.

Soviet novels are not peppered with scenes of burning passion, rape, homosexuality, incest, or similar items like western tomes. Soviet movies usually are pure as the driven snow. Love scenes are emotional but not passionate. Kissing scenes are rare.

Cheesecake photographs are virtually unknown. So are magazines featuring undraped or nearly nude females. Advertisements featuring curvy girls are absent.

Whether this absence of stimulation results in a low rate of sex crimes and sexual aberrations is not known. No statistics are released. However, in *Problems of Sex Education* Dr. Atarov claims that "a very harmful habit" among boys, masturbation, "is no longer the mass phenomenon it was before the revolution"—according to him, thanks to the unbreakable principles of Marxism-Leninism.

I can only note that when Russians arrived in Brussels for the 1958 Exhibition, they stocked up, goggle-eyed, on French pin-up magazines. Tiny telescopes showing nude girls also were popular souvenirs to take home to Moscow.

Russians also talk with amazement, and delight, about the bedroomy French movies that sizzled Moscow in 1960 during the influx of foreign entertainment.

Once an English scribe asked an official of the Soviet Writers' Union what he thought of the fuss in England over *Lady Chatterley's Lover*.

"We never print anything like that here," the official said.

"And what if you did? Wouldn't people line up to buy it?" persisted the reporter.

The Russian laughed and admitted, "Yes, they would."

There is some indication that the subdeb generation may be acquiring habits of its own. Public kissing and hand-holding was Just Not Done in Moscow—until young Russians saw other young people doing it during the 1957 Youth Festival.

Now occasionally I have seen young people kissing by the Moskva river wall, or walking arms around waists. A young man and his girl were celebrating International Women's Day at the National Hotel in 1961 by dancing with both arms around each other. When they kissed at the end of the tune, this was too much for an older Muscovite. "Why don't you just go find a bedroom somewhere!" she snapped.

As the Khimki boat shows, romantic couples have few places to be alone. There are not many private automobiles, not many quiet family sofas or porch swings.

The new Soviet society also found it had a problem about where people should get married. Many young Russians who believed in Lenin, not God, nonetheless were getting married in churches. One newspaper lamented, "The state has not tried to compete with the theatrics of the church."

The only alternative was the austere marriage license office. The American practice of weddings in homes is unknown in Russia. Russians shrug, and ask, "How can you be married in a small, crowded apartment?"

In 1960, a wedding palace opened in Leningrad in a former noble's mansion. Moscow followed suit in 1961. At the opening of the Moscow Palace, I watched one couple adjust their wedding finery in a dressing room, the girl in a short white dress and veil purchased at a newly opened "Newlyweds Shop" on Prospekt Mira. Then they walked into an elegant, paneled room. A city official read a simple ceremony. The only question he asked was, "Have you thought carefully about the step you're taking?"

After the wedding, not many of these couples move into their own apartment and start buying furniture as they would in most other countries. Except for favored scientists, writers, and politicians, many Russians in cities live in communal apartments at this writing. Following the war, the Soviet government poured millions of rubles, materials, and man hours into making arms and sputniks; and the common man the Party is supposed to pay so much attention to was forgotten as far as housing was concerned. Only in 1956 did the government begin to build apartments on a grand scale. The goal is everybody in a private flat by 1965. Meanwhile, families double up until, often, an apartment resembles a rooming house.

Most apartments are built like "railroad flats"—the rooms all open off a corridor. A family may live in one room, two rooms, or even three. All families in the apartment share the bathroom, lavatory, and kitchen.

The young man who brings his bride home is lucky to have a room alone. Often newlyweds have to sleep in the same room as the bridegroom's younger brothers or sisters, his grandmother, or even his parents. "You can imagine the frustrations, the problems," one Russian husband told me. "I know one couple who hardly ever are alone together, unless the rest of the family leaves the apartment for a Sunday movie. They feel so inhibited with his parents always around."

He said only rarely do people not from the same family live in the same room. On the other hand, often a couple will obtain a divorce but continue to live in the same room because they have no place else to go. Then it may happen that the man brings home a new mate, or prospective one. The original wife finds herself no longer in charge of "the household." And she may suffer the pain and humiliation of sleeping in the same room with her ex-husband and her replacement.

Often these cases wind up in court. One court case, witnessed by an Italian correspondent, involved a couple who had divorced and brought home new spouses. Wife No. 1 and wife No. 2 had tangled in a knife fight.

Being alone isn't the only problem. Russians tell of endless squabbles over who spends the longest time in the bathroom and who left a ring on the tub. Separate light bulbs are installed in some communal rooms by each user, and separate electric meters in each family's quarters. But gas use cannot be accounted for in such a way. The gas bill must be divided among families, with resultant tiffs which, I was told by Russians, pale differences between NATO and the parties to the Warsaw Pact.

The new "instant" prefabricated apartment houses are

supposed to provide 100,000 new flats a year in Moscow (in 1960 they managed only 91,000). The city's chief architect told me they may never catch up unless they devise even faster methods than prefabricated houses. The large teen-age group soon will marry and need more rooms. And the new apartments are made so hastily that foreigners predict they may not last long.

I visited half a dozen new apartment buildings. Hundreds march monotonously across the flat plain, surrounded by forests of building cranes which look like docile animals with entire walls dangling from their mouths. The cranes nudge into place walls complete with doors and windows including glass. Floors sail giddily through the air with bathtub, sink, and toilet attached. It takes eight workmen only one month to put up a fifty-apartment building. Two to six months are needed to paint the entryways and install utilities, wallpaper, people, and furniture.

I noticed many of the six-inch-thick porous clay-and-concrete panels that were taken off factory trucks already were chipped and cracked. The completed buildings look fresh but not very solid to me.

The similarity of the block-like buildings makes most of new Moscow resemble a monotonous housing project. Recently balconies have been painted in bright colors in an effort to relieve the conformity.

When I interviewed the chief of the Ministry for Housing, he said to me, "I inspected the architecture in Helsinki, and almost every building is different. Why? We have twenty to twenty-five different designs. That's enough."

The rent is one advantage of a Soviet apartment.

Citizens pay according to floor space, and utilities are so low the total comes to the equivalent of $3 to $10 dollars a month. We foreigners, however, pay foreign-style rents, from $60 to $140 for an unfurnished apartment, plus utilities.

When I was accompanying the American governors on their tour around Moscow in 1959, we were taken to a "model" apartment. It was furnished with modern-looking but modest couch, chairs, lamps, and tables in the living room and twin beds in the bedroom. Since then I have been in at least a dozen new Russian apartments and have never seen anything approaching that "model."

In most apartments the "living room" is a combination eating-sleeping-dressing-entertaining room. Furthermore, small-scale, modern furniture to match these new small rooms is still difficult to find in Moscow. The Soviet propaganda magazine that is circulated in many countries including the U.S., *Soviet Union,* in 1961 showed modern Lithuanian-made furniture. But a Russian man said to me as we looked at the photographs, "We never can find that in our stores."

The apartments of Russians the city architect took me to were furnished in what I was told is the "traditional" way. Each room had a bed or sofa-bed with big Russian lace-covered pillows propped on display; mammoth wardrobes, china closets, and big round tables with heavy, shiny varnish filled most of the room. The rug was hung on the wall. "We prefer linoleum on the floor. Rugs are dirty and unsanitary," one Russian husband explained.

I noticed that some apartments in the new buildings still are communal. In one new apartment I visited, one family occupied two rooms. The third room had a padlock on the door and a separate mailbox. I was told another person, or couple, lived in that room.

Many New York families have such living arrangements. But they are usually people on low or no incomes, often immigrants who arrive jobless and move in with relatives. People living in Russian communal apartments often have well-paid jobs.

After I'd lived in Moscow a year and a half, I got to know four Soviet couples. Through luck and connections, each couple finally wangled what the Russians call a "self-contained flat." Two of the husbands had built kitchen, linen, and dish cabinets, like the ones one sees in western apartments. They had bought some of the new half-modern Soviet furniture and were interested in western décor. In each case the couples slept on bed-sofas in the living room while their children and *babushki* slept in the other rooms. But at least their living rooms were decorated to look like living rooms. And nobody shared their kitchen and bathroom. I never have seen two such deliriously happy couples in Moscow.

"What do Russians want out of life?" I demanded of one Soviet husband during the 1959, early 1960 *"mir i druzhba"* period when Russian friends were comparatively easy to acquire.

"This," he said, pointing to his furniture. "Russians are concerned with their homes, with getting better and more modern furniture and lamps."

A Russian woman friend said fervently, "I want a *dacha* [country house] with a yard for my children. Isn't it wonderful that this is what we desire, instead of a world revolution as my mother wanted?"

I also visited a prominent Russian singer and her hus-

band. They had a new one-room apartment all to themselves, furnished in a modern style which the "in" set
here covets. In another country she might have had a
ten-room penthouse, but in Russia she is considered very
well off. Because of the shortage of telephones in the new
buildings, the neighbors kept dropping in to use theirs.
Sometimes her mother visits her, she explained, and sleeps
on a cot in the kitchen.

My friend Mikhail did not fare so well at first. One day
during the *"mir i druzhba"* period, we were having lunch
in a Leningrad restaurant. I told him I had finally been
invited to some Russian apartments and asked him why
he never invited me to his home.

He said he was ashamed of it. He and his 21-year-old
son slept in one room, his late wife's parents in another.
It was a communal apartment occupied by two other
families.

"The foyer is always a mess, coats here and there," he
said. "Besides, you are a foreigner. They would gossip.
There's no privacy."

"But you will be allotted a new apartment," I said.

"We'll never get one, that's just it," he said in despair.
"Our rooms are very large. We actually have more than
the eight meters of living space the government allots to
each person. We will never be moved."

"The Soviet press says everyone will have his own
apartment," I tried to reassure him.

Mikhail was forty-five. He usually looked fifty-five, and
that day he looked sixty. His son may have his own apartment and a better life, I thought, watching his bleak face.
But the communist emphasis on heavy industry instead of
people's needs has meant the sacrifice of Mikhail's life, of

his father's life. Two generations gone! I thought. His ability, his hard work, even his big salary—all for what?

Whether Russians will ever enjoy private lives is not yet clear. The Party still firmly goes on making plans for the "dwelling communes" citizens are supposed to live in under "communism," if it arrives.

"In each commune . . . one may locate on the ground floor a medical office, post office, laundry, and the like," one plan by architect S. Strumilin of the U.S.S.R. Academy of Architecture reads.

"One wing of the second floor could be used for children's apartments . . . the children's collective, guided by the experienced hand of the educator, can do more to inculcate the best social habits than the most loving mother . . . public forms of upbringing must be extended to the whole population within the next few years. . . .

"Each Soviet baby would be assigned to a nursery, then to a kindergarten, then to boarding school . . . the parents could visit the children's collective as often as rules permit. . . .

"The other half of the second floor could be tenanted by the aged. . . The third floor would consist of two- to three-room flats for the married, the fourth of separate rooms for students, working youths, and bachelors. . . ."

The commune apartments would not have kitchens. According to the party line, women want to be freed of kitchens. The apartments would have "niches" for warming "ready-made dinners, or they may want to prepare the meals themselves."

"But the great majority will be loath to waste time on such a thing and will prefer to meet their friends and join in friendly talk around the commune's public dining-room tables."

Privacy, not being known completely in Russia, may not be as highly valued as it is in a society where individuality is stressed. In fact, there is no word for "privacy" in the Russian language.

However, many Russians appear desperately to want more of a really private life. One Russian told me, "I don't want any 'joyful comradely communion' around a public dining table every night. I want my own apartment where I can relax and eat with nice modern dishes like the ones you have. Ah, just to be alone!"

11

The Comradely Arts

"What's the use of being a member of the Party? What hopes do you have of obtaining justice?" demands a young boy of the hero in a movie scene.

"I am against the vigilance, the suspicion . . ." broods the hero.

Then a friend calls out, "Stalin is dead," and the characters' shoulders droop in poses of relief. The camera switches to ice breaking up from a frozen river, the water slowly trickling over rocks.

Such anti-Stalinist scenes appeared mild to some western correspondents who saw *The Clear Sky* when it opened in Moscow in the spring of 1961. But Russians who flocked to see it told foreigners later it was "fantastic that they would put such a thing in a movie. . . ."

The ice-breaking scene epitomizes to many observers the slow changes we can watch taking place in some of the arts in the Soviet Union. Of course, the arts still are regarded chiefly as instruments of propaganda, and the long arm of the Party hugs them tightly. But at least the propaganda has softened during my tour of duty in Sovietland.

The film industry is in the throes of an evolution that has pushed some recent Soviet films into the circle of internationally acceptable art after decades of stagnation in "boy meets tractor" epics. *The Cranes Are Flying* was the first truly international Soviet hit since the Russian film virtually died under Stalin's reactionary hand. *Ballad of a Soldier* collected a prize at the San Francisco Film Festival and caused wet handkerchiefs all over Europe. *The Clear Sky,* directed by Grigori Chukhrai, who also made *Ballad,* is scheduled for foreign release; Soviet Ministry of Culture officials are already talking of entering it in international film festivals. *Romeo and Juliet, Othello,* and the second half of Eisenstein's *Ivan the Terrible,* once banned by Stalin, have found favor abroad.

Actually for Chukhrai and the other talented directors of the Russian "new wave," these successful steps forward involve a step backward to the Russian silent movies, which film historians regard as masterpieces.

I visited Mosfilm studio shortly after arriving in Moscow in 1959. I was excited to find in one building a little museum dedicated to the glorious age of Russian films, the twenties. The movies made during that decade were Soviet "propaganda" pictures, too. But few equaled the poetry and technical perfection of *Mother, Potemkin, Arsenal,* and many others. The Soviet artist in those days was not so inhibited in creating his work.

To me it was like visiting a shrine to see the original posters of those movies hanging on the wall of the little museum at Mosfilm. Many of the scripts of those great films are preserved there, as well as personal mementos of the productions. On a table are several scrapbooks containing scene sketches by the director Sergei Eisenstein.

"I am so surprised that you, a westerner, love those old films," said a woman who was showing me around. "Why, they're about our revolution."

I replied that "bourgeois" critics considered that the technique as well as the content of a work of art determines its merit. But my guide shook her head as if she did not understand.

A saying of Lenin's still hangs in a hallway of Mosfilm: "Of all the branches of Art, the most important is the cinema." I have seen that sign also in some Moscow movie theaters. Lenin meant the film was the most important art for "educating" citizens. Stalin took this seriously and in the thirties and forties was the country's No. 1 movie critic. He personally saw every Soviet movie in his private projection room in the Kremlin.

By the time Stalin died the country was turning out fewer than twenty films a year. Most of them were routine. Few saw the light of foreign movie houses. In most of the films party men were the stalwart heroes and American capitalists the shady villains.

During the liberalized Khrushchev era, movie production has boomed. Twenty-five feature films were produced in 1961 at Mosfilm studio alone. Soviet films are shown to 4.3 billion persons, and the country is building more theaters. As long as citizens live in crowded apartments, the movie producers do not have to fear competition from television. People in Russia really do want to "get out and see a movie," to borrow a one-time U.S. theater promotion phrase.

Down the hallway from that little museum at Mosfilm, directors are trying to capture those golden days of the Russian screen. Of course, all Soviet movies still fit the official requirements of encouraging the march toward communism. You can find a few modern movies that don't mention politics, such as *Seriozha,* about a little boy getting to love his stepfather. But in pictures with a modern setting, and even in most of the costume or historical epics, there's usually a communist moral.

Anti-war movies are politically safe. They allow for tragedy, heavy drama, poignant love scenes. An anti-war theme is acceptable "propaganda" in theaters abroad. Thus the most internationally praised Soviet films of the "new wave"—*Cranes, Ballad,* and *Clear Sky*—have all been anti-war movies.

Classics are also safe, such as *The Overcoat* and *Ivan the Terrible.* But in modern films the thread of the Party Line is not hard to find. One 1961 comedy tells about two "unmanageable" boy factory workers. A girl Komsomol (Young Communist Leaguer) is assigned to reform the scamps, and you write the rest.

A potboiler thriller I saw concerns an engineer building a bridge in Siberia; villainous bureaucrats try to ruin his plans. The Soviet version of "westerns" are action films, such as one showing Russian Communists on horseback pounding that-a-way as they "liberate" the Ukraine and establish bolshevik rule. A short comedy called *The Poachers* won an award at the 1961 Cannes Film Festival and probably appeared to French audiences to be a hilarious chase à la the Keystone Cops. To Soviet audiences back home, it echoed a campaign vigorously pursued in the press. The movie satirized "thieves of socialist property" who catch fish in the river and sell them at the markets for private gain.

Nineteen studios produce feature films in the U.S.S.R., and another eighteen make documentaries. Moscow is the "Hollywood," with three studios. Mosfilm's three buildings and ten stages are modest compared to the Hollywood film factories I used to cover. The office buildings are connected with the sound stages, so I saw actors in costume hurrying through the executive hallways. The outdoor sets depict onion-domed churches and fake Georgian villages instead of the western or old English streets on Hollywood back lots.

Mosfilm also makes movies for TV that run about ninety minutes. I watched two young actors enacting a love scene for a television movie—before an American Mitchell camera bought during the war. The director, a woman, looked like a friendly housewife. Instead of calling the Russian equivalent of "cut" at the end of a scene, the directors say the English word, "stop."

A Russian movie costs the equivalent of $325,000 on the average. Wide-screen movies, about 25 per cent of total production, cost more. Soviet directors referred to their wide-screen films as "Todd A-O," "Cinerama," and "Cinemascope" when explaining them to me. A film is in production about eight months. Studio party functionaries check the script before it is bought, and then the Ministry of Culture looks it over. Actual shooting time is about ninety days.

In some little ways, the Soviet film industry may have some advantages over that of western countries. Fan or scandal magazines have not yet reared their heads in Russia. The only two Russian film magazines are devoted to the serious side of the art. Newspapers do not devote space to movie gossip columns. There are no press agents trying to get some starlet to prance on Red Square for photographers; and no Schwab's Drug Store, Gorky Street branch, for the movie fringe mob to hang out in.

Movies open without platoons of publicity-seeking stars

in rented finery waving at hysterical teen-agers. Citizens sometimes ask Soviet film actors for autographs on the street and the players receive fan mail. But according to three top actresses I talked to, the mail doesn't nearly approximate the paper and time people spend writing to even lesser luminaries in America.

Players do not "dress" for their public. The Russians decided to join the film-festival circuit as a means of making-friends-and-influencing-people. At a cocktail party for the first Moscow Film Festival in 1959, several Russian film actresses stood around eating ice cream and were virtually unnoticed by the chattering guests (ice cream is the national passion and is served even at cocktail parties).

During Stalin's day a handful of antique actresses won most of the starring roles. Today Russian film factories swarm with pretty young things. Tatiana Samoilova, the fiery star of *The Cranes Are Flying*, is an intense, dramatic beauty. When I interviewed her at Mosfilm she was wearing a simple red sweater and blue skirt. In this land of braided hair and accordions, her hourglass figure is fashionable. She was make-up-less. The emphasis is on acting, not artificial glamour. Like most Russians, she was trained at a cinema institute, not discovered at a "corner vodka fountain."

What does it mean to be a Soviet "star"? Like ballet dancers, they have a better chance to get private apartments. However, Zhanna Prokhorenko, the star of *Ballad of a Soldier*, told an American reporter she shares her bathroom like many other Muscovites in a communal apartment. Soviet film stars do not own yachts but some have country houses, or *dachi*. Tatiana and the 250 other actors and actresses on contract at Mosfilm are paid the equivalent of $240 a month when they're not working and $300 or $400 when they are, plus bonuses. Ballet dancers make up to $900. Some actresses dress more fancily than other Russian women, but they are still quite modest by Hollywood standards.

Cheesecake in films is not included in party decrees. A blonde film actress, Inna Makarova, told me she saw Gina Lolobrigida on the screen and thought the audience saw "too much of her."

The Russian movie houses I have investigated during my Moscow stay bear little resemblance to the western flicker palaces. The *"kinos,"* as the Russians call them, are among the few buildings in Moscow which carry colored neon signs—but they are simple ones. The theaters do not have canopy-like marquees. Painted posters above the door depict the title of the film and list the actors.

Movie tickets cost the equivalent of 12 and 45 cents. The theaters have the usual ornate chandeliers but plain walls. Since a Russian can seldom be parted from his ice cream, they sell the stuff in movie houses, too. The seats are reserved. If you are late, you are refused admission, and no refunds are allowed.

Soviet policy for the theater arts follows the same outlines as films. As long as theatrical actors and directors stick to the classics, they win acclaim from both natives and foreigners. To me it was worth the trip to Moscow to see the Moscow Art Theater productions of prerevolutionary classics such as *The Brothers Karamazov, The Cherry Orchard, The Three Sisters,* and *Anna Karenina.*

I have seen some modern Soviet plays that were well produced and acted. But the plots put up such a struggle to fit the party requirements that they wind up short of satisfying to me. One play of the thirties, *The Aristocrats,* is based on the building of the White Canal by forced labor. "Anti-socialist" dregs, from aristocrats to thieves, are recruited to construct the canal and thus be "rehabilitated" by work. A prostitute is the heroine. The MVD officers who round up the workers are depicted as kindly men. In the end—you guessed it—the heroine reforms and marches on stage in a tailored Komsomol-type suit.

Some plays in Moscow these past two seasons have poked fun at bureaucrats, but that is approved sniping for the press and other media. Other plays may not have been tolerated under Stalin. A Leningrad satirist now mocks the works of various ministries, but not that of Mr. Khrushchev. A commedienne named Maria Moronova throws out such quips as, "This joke I can't tell—it hasn't been approved yet." A psychological drama, *The First Day of Freedom,* was shown in 1960, but its author is Polish.

Two satirical plays that were not produced under Stalin, *The Golden Calf* and *Twelve Chairs,* adaptations of the famous books by Ilya Ilf and Eugene Petrov, were popular in Moscow during the 1960 theater season. The objection in past years reportedly had been the central character in both plays, Ostap Bender. He is a rogue who seeks fortunes but won't work for them. He winds up with nothing, of course. But he is such an engaging fellow that he arouses amusement and a desire to imitate, not indignation, from many members of the audience. Those plays are the Bible of the "sophisticated" young set. Teenagers practically base their vocabulary on Ostap Bender's.

Such efforts indicate how difficult it is to create a good

work of art with a party politician looking over your shoulder. The Soviet playwright constantly is deluged with party instructions. Even Khrushchev preaches to the writers. In a 1960 lecture to writers, published in *Kommunist* magazine in 1961, the Premier of the Soviet Union told them their task still was to "devote your talent to the great cause of the struggle for communism and for realizing the policy of the Communist party." In another 1960 address he declared, "The supreme social mission of literature is to arouse the people to struggle for new victories in building communism."

At the 1960 meeting of the Soviet Writers' Union board, the Union secretary discussed the "solicitous attention which the Party and government are paying to the development of literature and the arts. Literary men must do their duty as writers as the Communist party teaches. . . ."

Playwrights who try to write not according to these preachings run afoul of party watchdogs. *Pravda* once said "the main drawback of plays is their failure to reveal the positive side in our life, to show the Soviet man at work . . ." *Literaturnaya Gazetta* complained too many authors wrote about men with "flaws."

The Russians are aware that such a dogmatic approach results in many modern plays that put people to sleep. *Pravda* said, "We have few new plays of great ideological and artistic merit. We have few new character portrayals or simply new plots."

The Russian theater is fascinating to many western observers even if we may regard the writing as absurd, for the acting is wonderful. The Stanislavsky "method" school of acting was invented by the Russians, and they know how to use it. Every bit player, every extra, plays with intensity and perfection.

The Soviet Union may be the best place in the world for an actor who wants to pull out all the stops. Russian acting is richly emotional. In a country where feelings run strong the theater has to be a notch broader to do ordinary life one better.

When I saw *The Aristocrats*, for example, the heroine put in a good two miles striding around the stage with jaw outthrust for three acts. In one hysterical scene, she cried real tears. She literally rolled on the stage, black velvet dress and all. She ripped the shirt off an actor's new Soviet manly chest. The audience cheered.

Another play often presented dramatizes decadent, pre-revolutionary life in Siberia fifty years ago. It could be called a western in Russian boots. In this epic, the hero steals his father's mistress, kills her to snatch money his father gave her, blames the murder on his best friend, has his father put into an insane asylum, takes dope, starts a forest fire, and orders the police to shoot striking workers at his mine. He ends it all—and the play—by jumping out a window.

The scenic effects in the Russian theater are flamboyant. Sets twirl on revolving stages. Snow flies, fires are astonishingly realistic. In *Anna Karenina*, the heroine throws herself under a train that roars right across the stage and stops short of the audience's laps.

Going to the theater in Moscow also means you get a meal out of the evening, even if the modern play you see is only about an inventor frustrated by bureaucrats. Plays at the thirty-seven theaters in Moscow have started at 6:30 since the introduction of the seven-hour working day in 1960. Most of the plays last until 10:30. There's no such thing as being fashionably late. Latecomers have to sit out the first act in the lobby.

As most theatergoers customarily don't eat dinner before 6:30, during the first intermission there's a wild dash to a room called the "buffet." Limp from the exciting play, the theatergoer devours thick salami or caviar sandwiches, cheese, beer, sweet Russian drinks, and even sweeter pastry. Then you rush back to your seat for another emotional hour. Or you promenade slowly through the lobbies in a well-defined "traffic" circle. Next intermission, everybody eats again. In fact, some foreigners don't understand a word of the play but give the caviar sandwiches their wild approval. After seeing one comedy about love at a machine tractor station, one foreign correspondent suggested the Russians shelve the play and just show the chocolate éclairs.

Russians love their theaters and fill them even for a piece about Komsomols harvesting wheat in the virgin lands. For almost four hours they sit with rapt attention, quiet except when an exciting moment occurs in the plot. Then they discuss this turn of events with each other and a loud whisper sweeps the theater.

Most of the theaters in Moscow and Leningrad are more ornate than those in New York; they sparkle with elegant chandeliers and gilded boxes. They have no marquees, merely posters out front, like the movie theaters.

After the play, Russian audiences usually waste little time applauding the actors. They head briskly for the cloakroom, that inescapable institution. In cold weather everybody bundles up in their brown cocoons of over-coats, scarfs, fur hats, and boots. Then, like a great brown wind, they surge into the snowy streets.

Russian classical operas such as *Eugene Onegin* are exciting, although many westerners find the singing below par. The news that the Russians finally allowed seven singers to be trained in Italy in 1961 was met with relief in many quarters.

In 1960 the Russians produced two "Italian" operas—that is, operas with Italian settings but sung in Russian. One, set in the twenties, concerns Fascists who dance to jazz in bars and skulk around churches while the Communists are true blue. The other is about a nineteenth-century revolutionist versus the church in Italy.

I asked an Italian correspondent who knows every coda in the La Scala repertoire what he thought of these two offerings. "Terrible," was his one-word review.

Vaudeville has added some fresh touches during the cultural thaw. Chorus girls stormed Moscow for the first time in an American-style music-hall variety show in Gorky Park in the summer of 1960. The revue was staged in an open-air theater which is one of the summer pleasures of Moscow. The girls, all pretty and under twenty, marked a big step in the westernization of the quiet Soviet capital. Appearing in colorful sweaters and snug toreador pants in one sailboat number, they might have been chorus girls in any western city.

Other acts differed little from their Las Vegas counterparts. Two comics in breakaway suits looked like a western burlesque team. Three boys and a girl did pantomime skits that could have passed in the West. A female quartet in short, fluffy, low-cut red dresses might have been inspired by the American "Ed Sullivan Show" that played in Moscow the summer before.

However, the long arm of Lenin's *Collected Works* still was in evidence. In one act the girls did their one-two-kicks in blue overalls like heroines of socialist labor. Comedians got in their quota of anti-American jabs. They blasted the American RB-47 that had been shot down a short time before and made fun of the abstract sculpture at the 1959 American Exhibition. Two male dancers dressed as American capitalists in formal morning suits gave "Heil Hitler" salutes before collapsing into grotesque forms like the cartoons in *Pravda*. "All American technique collapses," cried the announcer. Then came a patriotic ballet of Soviet soldiers waving a gigantic red flag.

Such variety shows may also remind some westerners in the audience of the long dead past. The choreography of those I saw was reminiscent of Busby Berkeley Hollywood musicals of the thirties. And the 24-piece band could be described as early Jan Garber.

The famous Russian dance groups, such as the Moiseyev and Bolshoi ballets, that play to standing room in foreign countries during the summer are all ours during the winter. Russians complain they have difficulty getting tickets, but a letter to the box office written by a foreigner usually can produce seats. I've often seen several Russians on the steps of the Bolshoi Theater trying to unload their own tickets a few minutes before the curtain goes up. Many Russians hang around the door hoping for just such a chance. When a foreigner approaches, a Russian invariably hurries over to ask, "Do you have any extra tickets you want to sell?"

An evening in the ornate red and gold Bolshoi Theater

can be memorable. Tears come to my eyes when I see *Swan Lake,* it is that perfect and beautiful. Russians appear as excited over their ballet as Spaniards are about bullfights. The audiences, especially students in the upper gold-encrusted balconies, cheer their favorites and toss them bouquet after bouquet of flowers as the stars bow over the footlights.

Russian dance companies may have the finest technique in the world, but their productions often look a little musty. Efforts are afoot to brighten and modernize them now that the internal political climate is warmer. The Bolshoi's *Stone Flower* had freshly designed scenery and costumes. The Moiseyev group has a brightly modern repertoire that even included a satire on jitterbugging for its 1961 American tour. When we correspondents saw the preview of the show in Moscow, the Russian audience cheered and applauded the wild jitterbuggers—but for the wrong reasons, according to party standards. They were obviously not scoffing at the dancing but enjoying the boogie-woogie music and dance steps never before seen on Moscow theater stages.

Many modern ballets, however, still are chips off the old communist bloc. In November of 1960, a Ukrainian ballet company visiting in Moscow displayed a new full-length ballet in modern dress, a rarity in the Soviet Union. Whitman Bassow, the *Newsweek* correspondent, and his wife telephoned to invite me to the première. The ballet, they read on the tickets, was called *Chornoye Zoloto,* or *Black Gold*—in other words, coal.

"Hmm," said I. "There will be little pieces of dancing coal."

There were, we discovered, as we sat in the glittering

red and gold theater boxes with some Italian and German correspondents.

The ballet, written by a Ukrainian, opened at a high-school graduation ball. A visiting Komsomol, who worked in a mine in the Donbas region, tells about what the program notes called "the grandeur of the miner's labor." He invites the students to go with him to build new Komsomol mines. As he talks, the entire back of the stage lights up with a scenic view of the future mines, smoke-stacks belching and machinery whirring. All the members of the graduating class clutch their chests at the sight and decide to go. Before they catch their train, they meditate in silence with heads bowed around a white statue in a park. Could it be—? Yes. It's Lenin.

With the hero, one of the students, off to the mines, the girl he leaves behind dreams of the mines. In a dream ballet, dancing flames and snakes represent forces of evil trying to prevent the mine from being opened. But young Komsomol miners leap with bravado and save the little pieces of dancing coal. As the curtain falls, the hero and heroine are reunited after he steps from the mine with the first piece of new coal in his hands.

One ray of hope: even Soviet critics wrote that this ballet was not exactly tasteful.

Moscow concerts of classical music are numerous and cheap, and packed with Russians and foreigners. I have often attended with diplomat, journalist, or tourist friends. But sitting alone can also be rewarding. At one concert by the noted violinist David Oistrakh, two young music students next to me insisted I go with them the next week to hear the noted pianist Svyatoslav Richter. At that time

I had never heard of Richter. Two years later Americans cheered him on his U.S. tour.

American conductors who toured the Soviet Union in 1959 and 1960 told correspondents they thought Soviet classical music by Shostakovitch, Prokofieff, and Kabalevsky was "first rate." However, when England's Lord Harewood toured Moscow music schools he reported seeing not one sign of experimental or "modern" music.

Other forms of Soviet art stir discussion among foreign observers. Most of the translations of Soviet literature I've read on long Russian winter nights sound like ordinary magazine stories; that is, they are technically proficient but hardly memorable. "Socialist realism" in painting reminds me of magazine cover illustrations, too. The paintings I've seen in Moscow that best caught the spirit of Russia were made by an American, Helen Lambert, the wife of New York *Herald Tribune* correspondent Tom Lambert. Mrs. Lambert exhibited her paintings on the indoor tennis court of the Indian embassy, mainly to foreigners. A couple of Russian artists who had been invited appeared very interested in the semi-abstract way she had portrayed their city.

The party fathers are finding it harder to hold down the tent against the stiff winds of change. Ordinary Russians laughed at the example of abstract art displayed at the 1959 American Exhibition. In fact, so many Americans back home objected to the display that conservative paintings of President Eisenhower's choice had to be rushed halfway around the world and hastily added to the collection. Nonetheless, I saw many artists and other citizens crowding around the abstract paintings to examine them and arguing spiritedly over the technique.

In the following year, 1960, the British held an art exhibition at the Pushkin Museum in Moscow. Again the biggest crowds congregated in the room where abstract paintings were on exhibit, but this time it appeared to me that fewer viewers jeered.

Stories began to circulate in Moscow about the new "underground" painters, who experiment in secret at home with officially condemned abstract techniques. A British correspondent reported in 1960 that the Artists' Union tried to inspect the studio of a well-known Soviet artist who was suspected of dabbling in abstract art on Sundays and selling the paintings to the small circuit of modern-art fans among the Moscow intelligentsia. The artist announced that under the new "socialist legality" a warrant is needed before an apartment can be searched, and that what he was doing was his own business. The Union dropped its demand.

After the American Exhibition closed, some of the advocates of abstract painting spoke up. "I believe in the decorative significance of abstract painting," the popular young poet Evgeni Yevtushenko wrote in *Komsomolskaya Pravda,* organ of the Young Communist League, in August 1959.

At the same time a reader wrote in *Literaturnaya Gazetta,* "We are lagging behind the West. Art has no further use for small-town realism. The leading artists in the West abandoned slavish imitation of real things a long time ago and have gone over to the world of impressions. We are just marking time on the same spot." The newspaper, however, condemned him as "a pugnacious ignoramus."

The strangest aspect of this battle to foreign observers

is that Russian painters like Kandinsky and Chagall were leaders of the abstract movement in art. The Soviet "explanation" of this is that Russians tried the technique and abandoned it as useless.

Since the influx of the various modern-art exhibits in Moscow, we've read vigorous campaigns in the press against abstract painting. "Modernness in art means portrayal of the current scene from the standpoint of our Marxist-Leninist ideology. A new form cannot be invented," one article stated.

Another article said, "We must fight for those few [young artists] who buzz like flies over the syrup of bourgeois fashions, to keep an alien wind from blowing them into a foreign bog . . . our enemies try to wiggle their way into every crevice, in order to confuse and defile the immature section of our youth . . ."

Even the first-rate Moscow circus often winds up plugging one aspect or another of the ideological line. The famous clown Popov told me seriously his job is to "help educate the people to communist ideals." When the new "heavy" ruble was introduced in 1961, the circus clowns built skits around the notion that the ruble is strong, the dollar weak.

Television can be another evening's entertainment for a Muscovite, and one in which the ideology is less noticeable. Two channels run continuously from 6:00 P.M. to midnight, and there are some afternoon shows. The programs include variety shows, movies, science documentaries, concerts, news, sports events, and occasionally interviews with American "defectors" and "spies." Some of the announcers are pretty girls like those who advertise soap and hair spray on western TV.

Moscow Radio is a world-wide propaganda operation the size of six NBC's which broadcasts in thirty-nine languages. Its No. 1 job is to spread the "faith." One main "A" station is operated for the home folks. Our office bought a loudspeaker which plugs into a special outlet connected to this station via a telephone line. As we can hear no other station on this static-free set, we call it "the Big Brother radio."

Moscow Radio is not like radio in other countries. One American correspondent calls it "a public-address system, with music." The Party announces its decrees, the government announces its notes. The "commercials"—advertising sales at stores, for example—are read off in one fell swoop each morning. Then no commercials interrupt the concerts. Of course, the station is one grand "commercial" for the Communist party, and these "sponsors" get plenty of plugs.

Concerts and spirited Russian folk songs are sometimes followed by equally spirited anti-American commentaries. Children's programs teach moppets to sing songs about Lenin and rockets flying to Venus. The Soviet popular songs which come over the air waves are mostly love ballads, but often one hears tunes about Komsomols and Lenin. In our office we chuckle to one another that it's as if in the U.S. the radio announcer said, "And next Doris Day sings, 'Ode to George Washington,' to be followed by Louis Prima's 'The Peace Corps Rock.'"

Moscow Radio has loosened up on music, however. Some western songs, and even whole scores of *My Fair Lady* and *Oklahoma!* crop up now and then.

Radio dramas are supposed to be "educational." One night on duty I heard a drama from a book called *Tonya* that describes the adventures of a Russian couple working at the Soviet embassy in Washington. The wife discovers she has to pay at a hospital. American girls tell her they can't afford to get married. The couple goes to a night club and finds it dull.

"I just received a letter from a friend in Moscow," the wife says, weeping on the husband's shoulder. "She goes to her factory rest home at no cost. Every week she goes to theaters and to the skating rink. Oh, how dull and tedious it is here in Washington compared to Moscow! I want to go home to Russia!"

Big Brother also features setting-up exercises every morning at eleven over the country's 28 million "wired" sets. The Russians apparently do not all flex their muscles to this program. On the beach at Sochi the Big Brother radio beats down on the sunbathers' ears all day. During my stay there when the exercise man began calling, "*Raz . . . dvah . . . tri . . .*" not one beach lover bestirred himself. However, I walked into a fish cannery in Murmansk at eleven o'clock one day to see all the workers bending their arms in unison under the direction of an unseen voice.

Any Russian is free to buy an ordinary radio. He can tune in on the second Moscow channel, which is devoted to culture; two channels beamed to other republics or around the world; or to the Voice of America, BBC, and Radio Liberty if unjammed. I have heard Russians in many Soviet cities mention the "Voice."

While the arts in the Soviet Union are being given a small breath of life, brave voices occasionally speak up to push the enlivening process along. On his seventieth birthday in 1961, the outspoken writer Ilya Ehrenburg delivered a beautiful essay that electrified Moscow's intellectual circles. It could be labeled an important footnote to Soviet history.

Ehrenburg, regarded by westerners as one of the few artists with the integrity and courage to express himself honestly, spoke of young Soviet people "who do not find the books which will give them wings." He spoke of Soviet paintings "which recall bad color photographs in opulent frames."

"I mentioned that, in 1907, I called upon Moscow children to become the trumpeters and drummers of the revolution," he said.

"Now the orchestra must have many instruments; the symphony of the new life cannot be played on drums and trumpets alone. Today these drums do not arouse us, they merely send us to sleep. It is time for this to be understood not only by the rank-and-file drummers, but also by the conductors of the orchestra . . ."

12

Alice in Wonderland

The Russians stage the most dramatic, bang-up parade in the world every May 1 (Labor Day) and November 7 (anniversary of the revolution). Twice a year in Moscow I watch half a million singing, chanting citizens carrying balloons, flags, and pictures pour into Red Square. Troops goose-step in perfect order, armored vehicles rumble through exhaust smoke over the cobblestones. The parade passes in review before the ruling party Presidium members who stand atop Lenin's tomb.

And who else sees this staggering sight in honor of the working man? Not the working man—unless he's in the parade; or unless he stays home to look at it on television. The "parade" forms outside Red Square and disbands immediately on the other side. Only visiting delegations, especially honored citizens, diplomats, and foreign correspondents are given tickets to enter the square.

As one American tourist described his reaction after the 1961 May Day parade, "It's a demonstration *of* the people, not a parade *for* the people. Furthermore it appears so religious . . . they carry photographs of their leaders as Russians once carried icons of Christ. And the party leaders on top of the tomb look like high priests to me . . ."

The longer I stay in Russia, the more I find the country intriguing, complex, and confusing. Sometimes I feel like

Alice in Wonderland, trying to figure out why the dormouse is sitting at the Mad Hatter's tea party with a bowl over his head.

For example, regularly in the Soviet press I read that "the Soviet people are carrying out their program of communist construction." But it's a "puzzlement." Sometimes things seem to us foreigners to be shifting the other way.

Because I expected Russia to look like chapters out of Marx, I was not prepared to see neon signs around Moscow with curlicued, Victorian, red and blue letters reading, "Save Money at Your Savings Bank." One in Leningrad lists the rate of interest. Capital making capital doesn't sound like communism to me.

"A few vestiges of the bourgeois influence must be stamped out," *Pravda* avers. But some members of this society keep coming up with private ideas for making more money. The press has run stories about speculators flying from Georgia to Moscow with scarce fresh vegetables jammed in suitcases; about a man who hired two workers and started a *valenki* (felt boots) business; about a printing-shop operator arrested for turning out Bibles and selling them on the black market.

One correspondent who delved into the black market in Moscow reported it has bosses, middlemen, and salesmen. Foreigners get offers on the street for their coats, suits, scarfs, dollars, records, and books. Once on a trip to Leningrad I discovered to my surprise that private buying and selling still flourishes at a "flea market" just as in Paris and Rome. I bought a lovely old Russian clock for the equivalent of $1.11. I have seen lace sellers operating right under the noses of the authorities inside shops in

Sochi and Leningrad. Men sell toys and souvenirs privately on the beach at Sochi as in any other country.

Decrees were passed in 1961 against speculators and "parasites" who do not work or who work illegally as private entrepreneurs. Yet private enterprise continues. One Russian wanted some cabinets built in his apartment. He went to a factory, buttonholed a departing worker, and hired him. The worker did the job after hours—with wood "borrowed" from his factory.

Russians can build private houses in the country now only if they are registered to live in that area and therefore do not occupy a Moscow apartment. Not only the housing shortage prompted this 1960 decree. *Kommunist* magazine, the Party bible, said "some people who own personal country homes at times make a profit by renting out rooms at excessively high prices."

Kommunist proposes that *dachi* should be "united as cooperatives" and public boarding houses built in order to stem the movement away from private week-end homes in the country.

Some persons come to Moscow with the hazy idea that Russia has little or no crime. How much there is remains a mystery. The Russians do not supply statistics on crime. In past years they've even refused to admit to visitors that there was any, a curious practice considering that crime stories are printed occasionally in the newspapers in order to emphasize the wrongdoing.

It takes only a little firsthand knowledge of the country to realize that crime in the U.S.S.R. is not yet extinct. Before a policeman could be stationed in front of the newly opened apartment house for foreigners on Kutuzovsky Prospekt, a young Englishwoman lost to thieves all of her filled suitcases and trunks. Souvenir hunters lift side mirrors, radiator adornments, hub caps, windshield wipers, window holders, and other odds and ends from foreigners' cars. The standard practice is to keep your windshield wipers inside the car and to put them on the windows only when it rains.

When *Newsweek* correspondent Whitman Bassow pointed out the theft of his radiator ornament to the policeman in front of our apartment building one day, the officer replied, "You lost it. It couldn't have been stolen!"

Another correspondent lost his hub caps to what the press calls "hooligans." "Are you sure a Russian stole them?" inquired the scribe's unbelieving Soviet translator.

Unconsciously lulled by the rain of propaganda about socialist morality, we carelessly left valuables around our UPI office-apartment. But several times it was robbed of cameras and money, just as if we were in New York or London.

"You mean a Russian entered your apartment, the apartment of a foreigner?" gasped one Russian acquaintance in disbelief.

The thief got in, through a small unscreened window with a broken pane on the side of the building unseen by our policeman at the entrance. One night I woke up to discover the burglar in my bedroom extracting four rubles from my wallet. He scurried to dive out the little window and I fled in my nightclothes outside to our policeman. Soon more policemen and detectives in plain clothes were swarming through our office-apartment. But they didn't act like the glinty-eyed heroes of American TV detective serials. They took no fingerprints, asked few questions, and wrote nothing down. They never telephoned later or came back. In fact, one detective stated that "as is well known" no thief could possibly have been in my apartment. Later, our Soviet insurance office showed me the police report. It said, "No evidence of theft was found. But a cat was seen in the apartment. It was the cat that Miss Mosby heard."

Except for thievery mostly of the petty variety, foreigners have not reported being involved in other crimes during my Moscow stay. I have heard Russians say, "If a Russian had a knife at your throat, he would drop it when he saw you were a foreigner." This is one country where a single woman usually can go where she pleases alone at night with little worry of being molested. I have never been whistled at or followed by predatory males. There appear to be relatively few attackers roaming the streets at night—or at least they give foreigners a wide berth.

The visitor to Russia is bewildered by other aspects of Soviet life that at times remind one of Alice's world "through a looking glass."

After all that talk about a "classless society," I was surprised to read that the Soviet press identifies citizens as belonging to the "workers', peasants', or intelligentsia classes." Many correspondents write with amazement that boats and trains have separate classes as in other countries. Some visitors notice as much class consciousness as in other European countries, or more. I was told that Moscow University students, for example, would not dream of working summers at manual jobs, as many American students do.

Once I heard a Russian man talking about a certain well-dressed Russian woman who hobnobbed with foreigners. "Where does she get off, putting on such airs!" he snorted. "Why, she's from peasant stock!"

Sessions of the Supreme Soviet are entirely different from legislative meetings in other countries. At times they seem like a play with the script written out in advance.

The Soviet newspapers regularly point out that their "parliament" is truly democratic because its members are milkmaids, machinists, and so forth. Why, in the United States, the newspapers say, not one Congressman is a "worker" or "peasant." Supreme Soviet members don't have to know anything necessarily about law or economics to be elected.

At the sessions in the Grand Kremlin Palace, the dark-eyed Armenian deputies, the Uzbeks in colorful square embroidered caps, the broad-shouldered Russian women all sit like dutiful pupils in school. Nary a question is raised from the floor. Never an argument rings through the hall. Periodically a vote is taken on some measure and all hands raise in unison. The deputies always unanimously agree on all the bills submitted by their leaders.

After the first day, the Turkmenians, Georgians, and others stop listening to every word of the speeches. From our balcony in the marble hall, we foreign correspondents, segregated from the Soviet press, can look down on rows of deputies' desks. Many members read *Pravda* during the speeches. The day *Krokodil,* the Soviet humor magazine, is published, many a desk sports one. By the end of the week's session, the deputies are busy wrapping and unwrapping their packages from Gum during the speeches and admiring each other's purchases. For many, those shopping sprees at Gum are a highlight of their trip to Moscow.

The Soviet system is riddled with confusing contradiction. Western observers report seeing practices in Moscow hospitals that would be regarded as unacceptable in other countries, such as allowing visitors into a room holding incubator babies. Few westerners submit to serious operations in Moscow hospitals after discovering local anesthetic is regarded as sufficient for many types of major surgery. Yet visiting doctors often laud some Soviet experimental work. And medical care is available to all at no cost, except for medicine. At a maternity hospital I visited, all guests had to put on white coats and caps. Yet at the red soft-drink dispensers now lining Moscow streets in the summertime, everybody uses the same glass. The customers wash it between uses in a cold-water spray. One big cloth towel usually is for everybody's use in public washrooms. But streets are kept clean. And usually buffet waitresses pick up your cakes and sandwiches with a piece of clean paper.

I like the fact that the Russians make culture and education fashionable. I like signs of special consideration for the working woman, such as paid leave for having babies, stores open until 8:00 P.M., and plenty of free kindergartens. Observers never have noted racial discrimination in hotels, schools, or restaurants. Despite all the cries from Africans at Moscow University in 1960, correspondents never could uncover a documented case of racial discrimination (we are all discriminated against in some ways because we are foreigners).

On the other hand, nationalities within the Soviet Union have their feuds and points of friction much like nationalities throughout the world. Some Russians talk patronizingly about the peoples of what some outsiders call their "colonies." A Komsomol pointed out that first party secretaries of Soviet Republics usually are of that republic's nationality, such as Uzbek or Georgian. Second party secretaries usually are Russian. "We Russians have to keep an eye on them," he said. "You notice those corrupt farm leaders exposed at the Central Committee meeting [January 1961] were not Russians but central Asians."

Georgians tend to dislike Russians, I was told by many Georgians when I visited Georgia. One Muscovite I met on the beach told me that a Georgian approached his hotel dining-room table and inquired, "Are you Russian?"

"No, I am Jewish," replied the Muscovite.

"Great!" exclaimed the Georgian with a smile. "Then I'll sit down and talk to you. I don't like Russians."

A young Georgian said to me in Sukhumi, "I never would marry a Russian girl. She would not know how to cook Georgian dishes. Our children would be neither Georgian nor Russian. I want to marry a Georgian girl to preserve our nationality."

If Soviets are not the "pitiful slaves of a police state" as some U.S. Congressmen and columnists have depicted them, neither are they dutiful sheep agreeing with every word in *Pravda*. It is not difficult to find free thinkers in the Soviet Union. They appear to be an unorganized negligible minority, but at least the Soviet Union harbors more free thinkers than the regime would like to admit.

"To the days when the authorities won't have so much authority," said a Russian at a table next to mine in the National Hotel restaurant, lifting his glass.

"If they unlocked the borders of this country, 80 million Russians would leave tomorrow," announced another

Russian, who joined a correspondents' table at the Budapest Hotel restaurant.

There are many dissidents among peoples the Russians "colonized," as correspondents who tour the Baltic countries quickly discover. In Moscow once I was standing in line at the big Kremlin museum to view the collection of gold Bible covers and jewel-studded eggs. A young blond man took me aside to ask in Russian, "Are you from Holland?"

"No, I am American," I said.

"I am Latvian," he said softly as we stared in the display windows holding the extravagant treasures of the czars. "We have Russian bosses. Things are very bad in Riga. I make 1,400 rubles [then $140 at the tourist exchange rate] as a bus driver. Look at my shoes! They cost 240 rubles. I have a brother in Brooklyn. Would you write to him for me? Oh, I want to go to America!"

On the rocky beach at Sochi, a handsome middle-aged Estonian said to me, "If they would just let us travel! Before the Russians came to Estonia, I traveled abroad and studied in London, but now . . . Of course," he added, "my son is studying to be a physicist. He might never have had that chance in the old days."

"We want to see Mexico!" two handsome Georgian men said as we sat together on the veranda of my hotel in Sukhumi. "But to get a passport to leave is almost impossible. What is Mexico like?"

Russians tell a joke about a promise Premier Khrushchev made in a speech that "soon all Soviet people will be able to travel to the moon."

"That's all very fine," said a voice in the hall, "but when can we go to Paris?"

A man with a ruddy face approached me when I was walking in Moscow. "How's life in America—better than here?" he demanded.

"Yes," I replied, "better."

He wore a shabby leather coat, quilted inside, and a worn shirt. He touched my wool coat and said, "We dress poorly here. Foreigners dress better. You are allowed to go only 40 kilometers. Go farther out and see how badly we live."

As a consolation I said, "You have better sputniks than America."

"Sputniks!" He spat on the sidewalk. "I would rather have clothes."

Taxi drivers are great talkers here as in other countries. One spat out the window when I congratulated him on a Soviet moon rocket. Another orated, "Everybody profits from socialism except the workers. The speculators, scientists, professors, Communists are rich. Workers have nothing! You foreigners have cultured, nice lives."

Another warned, "Pay attention! Communists are in Africa, India, and Latin America."

Some students openly say they do not like communism. Three students approached a foreigners' table at the Aragvy restaurant once, and later some of us westerners strolled with them down Gorky Street.

"We have no time for communism, it's a fake," one said. "Do you pray? Often we talk about having nothing to believe in . . ."

"What's wrong with the West?" argued another. "Why don't you quell the Communist party in the United States? Why didn't the American army interfere in Laos, Hungary, and Tibet?"

Some soldiers walked by in their breeches and black boots.

"*Vot*" (look here), said one student sarcastically, gesturing to the soldiers. "We're 'peace-loving' people. We just want to conquer all of Europe."

In Sverdlovsk during the 1959 Nixon tour a man approached me in the lobby of our hotel. He said he wanted to talk to me "because I haven't seen a foreigner for twenty years." He said his father, a minor government official, was shot during Stalin's purges of the late thirties. "Night after night we would lie awake in our apartment, hearing the footsteps and the knocks and wondering if our time would come," he said. "One night someone knocked on our door. They took my father away."

After Stalin died, Khrushchev ordered a rehabilitation period. This man was given a good position and better than average living quarters "to make up for Father's death."

"What is living in Russia like?" I asked him.

"Did you ever read George Orwell's *1984*?" he said. "That's what it's been like, until the last year or so. Big Brother was everywhere, although we think now those bad police days are gone and things are going to be different."

Since I expected to find a strictly organized Orwellian society in Russia, my initial reaction was that the country isn't like that at all. The longer I stay, the more it appears that the official veneer is very Orwellian, although the society underneath is very human and Russian.

"Hail to the Communist party!" shouts the red banner on the new apartment house. "Maintain standards of communist behavior!" warns the sign in the lost-and-found office of the Leningrad railway station in Moscow. "Forward to communism," proclaims the banner in the factory in Petrozavodsk.

In 1961 it was decreed that students who are Komsomols can reprimand teachers if the teachers do not teach correct communist principles. Party members are in control every place, from the courts to the ballet companies. Marshal Rodion Malinovsky, head of the armed forces, said in a speech that party members in the army and navy assure him "all the men of the armed forces are solidly united around the Party and its Central Committee. Our Party attaches extremely great importance to educational political work in the army and navy . . ."

On main streets, on side streets, in apartment houses are the ever-present signs designating an "*Agitpunk*," or agitation point. Here party agitators show films, give lectures, and hand out pamphlets.

Many outsiders find some Russian rituals and demonstrations intriguing. The arrivals and departures of Premier Khrushchev and other heads of government would be the envy of that master of mob scenes, the late film director Cecil B. de Mille. Groups of factory workers are taken to the airport in special buses. They stand between chalk marks as on a movie set. They wave and applaud and present flowers when Mr. K. or his honored guest walk by. We correspondents stand between chalk marks, too.

TV cameras grind away at most press conferences, no matter how trivial. The participants invariably march in for a grand entrance after the reporters are seated. For Khrushchev press conferences at the Kremlin, first the stenographers, as "supporting players," file in. They stand and applaud when the "stars" enter. The presence of the

cameras makes me feel self-conscious about standing up
to ask even a simple question.

The "mock trial" of Fritz Oberlander, an accused ex-
Nazi in the West German government, was the height of
press conference dramatics. The bizarre cast of characters
on hand to denounce him included an Orthodox priest
with a towering bejeweled white hat; Trofim Lysenko,
Stalin's pet geneticist, who has returned to court favor; six
Ukrainians and Volga Germans who had collaborated with
the Nazis, and a woman World War II pilot.

The press was supposed to be allowed to submit questions. But as a written question was read, the trial "director" would ignore it and order the next witness to "tell
more about Oberlander."

Russians often assume that everybody else's system is
carefully arranged, too. At the opening of Friendship University, Carl Mydans, then *Life* correspondent in Moscow,
was talking with some Soviet photographers. One asked
how a photographer happened to be on hand to make the
striking photograph of a right-wing student stabbing a
Japanese socialist in Tokyo. Mydans replied he understood the politician was speaking at a meeting to which
all photographers had been invited.

"That's not so!" cried the Russian. "The photographer
was there because the stabbing had been arranged by you
Americans!"

During the 1958 Brussels Exposition I told a Soviet
journalist that a temporary relief camp had been set up to
handle "defectors" among tourist groups from eastern
Europe.

"Hmm. Belgians seek to discredit Soviet pavilion by

staging provocation . . ." he mused, as if composing his news story for the day.

I told him I had seen the camp with my own eyes, that it had been established by the Red Cross. He would not be dissuaded from his conviction that the Belgian government had arranged the camp as a cold-war tactic.

Afro-Asian students from Friendship University in February 1961 marched down Khlebny Pereulok (Bread Lane) to the Belgian embassy to protest the death of Congolese leader Patrice Lumumba. The boys and girls were accompanied by Russian students who wore the unmistakable self-important air of young people given responsibility.

While the Africans and Asians shouted and threw milk and ink bottles over the embassy's white columns, the Russians tried to keep the demonstration from becoming too spontaneous.

"Be careful! That's not necessary!" one Russian youth near me in the surging crowd cried to an overexuberant Russian girl.

Policemen observed with a detached air while students heaved bricks through the windows. Not one policeman made one move to stop the students, except when some tried to get into the embassy. The police did allow a few to enter—apparently "stars" picked in advance to deliver a petition.

Extra police and Soviet correspondents had arrived near the embassy two hours in advance to "wait in the wings." Then the minute the "riot" ended, in walked Soviet repairmen from UPDK.

"We hear you had a little trouble," the UPDK man said

amiably to the Belgians. "Can we repair your walls and rugs?"

(When we reported this evidence of planning, and the broken windows, in our stories, the censor crossed out those lines.)

The demonstration over the counterrevolution in Cuba in front of the American embassy in April 1961 followed the same pattern. But whether or not the demonstration was organized in advance, the indignation of the participants appeared genuine. I observed the mob display from inside the besieged embassy. At one point I had to step out on a balcony to photograph the demonstrators below. It was a mighty unpleasant experience. Two thousand jeering faces looked up at me. Fists were shaken, signs waved. A rock zinged past my ear, and the window behind me shattered to pieces. All my theories about how friendly Russians are to Americans became a little wobbly at that moment.

Nearly every day I am puzzled like a wide-eyed "Alice" by the perplexing comparisons between what some communists tell me and what I see in real life.

Soviet journalists in Brussels assured me I'd find no beggars in the Soviet Union. They are rare; but twice on the train to Saltikovka, a suburb of Moscow, I saw old men begging with hats outstretched. Outside a Moscow church half a dozen old women beseeched me for coins so that they could buy "holy" water from the priest to take home to drink. After I left a café table in Leningrad, a little old woman hurried to my table to devour my half-finished *blini*. Perhaps these persons are too lazy to work or have used up their pension for the month. But whatever the reason, they exist.

"It's really almost like any other European country here, isn't it, despite the party propaganda?" one Russian intellectual asked me.

"In many ways, yes, but the fact that the Soviets say it's different is one reason that makes the Soviet Union seem so curious to us foreigners," said I.

Other Soviet journalists have looked me right in the eye and said there is no censorship or prostitution in the Soviet Union and that no Russian women smoke or drink. I have found out otherwise. Once a Soviet official confessed to Bud Korengold, "When I say 'it seems to me,' that means it's my opinion, and when I know for sure, I say 'maybe'." That type of response is why it can be so maddening to talk to Soviet officials.

Once I ordered a car from UPDK and was told the prices and terms. The car failed to arrive at our office at the appointed hour. "But we telephoned you two days ago to say we had no cars," the official insisted when I called to check.

A British journalist arrived from London on the $30-a-day Intourist plan that entitled him to be met at the airport by a limousine. No car was to be seen, so he thumbed a ride in another tourist's Intourist car. At the hotel, the Briton demanded to know why he wasn't met.

"We never send cars to the airport," the Intourist girl replied.

"Young lady, I just rode in from the airport in another tourist's Intourist machine!" said the bewildered Briton.

"No, you didn't," she insisted.

I truly felt like a befuddled "Alice" in a strange sort of Wonderland when I became involved in an odd incident during a tour of the Black Sea area.

First I visited Sochi, which reminded me of Forest Lawn, that celebrated cemetery in Los Angeles: the same clipped hedges, piped-in music, statuary (only in Sochi it's of Lenin and Stalin), the pseudo-Grecian urns. I rested for a while in a becolumned resort hotel sandwiched between workers' sanitariums with flapping banners reading, for example, "Needle Factory No. 60 Rest Home."

Then I traveled on a luxurious steamer farther south to Sukhumi, Georgia. The Georgians' spicy food, wines, and hearty spirits were such a relief to me from the quiet of Moscow that I wound up broke. I had left some money and most of my baggage at my Sochi hotel.

The few kopecks I had left in Sukhumi just paid the bus fare to the railway station, where I could catch a five o'clock train that ran along the sea edge (I had bought a round-trip ticket in advance). The bus was bulging with Georgians. Two handsome, mustached youths insisted on helping me inside. In the crush one of them leaned against me, laughing as the bus lurched along. At the next stop, two blocks later, they hopped off.

As the bus started up again, I saw my plastic handbag was open. My black leather passport case was missing— with not only my passport but my train ticket to Sochi, airplane ticket from Sochi to Moscow, Soviet internal passport, American passport, Foreign Ministry press card, International Driver's License, and Soviet automobile documents.

"My passport! My money! That man took it! Stop!" I cried out in Russian.

The other passengers shouted to the driver to stop. Some helped me look on the floor and under the seats. At the thought of what had happened, I burst into tears. One

Georgian boy got off the bus with me and carried my suitcase and my coat while I sobbed my sad tale. "I know that boy who took it," he said.

By the time we reached a traffic policeman, about fifty curious Georgians were trailing along behind us like persons following a parade. The officer telephoned for a police car to take us to the station, a two-story building in a courtyard.

First I repeated my story in English while an Intourist guide, summoned from the hotel, translated into Georgian. An officer wrote a report in careful Georgian longhand. I signed it.

Officers hurried in and out of the little reporting room. Everybody appeared agitated. Not only was I a foreigner, but an American—and what was more disastrous, a journalist!

As is well known, to use a favorite Soviet phrase, crime in the Soviet Union is not talked about very much.

But I had seen one. They acted as if I had uncovered one of their atom-bomb factories.

One of the chief's assistants took me aside. "Do they have any thieves in America?" he asked in Russian.

"Of course," I answered. "There are such people in all countries."

"But you will think ill of our Georgia," he began, but I interrupted, "Not at all. I like your people."

Finally I was ushered into the police chief's large office containing a large desk, a table, and several chairs. My escort from the bus was there. After some conversation in Georgian, the translator told me, "The suspected thief is a well-known hooligan. They even know where he lives."

The police chief wore a shirt with no jacket in the heat.

He looked to me like an Arizona sheriff. He said, "You'll get your passport case back, don't worry. But I want to give you your documents myself. You must stay here one more day and not return to Sochi yet."

The police chief appeared determined to show an American that his staff could surpass American policemen any time at catching pickpockets. Back to the hotel I went. Intourist promised to pay the room and board bill. I did not mind another warm, pleasant evening on the veranda, talking with the friendly Georgians and watching citizens promenade eight and ten abreast down the middle of the street.

The next morning the police chief said his officers waited all night at the suspect's home but he never returned. While the search continued, he wanted me to inspect a "line-up" to help identify the suspect. I thought this odd as the suspect was known.

Five men walked into the room and stood before a potted palm. I assumed they were suspected thieves rounded up by the police as in an American line-up.

"The suspect is not in this group. We want to confirm his identity. Just tell us if one of these men resembles the suspect in size or expression or facial characteristics," the chief said.

I selected a slender young man with a mustache.

After this performance, everybody thanked me for coming. Again came the question, "You will think badly of Georgia, no?"

"No," I said wearily. I was told to come back at three.

On the way to the hotel the translator told me that line-up consisted of some of the town's leading citizens. The one I picked as looking like the thief was a prominent dentist. I had a brief mental picture of the stocky, ruddy-faced chief calling up his pals around town to drop in at the station to act in a line-up for an American female correspondent whose passport case had been stolen.

After lunch, the police chief said they still had not found the passport case. But they were hopeful. In the midst of his speech, the telephone rang: long distance; a village outside Sukhumi.

"Your passport case has been found. Turned in to a police station. It will be brought here," the chief declared with a smile. "Come back at seven."

I happily thanked everybody and hurried to the hotel to pack my bag. The guide ordered an Intourist car to pick me up at 7:30 at the police station to drive me to Sochi. (My train ticket was useless. It was good only on the date stamped.)

At seven the chief, his aides, the city prosecutor, the Intourist translator, and I assembled in the chief's office for the finale.

"You are an American correspondent," the chief began in an official-sounding voice. He paced around the room. "You probably will go back to Moscow and write about crime in Georgia." He adjusted the drapes and sat down behind his desk. "We have recovered your passport case," he said, watching me carefully. "We do not rule out the possibility of theft. But it appears you lost it on the bus. It was found by a man who wrote a letter explaining he did not have time to turn it in right away."

I was stunned. I tried to remember the events of the day. Having lost many objects in my life, I thought such a mishap was possible. "I don't understand," I spoke up.

"We looked under the bus seats. Where did the man say he found it? Will you read the letter to me?"

The chief did not answer. He gave me a paper and pen and told me to list the objects as he returned them to me. Because I had stuffed even money-changing receipts from Frankfurt into my passport case, the listing took fifteen minutes.

Then he told me to write, "I lost my passport case on the bus. The police made every effort to find it, treated me kindly, and returned everything to me in good condition."

My cheeks burned with embarrassment. The Sukhumi police had worked so diligently, turning the town inside out, and I had only dropped the passport case out of a bag whose clasp was loose. . . .

The prosecutor said the case was closed.

"Wait a minute," I said. "I still don't understand. What did that person write?"

The translator picked up the letter and read it. The writer, a schoolteacher, said he found the passport in a public toilet opposite the Sukhumi post office. He said he took it home because he was in a hurry. The next day he turned it in to his village station.

"Where is the post office?" I asked.

"At the first bus stop after you got on," the translator said.

"That's where those boys got off!" I said. "One of them took my case, saw it was a foreigner's, and became frightened. They left it in the toilet, knowing it would be found."

The police chief nodded in cheerful agreement. "Yes, that's probably what happened."

The chief, the prosecutor, and the other officers stood up

and began gathering their documents and talking to each other.

"Listen!" I turned to the Intourist translator. "Why did you let me write 'lost' in that report? I didn't lose that passport. It was stolen and you know it. Tell him I want that paper back."

But the Georgians had started for the door. They were offering their hands and wishing me a good journey. Everybody made noises about Georgian-American friendship. Should I make more of a fuss? The Intourist car was waiting.

A downpour of rain steamed the hot streets. With many smiles I was seen off.

In Sochi the airline wanted to charge me double for my ticket to Moscow because I had missed my reservation. I produced an "excuse" the police chief had written for me to the airline, and discovered, upon translating it, that it said I was delayed because I had "mislaid" my passport case.

Only on the plane did I finally face the fact that I had committed a cardinal stupidity: signing a paper without making sure what I was signing.

At the UPI office, Henry Shapiro smiled. "You'd better not write a story about this or they'll produce that paper you signed."

Later when I told the story to my friend Mikhail, he laughed. "You idiot," he said. "The whole thing probably was made up. They undoubtedly caught the thief immediately. They found the passport immediately in the toilet, or maybe on the thief.

"They were afraid of what you would write. You will have to tell the Foreign Ministry about this, and the report will filter down, down, down, until finally the police chief is fired for allowing pickpockets in his community. He was scared.

"So he stalled, showing you the line-up to make you see how efficiently they worked. Then he staged that phony scene of having it turned in to the police station a day later."

I had telephoned Henry Shapiro from Sukhumi to inform him of the mishap, and he had notified both the Soviet Foreign Ministry and the American embassy. So I had to write a report to the ministry about the recovery of the passport case. This time I stated exactly what had happened—that it apparently was stolen.

Weeks later a Soviet journalist I knew stopped me at the Central Telegraph Office. "I just returned from Sukhumi," he said. "The Intourist guide at the hotel said the police chief received a copy you sent him of the letter you wrote to the Foreign Ministry. He doesn't understand why you didn't stick to the official version, that you lost your passport case on the bus . . ."

"Official version? Lost?" I burst out laughing.

What a strange country! As Alice in Wonderland said, "It gets curiouser and curiouser!"

13

The Party Line

One of the nicest advantages for a foreigner living in Moscow is that we're treated almost the way movie stars are in America.

If I'm waiting in the usual queue to have my hair washed at a beauty shop, I'm often whisked to the front of the line after the manager sees I'm a foreigner. Salesgirls sometimes pull out the best goods for us: head waiters bow us to the best tables.

Russians for centuries have nurtured this double-edged attitude toward foreigners. On the one hand, we are regarded with suspicion and segregated. Yet we are given the best of everything, admired, and stared at.

Nowhere is this more evident than at night when foreigners gather for the diplomatic social merry-go-round at embassy receptions. Policemen blow whistles and wave Russian traffic away from the embassy doors. Black shiny Cadillacs and Rolls Royces and Mercedes Benzes with the "D" for diplomatic license plates roll up. Foreigners, elegant in their evening finery, step out and sweep inside. And all the while Russians line the sidewalk across the street and on either side of the entrance, like celebrity-watchers outside a London theater or a Hollywood night club.

They stand, silent and dark, on the curbing, bundled in

their shawls and fur caps and heavy coats and boots. They stand, stolid and staring, much as they must have watched in bygone centuries the rich boyars in their furs and silks sweep into these very same mansions.

At first I had the urge to touch their arms and say, "Look, we're nobody." But we are "somebody" in a country which has no royalty or wildly feted movie stars, no film premières or celebrities' haunts on which the people can vent their curiosity.

When I flew across the steppes to faraway Novosibirsk, in Siberia, with the then Vice President Richard Nixon, he and his entourage were invited to the local ballet theater. The crowd outside looked like one for the première of an Elizabeth Taylor epic on Broadway. They not only applauded Mr. Nixon and his wife to display their yearning for peace, but when I rolled up in a taxi with two Washington correspondents we were cheered too. Foreigners in Siberia are a rare sight. Men stuck out their hands for us to shake. People touched me and applauded.

The scene of the embassy receptions in Moscow is splendorous. The embassies are housed in ornate mansions, gilded, tiled, chandeliered, and carved. They were the homes of pre-revolutionary nobles and rich businessmen, and make a startling contrast to the log houses of the peasants and the wedding-cake architecture of the Soviet regime.

The ladies at the parties should be in powdered wigs and hoop skirts to match the surroundings. At least they turn out in their Paris best—although underneath many lovely Balenciagas and Diors woolen bloomers dangle to the knee. In this land where it's cold for ten months and mansions and palaces are chilly, not many women go without their winter underwear, even to the fanciest party—but it's black, of course, for evening.

The women often arrive in fur-lined boots, carrying their slim-heeled evening slippers in their hand. (This is a Moscow custom. Theaters and restaurants usually have "changing" benches where ladies may sit to change their boots.)

These receptions may sound gay, but they are also "work." The Foreign Ministry does not hold regular press conferences or briefings and rarely gives out news. Government officials are not available to the press in their offices in this stronghold of secrecy. So embassy receptions and parties provide virtually the only chance both diplomats and correspondents have to hear official opinion at first hand or to catch a real live Soviet official to interview.

These parties are in some ways like Hollywood cocktail parties I used to cover for UPI, only much more exciting and worth while. In Moscow, too, they are "shop talk" parties. But instead of discussing Zsa Zsa Gabor's latest husband the party-goers talk about whether First Deputy Premier Anastas I. Mikoyan is moving up, down, or sideways, or what the last two words in the second paragraph of the day's *Pravda* signify. Instead of meeting press agents and starlets we share the canapé table with Premier Khrushchev, an assortment of Soviet generals, and ambassadors conversing in a dozen languages.

Each reception—and they can average three a week—follows a traditional pattern. Ambassadors and Soviet leaders stand on their private side of the hors d' oeuvres table to conduct their "business." By unspoken agreement, correspondents leave them alone during this time. As the evening nears an end we encircle our prey. When the victim is between conversations with diplomats, we pounce on him with questions.

A reception at the Kremlin combines the aura of intrigue around the Soviet regime with the dramatic splendor of old Russia. For my first, I was driven by our chauffeur over the one-time moat through the ancient Italian-designed gate, past the policeman, and into the three-block-square walled compound that is the Kremlin.

The reception was held in St. George's Hall of the Grand Kremlin Palace where the czars had their lush private apartments. A battery of stony-faced individuals checked my invitation and press card at the front door. Then I walked up a long red-carpeted staircase where once trod the Russian czars. At the top hangs a gigantic painting of Lenin exhorting the peasants, a reminder of a newer era.

St. George's Hall, the former ballroom of the czars, is a staggering sight, with its mammoth gold filigree chandeliers and its white walls covered with the names in gold of Russian soldiers decorated for bravery. The hall, the size of a football field, was filled with buffet tables laden with the usual delicacies people eat at Moscow parties: smoked salmon, caviar, fresh fruit (if in season), little cakes, wines, and soft drinks (vodka was banished from official Kremlin receptions in 1960 as part of the sobriety campaign, but it's available sometimes in side rooms off the main hall).

Safely behind an hors d' oeuvre table stood Premier Khrushchev, the other Soviet leaders, the ambassadors, and the honored guest of the evening, the Italian president. Farther back is a stage where the Red Army Chorus entertained.

After the guests had chatted and eaten for approximately an hour, a bell was rung signifying time for speeches. Premier Khrushchev spoke into a microphone to welcome the guest. Then the Italian president took his turn, with time for each speech to be translated.

The end of the party was indicated when Premier Khrushchev and the other Presidium members filed out of the hall through mammoth golden doors. Gradually the guests drifted away, down the red-carpeted stairs to the *garderobe* to claim their coats and furs. A man at a microphone ordered the chauffeurs to drive their cars to the grand entrance, calling out, for example, *"Machina Britanskovo Posla"* (automobile of the British ambassador.) For mine he intoned, *"Machina Yew-naited P-r-ress Internashunn-all . . ."* As I stepped out of the Grand Kremlin Palace, Victor, our office chauffeur, held open the car door with a flourish. Below me the lights of Moscow glowed over the black silhouette of the Kremlin's ancient walls.

Just like Catherine the Great tonight, thought I.

The most exciting Kremlin reception I've attended was the one for Yuri Gagarin, the world's first cosmonaut. Pretty little girls holding garlands of flowers lined the red-carpeted stairs leading into St. George's Hall. As Major Gagarin strode in his military uniform into the room full of celebrated guests, golden trumpets sounded. The nation's top entertainment stars turned out in a program to honor the pilot. Ballerina Maya Plisetskaya twirled, the Red Army Chorus sang, and pianist Svyatoslav Richter played.

Our "night work" also includes private dinner parties at noncommunist embassies, plus that of Yugoslavia. We seldom receive invitations from communist embassies.

When I received my first invitation to an embassy black-tie dinner party, I had visions of at last hearing from those "diplomatic sources" that I'd been reading about in foreign news despatches.

During dinner the guests indulged in small talk. They were seated according to languages. Speaking only English and fair French and Russian, I was placed between an American-speaking American and an English-speaking Frenchman. On the latter's other side was a German woman who spoke French, and so on.

Dinner offered fresh meat, fruits, and vegetables flown in from Copenhagen—what I saw of them. On an assembly-line basis, in rolled fish with white wine, salad, meat with red wine, dessert with champagne. If you weren't ready for the second helping when it came around, you missed it.

After dinner, the diplomats drifted together and began to talk about a mysterious submarine then reported trapped near Argentina. But the hostess firmly led me in the other direction. I had to sit with the diplomats' wives. It's the custom for diplomats to exchange news minus the ladies after dinner. Instead of hot tips about the submarine, I heard, "My husband and I go for walks if we want to talk, there are so many microphones in our embassy . . ." and, "There wasn't a *thing* in the antique shop today . . ."

One ambassador's wife told me diplomats and their families hesitate to make Russian friends for fear the Soviet authorities will suspect them of forming "spy" contacts. One of the ladies was astonished that I had a few personal Russian friends. Most embassy personnel move exclusively on the diplomatic circuit. Another embassy wife told me that in her three years in the Soviet capital she had never been inside a Moscow restaurant.

Finally the diplomats joined their ladies. At last I could hear what diplomatic sources were saying. But they turned to me. "What do you hear about that strike in Karaganda?" "What did Khrushchev say in his speech today?"

Then I knew what "diplomatic sources" were: correspondents tell diplomats who tell other diplomats who tell other correspondents!

Members of the press corps entertain each other and other foreigners at dinners at home. The meats, fruits, and vegetables imported from Helsinki and stored in the deep freeze in our office are saved for guests. Or I cook out of cans or make spaghetti suppers. One night in my living room I counted people from Holland, England, Italy, and France, speaking a variety of languages.

The best big party given by a correspondent during my stay in Moscow still is nostalgically recalled as "The Great Voyage."

Joseph Michaels, then NBC correspondent in Moscow, decided to rent a boat on which to give a welcoming party for his replacement, John Chancellor. Michaels wrote letters night and day to UPDK. The unusual request—foreigners usually don't ply the river—filtered up to the Foreign Ministry. Permission was granted a day before the event, which was fortunate, the host already having sent engraved invitations to ninety guests from the foreign colony.

Foreigners in black ties and evening gowns pulled up in limousines to the boat dock at suburban Khimki. The Russians didn't quite know what to make of this spectacle.

Some thought a regular boat was at dock and occasionally a peasant with his knapsack had to be detoured back down the gangplank.

At the last second somebody discovered there were no ice cubes on the boat. Back to Moscow to the Metropole Hotel rushed the NBC Soviet translator, Yuri, breathlessly demanding ice. The reply was standard: "Write a letter." The translator sped to the NBC office, wrote a letter, decorated it with various official-looking stamps, and hurried back to the dining room. He immediately was awarded two sacks of ice.

When Yuri returned to Khimki, he saw the big steamer pulling away from the dock. Hailing a passing police launch, he shouted the equivalent of "Follow that boat" and caught up with us. He was hauled aboard via a ladder.

The boat was big enough for 750 people. It could have made the trip to London. In the salon a hired Russian band at first played gentle waltzes. After two numbers the boys in the band confessed to one of the French correspondents that they'd always wanted to try "viskey." Out came the Scotch. The music soon changed to some of the wildest rock 'n' roll heard this side of the world. The captain got so carried away he steered our boat far past the 25-mile limit for foreigners before turning back. The party was a smash success.

Such events are a principal source of relaxation. This is a city of make-your-own fun. Moscow doesn't sport night clubs.

I can do without them. But I confess I miss coffeehouses and little intimate restaurants. The only interesting example I found of the latter is one called the Artists' Café near the Moscow art theater where some of the smart young set, such as Deputy Premier Anastas Mikoyan's son, hang out.

There are a few *pivnaya,* or beer saloons, still open in Moscow, and two hotels have sweet liqueur "bars." But there's no bar in the western sense.

You can dance in most hotel dining rooms to Soviet "jazz" or popular tunes. Growing better every year. In a few hotels even American jazz has broken out. You don't hear real western jazz on the radio. Despite strenuous efforts, the Americans have not yet persuaded the Russians to accept jazz artists on the cultural exchange program.

But in the National and Budapest Hotels, young lively bands play "Honeysuckle Rose" and "How High the Moon." Beginning with the arrival of the American Exhibition in Moscow, the bands began to get jazzier. In 1960 the National band shook the chandeliers with rock 'n' roll, the Charleston, and music fairly close to "cool," or progressive, jazz.

This band was so "cool," in fact, it was transferred to the Budapest Hotel about the same time the *stilyagi* customers were also moved there from the National.

The more subdued replacement band at the National also shows promise. In 1961 it acquired a young girl pianist. She looked more like a medical student in her simple dress as she bent earnestly over the keyboard, her brown hair falling over her forehead, her make-up-less face serious. She imitates George Shearing, the American jazz pianist. In the audience one night was Hollywood night-club owner Gene Norman. He summed up the state of Soviet jazz playing in 1961 as he listened admiringly and said, "She almost makes it."

These band members like to chat with foreign dancers on the floor. They know more about progressive musicians than many Americans—"Gerry Mool-i-gan, Shortee Rozhers," they will say. Their arrangements are taken note for note from Glenn Miller, Errol Garner, Teddy Wilson, and other artists—taped from the Voice of America.

In fact, almost every Russian I've met has a tape recorder, not a phonograph, at home. Why a phonograph when the local records are not to their liking? They tape music from the "Voice" instead.

Dining out in Moscow can be summed up this way: the food is not as spectacular as Soviet spaceships. Most foreigners agree that good Russian food is served nicely in the National Hotel, which has elegant czarist-day décor and a view of the Kremlin to go with it. But even those dishes often leave a lot to be desired. The tastiest items include caviar, vodka, sturgeon, mushrooms cooked in sour cream, roast grouse, fresh cucumber salad, and ice cream. Chicken Kiev is a traditional Russian dish but I've eaten better at Chasen's restaurant in Los Angeles.

A typical dish in an average restaurant is a small steak or piece of thin roast chicken, hunks of potatoes drenched in grease, and peas and carrots. The latter vegetables look as if they have been boiled, beaten, hammered, and flogged until they are without vitamins as well as taste. The result is coated with a white sauce and served in heavy little pastry shells.

There's a "Chef's School" in Moscow that teaches its students to prepare food that way!

The first thing most of us foreigners do when we get

"outside" is head for the nearest restaurant and eat, eat, eat.

Sometimes visiting journalists happily report the menu in their hotel has 85 dishes and 50 wines. Just order one! Most of those dishes simply are not available.

I was fascinated by the first Russian menu I saw aboard the train coming from Berlin. It was even more fascinating to arrive in Moscow and see the identical menu in all Intourist hotels and restaurants. The restaurant trust is all-pervading. It's one of the Orwellian touches in the Soviet Union.

The restaurant in Moscow generally regarded as the best is the Aragvy, which doesn't serve Russian food, but Georgian. There you can order excellent *shashlik* and chicken *tabaka,* pressed between bricks.

Moscow also has restaurants for the other Soviet republics, such as Armenia. Tourists say the Ukraine Hotel sometimes has good Ukrainian food. But there the infiltration of "foreign" food stops. This is "made in Russia for Russians" territory.

I ate with two Germans at the beautiful pre-revolutionary dining room of the Berlin Hotel. The menu listed German dishes but my friends judged them as Russian. Once East German beer appeared but has seldom been seen since. I've never yet been able to get Prague ham and beer at the Praga restaurant in Moscow. I thought surely there must be many wonderful restaurants in Moscow run by the Russians' staunch friends, the Chinese. There is one, in the Peking Hotel. The food is served by Russian waiters to music by a Russian orchestra. And who is cooking all this Chinese food? Somebody with the fine, old Chinese name of Vasilyev.

The same Russification is evident at other "foreign" restaurants. When a new restaurant opened in the Budapest Hotel it was the biggest news for the press corps since Khrushchev came to power. Foreigners hurried over to eat while the Hungarians still were in the kitchen. Dry Hungarian wine, Hungarian goulash, stuffed cabbage, pâtés and salami, ah . . .

Two months later the Hungarian cooks went back to Budapest. Now the Budapest serves the same food as all the other restaurants.

The day the new Warsaw Hotel opened near Gorky Park I found the Polish designer surveying the dining room. I was sure he was from Warsaw. He was wearing a slack suit with hand-stitched lapels and seams, a yellow shirt, and a jazzy tie.

"The Polish cooks can stay in the kitchen only two months. Then the Russians say they must return to Warsaw," he sighed. "I had wonderful designs for the hotel but they changed those, too."

His idea of low-hanging "funnel" modern lamps was Russified into a chandelier that looks like a row of floodlights in a TV studio. The Russians think *every* room, even a subway stop, has to have a chandelier.

He was able to install a small bar after an argument. His little shops in the lobby were supposed to sell souvenirs from Poland. *Nyet!* Russian souvenirs only!

Nonetheless, this hotel was the first modern-looking hotel in Moscow, although a modest affair.

I had the best meal I've eaten in the Soviet Union— and one of the best in my life—in a roadside restaurant in the mountains of Soviet Georgia. I was traveling by Intourist limousine from Sukhumi, Georgia, to Sochi, Russia, after that strange passport affair. The Georgian chauffeur and a jolly Armenian friend he brought along for the return trip insisted I be their dinner guest.

We ate a dish called "mother"—hunks of tangy goat cheese stuck in a bowl of hot mush; a circular loaf of warm Georgian bread; juicy, tender *shashlik* on a spit; and a spicy red bean and onion dish. Our table was loaded with other delicious cheeses and wines that Georgians don't export to Moscow. We drank two bottles of wine apiece, with numerous glass-clinking to Georgians, Americans, Armenians (but no Russians), their mothers, my father, etc.

It was a gay and remarkable evening, and not just for the food. The stout, mustached Armenian decided that because I did not speak Russian fluently I would understand him better if he shouted. And so he did, asking about this San Joaquin Valley in California where his relatives lived.

In Georgia you can tell the progress of a party by the number of empty wine bottles traditionally placed on the floor by each table. After six empty bottles graced our floor, the Armenian and Georgian with relish started in on their third bottle apiece.

"But you are driving," I protested to the chauffeur.

"A Georgian can drink three bottles of wine and drive, but not four," he explained with dignity.

Back we whirled to Sochi in the pouring rain on a road that wound through the steep mountains. The driver entertained me with soulful Georgian songs and to my surprise negotiated every curve quite soberly.

As a change from Russian restaurants and theaters, foreigners can dine on hamburgers in a real American snack bar and drink Scotch in an American night club in Moscow. Both establishments are part of the American embassy and are operated for foreigners only.

The snack bar was built in a garage behind the embassy and is furnished with tables, chairs, and equipment left over from the 1959 American Exhibition in Moscow. An Italian cook prepares the cuisine. His *lasagne* and spaghetti are popular, not to mention American treats such as hamburgers, pancakes, and Coca-Cola.

The night club is "The American Club," run by embassy military personnel in their quarters. It looks like any military club—a simple bar at one end, a juke box, tables, and chairs. But it has a monopoly on Scotch and foreign dance music among the "dazzling" night spots of Moscow. So it is a popular place with foreigners. Twice a week American movies are shown on a 16-mm. machine, and once a week the guests cut loose and play bingo.

The British embassy has a smaller club, where the embassy staffers and their wives serve beer and whiskey. They show movies and even provide a dart game to make Londoners feel at home. On a bulletin board are posted such notices as: "A man has a severe case of frostbite because he did not like his fur hat with the earflaps down. Let this be a warning!"

Although this may sound as if the night life of the gods in Sovietland is dull, on the contrary the constant parties in restaurants, embassies, and apartments make life very lively during the few hours I can manage off from work. The foreign press corps and diplomats are a congenial group, and many have established a sticking-together-through-it-all camaraderie. Some diplomats sail from luncheons to teas to cocktail parties to suppers virtually daily.

In the wintertime, ski parties are organized and you can skate right on the sidewalks in the many parks or at regular skating rinks.

One day the temperature in Moscow hovered around 22 degrees below zero Centigrade. So I went for a swim. What else would you do in this topsy-turvy land? The Russians have what they proudly bill as Europe's largest outdoor heated swimming pool, opened a few blocks from the Kremlin in 1960. The pool is not hard to find on a wintry day. Steam billows up from it as at hot springs in Yellowstone Park in Wyoming.

After building up my morale, I walked on a heated floor from the dressing room to a small indoor pool. A dive under the half wall, and there was the blue sky barely visible through clouds of swirling steam. The water was like a lukewarm bath, 27 degrees Centigrade. I kept moving so that it washed over my face and arms. I didn't even feel as if I were swimming outdoors in the heart of the severe Russian winter—until I saw the pool ladders and diving board encrusted with icicles and thick frost. Around the pool stood spectators, wrapped in heavy clothing to their eyebrows as protection against the numbing cold.

"Do you have anything like this in America?" demanded the dressing-room attendant.

When I admitted we didn't, she chuckled, "Ho, ho! Russians are strong people!"

The long winter from October to April is depressing to many foreigners and natives alike, and everybody's spirits soar when the sun comes out. The Russians emerge from

their winter cocoons of fur. A community garden committee spades the front lawn of our apartment building
and carefully prunes the trees. The Russians haven't invented golf yet, but there are some tennis courts. Coat-
less young people stroll, six and eight abreast, in the
streets, playing accordions and softly singing. This is the
time to head for the river. Swimming parties on the
Moskva and Volga rivers are our summer fun, and range
from midnight dips with champagne to sunning on the
many well-kept river beaches around Moscow.

My favorite swimming place is a spot near Arkhangel-
skoye, a beautiful palace of the noble Usupov family which
is now a museum. The road from Moscow winds through
picturesque villages. Sometimes the car nudges by a
funeral procession, a little band playing, mourners carrying floral wreaths and the body in an open coffin high
above their heads. After passing the palace, the car
bounces over a dirt road to the wide, mud-colored river.

The grassy bank is an excellent site for Russian-watch-
ing. The lucky ones with cars pull picnic hampers out of
the baggage compartments just as in other countries.
Once a Russian wandered over to our group to inquire
in English if we would give him a copy of the New York
Times. Another day a bus rolled up with a party from a
factory. The group included a "games leader" who kept
trying to organize the holidayers into folk dancing and
songs.

An afternoon on the river is wonderful relaxation from
the 24-hour strain of covering one of the world's hottest
news centers. There is something also very Russian to
me about spending a day in the country; the quiet fields,

the slow-moving water give a feeling of the vastness and greatness that is Russia.

Little hotels in the country that accept foreigners are scarce. So UPDK maintains three *dachi* and a small hotel for us about a three-hour drive from Moscow. This foreign compound segregates us from the natives; but one week-end I spent there I wandered down the road to a nearby collective farm to watch shy, smiling farm girls storing wheat in a barn. Permission to go to this hotel is necessary, since the "resort" is far past the 25-mile limit allowed us.

The hotel has ten bathless rooms with a communal bath-room, a beach on the Volga River, a large motorboat, billiard room, TV room, and a dining room serving fresh fish from the river. Each *dacha* has two bedrooms, a living room and a bath, and a kitchen equipped with the works, including refrigerators.

It's comfortable, pleasant, and reasonable ($15 a day for a *dacha*, $5 for a hotel room). At one week-end *dacha* party some capitalistic foreigners meditated what they could do if only: "Remodel a couple of log peasant houses on the river into a small hotel . . . Decorate the dining room in peasant style, hire folk dancers as a floor show, a *troika* for rides in the wintertime, and import a chef from Paris who knows how to cook Russian food; . . . Ah, we'd be rich . . ."

14

Just the News That's Printed to Fit

On the morning of January 7, 1961, a newspaper scandal erupted on the pages of *Pravda*. The Communist party organ accused one of Moscow's regional newspapers, *Znamya Lenina* (*Lenin's Flag*), of making "a crude political mistake."

Pravda charged that *Znamya Lenina* had been "entertaining."

The little regional paper had printed photographs of reindeer one day instead of a letter from Premier Khrushchev to a communist-brigade buckwheat grower.

To "eliminate these shortcomings," the Moscow Communist Party Committee met and voted to send *Znamya Lenina* a couple of new staff members: "politically prepared personnel."

Soviet newspapers are supposed to instruct, not entertain. Their unique operation entertains some western observers, however. Sometimes I get so angry at the Soviet press I feel like throwing it across the room. Nonetheless, one of the best diversions in Moscow for me has been perusing the Soviet newspapers and Tass, the Soviet news agency.

I have saved a few choice examples of how reality is often viewed through Leninist-colored glasses. The Belgian embassy was stoned following Patrice Lumumba's death in February 1961, by foreign students, accompanied by Soviets, and then by a crowd of 2,000 Soviet students. Tass ignored the Soviet student group and reported that the demonstrators were "students from African, Latin-American, and Middle Eastern countries." The news agency added, "hundreds of Soviet citizens passing near the Belgian Embassy building at the time added their wrathful voice of protest to the voices of the demonstrators."

The end of direct censorship in the Soviet Union in March 1961 was not publicized in exactly the same way by Tass as by the western news agencies. Since, as is well known, censorship never officially existed, the Tass reporter had an easy job. While we correspondents filed thousands of words, he simply reported, "Beginning with today, foreign journalists accredited in the Soviet Union may use any telegraph office and any telephone for transmitting their despatches, the foreign correspondents were told today by chief of the Press Department, Mikhail Kharlamov.

"The foreign journalists may transmit their despatches over telephones from private homes, hotels, etc. This measure has been prompted by the fact that the number of correspondents of foreign newspapers, news agencies, and magazines has greatly increased in Moscow of late."

End of story.

The Soviet press is unlike the press in any other part of the world. It is devoid of comic strips, crossword puzzles, gossip columns (or any columnists), headlines about murders and celebrities, advice to the lovelorn, or other "entertaining" items. It publishes serious political news and commentaries, ideological lectures, and scientific articles that are not written for the twelve-year-old mind like those in many western newspapers. Satires, discussions on literature and art, and serious poems are also printed in the Soviet press, which has the over-all tone of a lecturer rather than of a chronicler of life in the country. Tourists say that the character of the press is one factor that makes the Soviet Union seem so confusing. One tourist, upon reading an English digest of the Moscow newspapers, said, "If we only read, 'Man bites dog on Gorky Street' once in a while the Russians might seem human instead of so frightening and political."

Virtually every story carries a political moral, one way or another. One western correspondent describes the Soviet press as a house organ. He says the newspapers resemble a company sheet put out by, say, the Happy Hairpin Company for its employees. There are stories about the Happy Hairpin president and his staff, their statements and travels; and of course much newsprint is expended to show how kind the Happy Hairpin Factory is to its employees.

"I don't comprehend your newspapers," I confessed during an interview with Alexei Adzhubei, who has had an understandably meteoric rise in the Moscow newspaper business. We sat in his large private office overlooking Pushkin Square and the towering statue of the great Russian writer.

"Our newspapers are not like yours," he replied. "The purpose of the Soviet press is to inspire the people to work."

This is an understandable goal in a country which is trying to overtake the rest of the world. Get-to-work is the subject of numerous daily articles in every one of

Moscow's newspapers—and, as noted before, eleven publish daily in the morning; six, three times a week; two, twice a week; two, once a week; and two, daily in the evening. A newspaper such as *Sovietskaya Russiya* will preach, for example, "Cattle breeders must first of all increase the number of cows by 20 to 25 per cent . . ." One of the most famous women in the Soviet Union is somebody the rest of the world never heard of, Valentina Gaganova. She has been written about here more extensively than Elizabeth Taylor in America—because she helped slow textile workers work faster.

But the press has another purpose which Adzhubei did not mention. It also promotes the sponsor of the house organ, the Bolshevik Communist party, and helps keep it and its policies in power in the Soviet Union.

Even *Krokodil*, the Soviet humor magazine, is part of the educational program. I asked the editor what was the purpose of his witty cartoons and stories.

"We fight against supporters of the cold war and against all that which hinders fulfillment of the seven-year plan," he answered, and he wasn't trying to be funny.

Only Bolshevik communist newspapers are printed. Lenin closed all but the Bolshevik press in 1917 in a "temporary" order, to be "revoked when normal conditions of public life are re-established." Apparently those conditions never have returned.

Thus while the newspapers carry no advertising as we know it, except for theater and store ads in one evening paper and wholesale ads in technical journals, they devote much space to indirect advertising for the "sponsor." "The wisdom and perspicacity of the Communist party, its correct leadership, the sedulous labor and dedicated effort of the heroic working class, the glorious collective-farm peasantry, and the people's intelligentsia have transformed our homeland into a mighty socialist state," utters *Pravda.*

An army officer wrote in one newspaper, "The Soviet people, including all the men in the army, know well enough the source of all progress in the Soviet Union is the wise policy of the Communist party. It is owing to [the Party's] constant concern and attention that the world's most advanced school of rocket engineering emerged in this country . . ."

Reports *Politicheskaya Samobrazovaniaya,* "The future of art largely depends upon the establishment of communism, the most humane and just system on earth."

"It is only under socialism that the problem of prolonging life has at last seen its way to solution," writes a doctor. "The absence of unemployment, sweeping housing construction, the steady improvement of conveniences for the working people . . . have facilitated the prolongation of life in the Soviet Union."

From the din set up on International Women's Day, a communist holiday, you'd think the Communist party not only invented the idea of working women, but invented women themselves.

The Party Line is interwoven into every article, whether the subject is the raising of cotton or the presentation of a new ballet. Party preachings like religious sermons rain incessantly down on the reader. Lenin often emerges as a gentle, fatherly, Christ-like figure. "V. I. Lenin loved children and dogs," *Moscow News* wrote tenderly on his birthday.

It sometimes requires second thoughts for westerners to figure out what a news story is about. The highly publicized introduction of the new "heavy" ruble turned out to be a devaluation of the official rate. The Soviet press daily told its readers that the ruble is "the world's strongest currency," while the "decrepit dollar" is fading away.

The Soviet press also announced, "The gradual abolition of the income tax, started in 1960, will result in no more taxes at all by 1964. Mankind never has known anything like it in all its history!" No mention is made of the sales tax. A pair of British shoes that cost $5.60 in England sells for $25 or $30 in Moscow—a "tax" paid by rich and poor alike.

As noted before, statistics on crime and the like are not yet published in the press. During the Party Central Committee meeting in January 1961, the hierarchy confirmed what some western observers had suspected all along, that many agricultural figures have been faked. Later *Economicheskaya Gazetta* reported that some industrial statistics have been juggled, too.

Soviet planners also do not compute statistics in the same way as is done in other countries. Wet and waste wheat is counted in wheat production figures. What is called a "doctor" here in medical propaganda is not a "doctor" in western countries. A person can earn the title here with three years less schooling than in the U.S. The Soviet press hails the Lenin Library as the world's biggest. But an American librarian who visited the Lenin Library told correspondents, "Why, they count every magazine and pamphlet, instead of bound volumes."

Americans are often criticized for boasting, but the

Soviet press can sometimes beat even Texans. Everything the Soviets make is proclaimed as the world's biggest, from the world's highest structure (a new TV tower) to the largest thermoelectric station. "The Soviet Union is ahead of capitalist countries both in absolute volume and per capita production of perfumes," said Tass, for instance.

The day Moscow newspapers declared "Soviet perfume is better than French perfume" was bad enough for the French correspondents. But when one newspaper held that "soon the world will be looking to Moscow to find out what women should wear," I thought the Agence France Presse scribes would choke.

Such occasional overenthusiasm on the part of the so-called journalists is not always matched by other people in the Soviet Union. While the Soviet press billed the opening of a Circarama theater with a 360-degree screen in Moscow as the first of its kind, at the preview for the press the film producers honestly noted that the first such screen was built at Disneyland, California.

An Italian correspondent, Alberto Ronchey of *La Stampa* in Milan, was electrified to read one day in 1960 that a painting in the storeroom of the Pushkin Museum had turned out to be a Botticelli. Now it hung on the museum walls, claimed the newspaper.

Ronchey raced to the Pushkin Museum. The amazed director said that (1) he was not sure the painting was a Botticelli, and (2) it was not being hung in the museum because he didn't think it was very good.

(Ronchey wrote a story relating exactly what had happened. The censor never passed the copy.)

Ferreting out what outsiders consider the real news takes careful scrutiny of every word in Soviet newspapers. The front pages usually are splashed with party decrees and long stories about milkmaids who overfulfilled their production quotas. Or a "hot" story: "The Central Committee of the Communist party of the Soviet Union in a message to the Central Committee of the Communist party of Georgia congratulated it upon the fulfillment by the republic of her socialist undertakings with regard to the sale of tea leaves to the government."

In a three-line story we read that "Comrade A. Kirichenko has been appointed First Party Secretary in Rostov," signifying the downfall of an important member of the Party's ruling Presidium. The firing of Nikolai Belyayev as First Party Secretary in Kazakhstan was uncovered first when Tass left off his title in listing several officials who had received medals.

Omissions and distortions in the Soviet press result in a one-sided picture for the reader. True, after studying the newspapers here, some observers opine that the western press is guilty at times of distortions and surface reporting. But this may be due to ignorance, sloppiness, or superpatriotism, not to a carefully planned party-government policy as in the Soviet Union.

For one thing, the advantages of life in the outside world are not mentioned in the Soviet press.

Soviet readers were not told that the Soviet Union was giving aid to communist forces during the Laos crisis of 1960–61. After the cease-fire, *Pravda* did say that Soviet planes had been sending in food. Nor have readers yet seen one word in their papers about the speculation trial of Olga Ivinskaya, friend of writer Boris Pasternak; nor mention of the two trials of alleged Soviet spies in London in 1961. The 1961 trial in Israel of accused ex-Nazi Adolf Eichmann was scarcely covered.

There is a good deal of "undersweeping rugwise," as we say in abbreviated "cablese." One Sunday afternoon, Moscow television carried a spirited football game. Toward the end, a horde of irate fans rushed from the bleachers onto the field to chase the referee. Suddenly the TV screen went blank and a voice intoned, "And now— some Russian folk songs!"

We combed the newspapers for days to find out what had happened. Not one word. Not even the score of the game. Not even a story that the game had taken place. Playing up such spontaneous group violence is not party policy. Weeks later one newspaper carried an item that ten persons had been jailed for "hooliganism" at a football game.

In October 1961, the Soviet press erupted in rage because a Soviet woman tourist had been questioned by Dutch police at the Amsterdam airport. The Moscow newspapers never mentioned that she was involved in the airport incident because her husband defected to the West. In fact, the Soviet press never even mentioned she had a husband.

Similarly when a Soviet rocket with two dogs aboard burned up in 1961, this fact was mentioned in the last line of a Tass communiqué. Otherwise the newspapers were silent about the failure.

We correspondents filed hundreds of thousands of words, pictures, and film footage to foreign newspapers and radio and television networks about Yuri Gagarin's historic flight. But when the first American cosmonaut took his 15-minute ride into space, the Russian press did not reciprocate. The day of the flight, the Soviet press did not mention it was scheduled. Instead, the papers printed a story about how the American astronauts planned to buy property with money reaped from their venture. After the successful launching, most of the newspapers carried only the brief Tass announcement. During the next few days some newspapers printed a Tass commentary and interviews with Soviet scientists who pointed out that while the American flight was an achievement it was inferior in every way to Gagarin's. Not one photograph of Alan Shephard has yet been printed in the newspapers; not one film of the flight has showed up on television.

The Soviet press was silent on the flight of the second American cosmonaut, Virgil Grissom. Then the Soviet newspapers had a field day reporting the loss of Grissom's space ship.

Soviets who want to fill in the gaps in their knowledge of current events try to listen to the British Broadcasting Corporation and Voice of America broadcasts in Russian (often jammed) or English (usually not jammed). Non-communist publications are not sold within the Soviet Union, but Soviet journalists see a Tass digest of the foreign press. Journalists can also subscribe to western publications at their offices.

A Moscow grapevine operates among the "in" set with surprising speed. When I complained to a Communist that reports of rocket failures, most airplane accidents, and many government intermural battles are conspicuously absent from the Soviet press, he explained, "We don't want outsiders to know about our difficulties. And, as far as the Soviet people are concerned, sooner or later we all find out what is happening, anyway."

Typed copies of articles published in the *Manchester Guardian* and the New York *Times* about Soviet-Chinese differences during the November 1960 communist "summit" conference circulated among some Muscovites. So did a report that the Russians had withdrawn their technicians from China, an item that never saw the light of *Pravda*.

Many Soviets apparently are well educated by their press. Once in the National Hotel café two Russian teen-age girls sat at my table. During our conversation I pointed out to them a speculator who the day before had tried to buy dollars from me.

"I don't believe that," said one girl indignantly. "Why would he want to buy dollars? Our press says the ruble is stronger."

But many other Russians understand they have to read between the lines. When I asked one if he had heard of the 1960 drought in China, he said, "No, but *Pravda* might say the Soviet Red Cross contributed money to the Chinese Red Cross, and we would guess why." (The drought finally was mentioned in a Sino-Soviet trade agreement as a "calamity of nature.")

Some readers of the Soviet press complain over the way Papa Party tells them the story of the stork, so to speak. I almost fell out of a Moscow taxicab when the driver related what I thought was strictly a foreigners' joke about *Pravda*, which means "truth," and *Izvestia*, which means "news": "There is no truth in *Pravda* and no news in *Izvestia*."

A Soviet journalist once told me that a letter sent to his

newspaper said, "If you don't want us to listen to the Voice of America and BBC, why don't you give us the western point of view?" The writer signed his name, but the letter was not published.

Radio Moscow and the Soviet newspapers have no intention of doing that yet, if ever. But a more liberal policy resulted in the printing of President Kennedy's inaugural address in full. The Ukrainian press revealed an earthen dam collapse in 1961, and it's rare that a major internal disaster has been printed. The lively Soviet press outpourings on Gagarin and Titov were unprecedented, old Muscovites say. Although the "personality cult" is condemned by the Party, Gagarin and Titov became the object of one. Many of the newspapers looked temporarily almost like western tabloids, with lively headlines, entire pages of photographs devoted to the spacemen, and—in regular "bourgeois style"—interviews with their wives and other members of their families. In fact, later a *Pravda* journalist writing in *Sovietsky Pechat,* a publishing trade magazine, complained that some Soviet reporters in a wild competitive scramble barged uninvited into Gagarin's apartment and absconded with the family photograph album and personal letters. "Some Soviet newspapermen were carried away by some strange, completely impermissible ecstasy, and instead of covering the event in a businesslike way, tried to create sensations," wrote the *Pravda* correspondent.

Alexei Adzhubei brought a fresh, western look to *Izvestia* when he became editor. The theretofore old-fashioned building blossomed out with modern furniture and even a bar for executives that was the talk of the town. The newspaper acquired a livelier make-up and a Sunday supplement. On the first day of spring in 1961 the supplement printed what Russians say was the first nonpolitical, non-party-lining editorial in Soviet history. It was about spring, and it was the sensation of Moscow. One day *Izvestia* even printed a picture of a girl in a bathing suit on water skis. Because of poor reproduction methods, the paper's photographs still look as if they were boiled in formaldehyde, but there are more of them.

Izvestia printed the full text of editor Alexei Adzhubei's November 1961 interview with President Kennedy. But not even a summary was given the millions of readers of other Soviet publications.

The good, gray, grave *Pravda* remains the same, however.

Although the Soviet newspapers may be short on what westerners regard as complete information, they are long on unsurpassed colorful language. The feeling for drama and the broad emotions of the Russian people fairly sizzle in their newspaper stories. For instance, I will cherish forever this lead from *Izvestia*: "Like a flash of lightning in a tropical storm, the brutal murder of Patrice Lumumba and his comrades-in-arms showed to the whole world the monstrous grin of the colonial butchers."

What is sometimes dull political fodder in other countries becomes the subject for passionate reporting in Russian papers. The Soviet people "boiled with wrath" over Lumumba's death, according to the press, and Dag Hammarskjold was called everything from a "dog" to a "blood-stained murderer." The Soviet delegate gave a "pithy" speech at the Geneva Nuclear Test conference.

And always "the soil of Africa burns beneath the feet of the wretched colonialists."

In 1960 when the anti-West German campaign reached a peak, *Pravda* printed a letter from a worker advising "that fox Adenauer to defecate [only a Russian four-letter equivalent was used] in his pants."

Foreign correspondents often are severely lashed. When Edouard Bobrovsky of *Le Figaro* wrote that Vladimir Ilyushin, not Yuri Gagarin, was the first man into space, *Izvestia* charged the scribe was "wallowing in his ink-well . . . a Lilliputian trying to build a paper ladder to crawl over the Soviet Gulliver . . ."

Some stories might reap a harvest of libel suits if they were printed in other countries. *Izvestia,* for example, lit out after Marilyn Monroe because she divorced playwright Arthur Miller. His plays, *Death of a Salesman* and *View from the Bridge,* are highly popular in Soviet Russia and regarded as exposing the evil ways of capitalist life. Assuming she tossed Miller aside, *Izvestia* scathingly listed the symbols of the American way of life as "chewing gum, Coca-Cola, and Marilyn Monroe." "Marilyn's path to the stars is as ruthless as was old Rockefeller's to Wall Street," said the party organ, neatly killing two capitalist birds with one sentence.

The paper went on to give a biography of Marilyn which was almost as fanciful as the one the Hollywood studios furnished at the beginning of her climb to fame. *Izvestia,* the spokesman for the government of the Union of Soviet Socialist Republics, proclaimed that Marilyn had "posed for pornographic magazines." When, according to *Izvestia,* Marilyn's "contracts grew more and more infrequent, and poverty knocked at the door," she "created another sensation. She married Joe Di Maggio. But Di Maggio's happiness soon came to an end. He had wanted a wife and family and never suspected he was being used for publicity purposes by a heartless woman . . ."

Then, when Marilyn, described as "a tasty bit of meat," began to "lose favor" again, she married Miller, charged *Izvestia*. "She exploited him mercilessly," the newspaper continued. "He wrote scripts for her and turned her into a real actress. And Marilyn paid him back by throwing him over. The dream of millions cannot belong to only one man, she told newspapermen. She still is clambering toward the stars, leaving another smashed life in her wake."

Until this story appeared, incidentally, only a few Soviet journalists who had access to western publications were aware of Marilyn's fame. Somehow the same journalists also knew that I had broken the story of the nude calendar. Over and over again I have been asked by various Russian scribes to tell about that scoop and relate what Marilyn is "really" like.

In addition to its extravagant language, some other touches entertain detached observers of the Soviet press. After every rocket launching, with the unswerving regularity of the rising sun each Soviet newspaper is splashed with drawings, cartoons, and little poems. Many of the drawings show the "new Soviet man" in overalls, eyes fixed on the horizon, while around him whir rockets bearing the hammer and sickle label. Surrounded by praising comments from scientists and workers from, say, ball-bearing factory No. 27 in Minsk is the usual poem, such as:

"Dear Venus, I have a lot of questions to ask you.
You won't be tired of them, will you?
Maybe you have people down there, Venus?
And what symbols on your coat of arms?"

Soviet newspapers have an aura of conformity about them because they all are devoted to the Party. The editors meet to plan press-wide support of some aspect of party policy. Before Premier Khrushchev makes a trip, both the press and radio usually drum steadily on the theme of Friendship with India, or wherever he's going. Campaigns against religion, drunks, nationalism in the Baltic states, idlers, abstract art, and snoopy foreigners are old favorites. Anti-American propaganda is a timeworn but durable device. Articles cry out about "the dark and repugnant abyss of America's hunt for the dollar," and so on. Often an entire issue of a magazine, such as the Sunday supplement of *Izvestia*, will be devoted to the ills of American life. While constantly emphasizing America's dreadful side, the press also persistently prods the Soviet people to work harder so that they can "catch up with and surpass" the high living standard and productivity of America. Observers wonder if this paradox does not result in schizophrenia on the part of some readers.

Soviet leaders act surprised when American diplomats in Moscow point out that relations might improve if the press toned down its steady anti-American campaign. The Soviets have the attitude that the campaign is for internal use only; why, they say, it has nothing to do with intergovernmental relations.

The press also features many one-shot campaigns. If any "letters to the editor" are needed to bolster the spread, they can easily be ordered up from party functionaries in factories, offices, etc. Some of the letters sound as if they were written by *Pravda* correspondents. For instance, *Pravda* reported that "A. Petrov, a laboratory assistant at a Moscow research institute, calls 'Tshombe, Kasavubu, and Mobutu traitors to the Congolese people, who committed a black crime when they stained their hands with the blood of the best sons of the Congo with the open connivance and support of the U.N. Secretary General. However, the colonialists miscalculated. The wheel of history cannot be turned back and it is impossible to force the courageous Congolese people to their knees. Your days are numbered, Messrs. Colonialists! Freedom for Africa! Kick Hammarskjold, a bigot and hireling of the colonialists, out of the United Nations.' "

Before the American Exhibition opened in Moscow, the Soviet press united in an extensive campaign to prevent the people from believing all they were going to see. Article after article tried carefully to counter every section of the exhibition, from medicine to abstract art. Muscovites read stories daily about "rising prices, growing inflation, taxes, mass unemployment" in the United States. The $13,000 "typical American home" of the show was ripped to shreds in print. ("It *was* typical," I have told at least twenty inquiring Russians since.) The same don't-you-believe-it barrage hammered away at the 1961 French Exhibition in Moscow.

The rescue by an American aircraft carrier of four Soviet soldiers adrift for seven weeks in the Pacific Ocean was the subject of another one-shot campaign. The boys were lost in January of 1960, but the Soviet press said not one word while the search for them was going on. The

U.S. Navy announced the rescue March 8. *Izvestia* printed the story March 12. For the next few weeks the entire press was saturated with the saga of the soldiers.

We foreign correspondents were awed by the stream of stories. They were angled on two themes: (1) the boys were anxious to get home ("Our four noble boys are hurrying home to their motherland," the newspapers repeated again and again); (2) the boys survived because the Bolshevik Communists are in power. "The soldiers demonstrate the exceptional modesty, calm, confidence, and strong character of the Soviet Man, the man of the new world, whom the Communist party has fostered," said *Pravda*. "Our soldiers' courage is due to the fact that they were brought up under the glorious traditions of Lenin's Communist party," heralded another journal. Nobody mentioned that they had been sheltered in a boat, or that they were young and used to a hardy life.

Article after article pointed out that capitalist-bred men collapse under stress and fight over the last crumb of bread. *Pravda* cited as an example the American airmen of the "Lady Be Good" bomber which crashed in North Africa during World War II, leaving only a diary "replete with despair, horror of death, and sorrowful prayers."

The press reported that Premier Khrushchev telegraphed President Eisenhower to thank him for the rescue. Khrushchev thanked the mayor of San Francisco, George Christopher, for receiving the heroes. The Soviet Minister of Defense thanked the American Defense Secretary. Khrushchev thanked the four soldiers for their "heroic exploit." Each of the four soldiers' parents sent telegrams to Khrushchev thanking him for thanking their boys. Then the four soldiers sent telegrams thanking Khrushchev for, etc., etc.

The telegrams were written in *Pravda* style. A *Pravda* man was accompanying the boys home.

Soon the press was inundated with eyewitness accounts signed by the boys but carrying the journalistic flavor of that *Pravda* escort. One article underlined the boys' "passionate desire to return home soon, in the family of the Soviet people." Another declared, "We shall be our Motherland's devoted sons, to our last breath!"

While the boys still were on the high seas en route home, their "eyewitness accounts," signed by them, already were selling like *blini* on the Moscow book stands. This was too much even for some of the Moscow newspapers, which complained things were being overdone.

Songs were written in honor of the boys. Poems such as the following were abundant:

> "No strength because of hunger
> Their rudder is powerless in the waves
> Only the light of their motherland
> Shines in the heart of the young Komsomols."

When the soldiers arrived at the airport in Moscow, a party leader made a speech. Another party man made a speech. An army man made a speech. Nobody asked the four heroes to say anything.

The campaign was the most wondrous piece of press agentry I have ever seen. I take off my fur hat to the Soviet press.

Newspapers in the U.S.S.R. are very frank about the role their journalists play. As *Economicheskaya Gazetta* put it, "To continue to be the vehicles of Lenin's ideas, active propagandists of the policy of the Communist party

—in this Soviet journalists see the purpose of their life and work."

During the period of liberalization in the U.S.S.R., many Russian journalists have begun to act more like western journalists. Some who have toured foreign countries with Khrushchev or seen foreign correspondents in action now run faster, ask more questions, and elbow their way to be first, as do their western counterparts. Many Soviet journalists try to write accurate reports and still keep within the allotted propaganda framework.

One day late in 1959 during the "*mir i druzhba*" era, one of *Pravda's* top reporters telephoned to ask if I would accompany him around Moscow before New Year's Eve to feel the pulse of Russian friendliness toward Americans. He promised me a ride in Khrushchev's helicopter—an offer that sounded too exciting to pass up.

First we were driven in *Pravda's* chauffeured limousine to Moscow University to watch a holiday show staged by some chemistry students. Later at a students' dance and in the university cafeteria we were surrounded by students asking questions about America.

The next day the *Pravda* man and I toured a machine-tool factory. I was besieged by workers who popped the usual questions at first: "Why do you have bases overseas?" "Why won't you get your troops out of West Berlin?" But then soon came curious queries: "How many hours do Americans work?"

As we left, the *Pravda* man said, "Now, wasn't everybody nice to you? Will you let me quote you as saying, 'There is no iron curtain in Moscow'?"

"I can't say that as long as we have censorship and other restrictions," I said.

Days later his story appeared. He wrote that "a lively, not unfriendly conversation" took place between me and the factory workers. He did not mention iron curtains. He quoted what I said accurately; but he omitted most of my answers to the workers, and my remark on censorship.

Manning the propaganda machine that sends the Soviet message and version of world news to countries all over the world is another job of Soviet journalists. A Tass English-language machine that transmits Tass copy abroad stands in our office. From reading the copy, one would think little but strikes, peace marches, bread lines, airplane accidents, mine disasters, and Communist party meetings take place in countries abroad. News about Soviet scientific, agricultural, and industrial accomplishments and about the wisdom of Soviet foreign policy hums soothingly over the wires. Western countries are painted as evil enemies of the newly independent Afro-Asian countries (the Soviets do not call the latter "capitalist countries"). The Socialist Camp is pictured as always on the side of "the people." The propaganda writers capitalize easily on western mistakes, and benefit skillfully from such events as racial difficulties in the United States.

To win friends around the world, Tass will even embrace the Russian Church. The Soviet press attacks the clergy as rapists and embezzlers for the benefit of the home folks; but propaganda directed to Moslem countries in Africa and Asia and to Catholics in Latin America may quote Russian bishops as calling for disarmament or the like.

One Russian Easter morning, Bud Korengold and I were sitting around the UPI office reading the Sunday papers. We were eating *blini* that my maid, Tonya, had made, soaked with sour cream and tasty gray caviar.

"Christ's resurrection is a myth," I began to read from one newspaper. It berated believers who still crowd the churches, particularly on Easter.

Korengold picked up copy from the Tass teletype in English that goes abroad. "Today in churches throughout the Soviet Union people gathered to hear the Easter message read by the patriarch of the Russian Orthodox Church," the Tass despatch began.

Propaganda that goes out by mail includes magazines on all subjects. Once I asked the Cultural Committee to let me tour the office of a woman's magazine in order to do a story on the *McCall's* of Moscow. I was puzzled to find at the office of the magazine, *Soviet Woman,* people preparing an issue in English, Chinese, German, French, Hindi, Hungarian, Japanese, Korean, and Spanish.

"We soon will begin to send copies to North Africa," the editor said.

"Why?" I asked.

"We have had many requests from people there who wish to read it," was the reply.

Moskovitchi say they have seldom seen this magazine on their newsstands. It is purely a propaganda medium for consumption abroad. Each issue contains a feature called "Lessons in Communism," plus articles claiming that while seamy conditions exist for women in capitalist countries a better life is given women in the U.S.S.R. Some stories describe how Soviet men and women receive equal wages with five months off with pay for women having babies (true), or how easy it is in Moscow to telephone to have your laundry delivered and windows cleaned (not quite true).

Many correspondents arrive in Moscow with the best

wishes toward the Soviet people and an open mind toward their system. But within a few months many aspects of Soviet life for foreigners drive the most cheerful scribe into fits of the blues.

The traditional isolation of the Russian from the foreigner is only one depressing factor. An abyss still yawns between Russians and even scribes fluent in the Russian language. An American correspondent in Toyko who came to Moscow told me newsmen in that alien culture do not feel as isolated as those stationed in Moscow.

Undoubtedly the worst aspect for many correspondents is the Soviet press. One Swedish correspondent heading for a vacation at home said, "It's reading those papers every day. I can't stand it."

I didn't realize how the steady drip-drip of Soviet propaganda was wearing down my own peace of mind until I took my first trip "outside" after a year and a half in Moscow. The colored neon lights of Stockholm below the airplane were dazzling. Then came the city itself; filled with beautiful slender women in high heels and short skirts, smart suits, and lovely hats. Bananas, tomatoes, lettuce, grapefruit, all foods in the grocery stores. People smiling, filling cafés and smart restaurants. And the noise! Young people talking and laughing on the street, music booming from a coffeehouse. It was such a change from quiet Moscow I wanted to scurry to a corner and cover my ears with my hands.

It took about a month for me to get my mind back in focus. Furthermore, only after many days did I get over the feeling of being watched, and wondering if the car at the corner was following me.

Most correspondents experience this impact. Some are

then doubly furious at the Soviet press for the way it pictures the outside world.

Within a few days of exposure to the Soviet press again after returning to Moscow from abroad, I felt "suspended" in another world, floating once again in "wonderland."

15

The Powers Trial

In the early afternoon of May 5, 1960, the Soviet-American *"mir i druzhba"* era abruptly came to an end.

I was sitting in booth No. 10 at the Central Telegraph Office in Moscow, dictating to UPI in London a story about the abolition of Soviet income taxes at a session of the Supreme Soviet. In the back room of the CTO, other foreign correspondents were clustered around a radio, taking notes in relays of Premier Khrushchev's speech before the Soviet-style parliament. We rival correspondents peacefully coexist, and to get basic information for such stories as Khrushchev's speech we even team up because our staffs are too small for adequate individual coverage.

I had just hung up on London and emerged from the telephone booth when a correspondent in the back room shouted, "Khrushchev says they've shot down an American plane!"

Many correspondents hurriedly drove the eight blocks or so to the Kremlin to join others in the press gallery watching the session of the Supreme Soviet. The sight of the Premier waving photographs of the American U-2 airplane as he stood before a statue of Lenin was like a dream—or, rather, a nightmare.

So was the thought that the pilot, Francis Gary Powers, was in Moscow. Nearly every day after that I drove from the Central Telegraph Office to the UPI bureau past the Lubiyanka prison, famous as a detention center for political prisoners in the thirties. It was chilling to think that a fellow countryman was sitting behind bars in that ordinary-looking stone building, perhaps looking out at my white sports car purring by.

The censors, then still in operation, allowed us to write that Powers was imprisoned in Moscow. But we could not say "in Lubiyanka." Some correspondents reasoned that the very name has such a bad connotation for Russians that they don't want it published.

Powers' unexpected arrival in the Soviet Union suspended the peace and friendship honeymoon. It had begun, more or less, with Prime Minister Macmillan's trip to Moscow in February 1959 and with the opening of the American Exhibition in July of the same year and that was at its warmest during Premier Khrushchev's first visit to the United States the following September. After May 5, 1960, relations between the Soviet Union and the U.S. plunged to what veteran Soviet experts called rock bottom.

Some Americans in Moscow felt defensive, others embarrassed, others sorry, and some antagonistic over the U-2 incident. Many were deeply worried as to where the trail would end.

The first few days after Powers landed uninvited in the Soviet Union, we watched carefully for the Russian reaction. Officially contacts froze at first. Before the U-2, the ice had thawed to such an extent that Soviet officials were even attending private dinner parties in American diplomats' apartments right inside the American embassy. A diplomat told me at one such party that this had never happened before during the period of the cold war.

But following Powers' unscheduled visit, some Soviet officials sent their regrets to an American diplomat who had earlier invited them to a dinner party set for May 7. Invitations to other private dinners at the American embassy were refused by Soviet officials.

Yet two months later came the sure sign that officially the Soviets did not want to shut the door completely. Deputy Premier Anastas Mikoyan and Party Secretary Frol Kozlov showed up at the American embassy July Fourth party along with a contingent of other Soviet officials. In fact, it was one of the best July Fourth turnouts of Soviets that many foreigners in Moscow could remember.

On a personal level, correspondents encountered the same pattern: it was difficult to make new friends with Russians; and social contacts with already established Russian acquaintances lessened. One day in May a Russian friend told me he was on his way to a Russian party. He couldn't take me, he said, "because you are in a dangerous profession. You ask too many questions."

Bud Korengold of our office had a chronic complaint that respectable Russian girls were hesitant about dating foreigners, particularly Americans. Shortly before the U-2 incident, Bud finally found a female Soviet friend. But after Powers was added to the foreign colony in Moscow, the girl told Bud her co-office workers had advised her against going out with an American. She also said with alarm that "somebody" had been asking her neighbors questions about her.

Some Russians who had personal relations with foreigners seemed not to want to give them up altogether. I had had a luncheon appointment for the day after the

U-2 incident with my friend Mikhail, who was coming from Leningrad to Moscow on business. I wasn't sure he would show up—but he did. "Everybody I know is dismayed because things had been going so well," he said.

Later another Russian intellectual I saw said, "My friends have expressed shock and regrets. But I've also heard admiration for what a fantastic machine that U-2 is!"

Foreigners could distinguish some curiosity on the faces of Russians who crowded on long lines to see the U-2 wreckage that the Soviets carefully put on display in a chess hall in Gorky Park. The people were indignant, yes, but they still like to look at machinery. The black airplane and its intricate parts, the poison "pin," the gold coins and other spy apparatus all made quite an imposing sight. Intourist put the U-2 exhibit on the city tour of Moscow for tourists, and the show came to be known around town as the American Exhibition No. 2.

One day I went to Gorky Park to copy down remarks that Russians and foreign tourists alike had written in a comment book near the exhibit. Every time I tried to read the book, two teen-age Russian girls indignantly snatched it away as if I were another U-2 spy. It was one of the few times during my stay in Russia that anyone appeared actually hostile to me. But I understood their patriotic fervor.

Some Russians were frightened. The day after the U-2 landing was revealed, word got around that anti-aircraft balloons were being erected over Moscow to snare American bombers on the way. Russians could be seen on Gorky Street and Red Square, staring at the sky and discussing the situation with apparent anxiety. (This incident also demonstrates that, despite Soviet progress in science, Russians are just as prey to rumors and old wives' tales as people in other countries.)

The consternation of the Soviet people over the U-2 was even more obvious to me during a few days' vacation I spent that summer of 1960 in Sochi on the Black Sea. After collapsing for two days' sleep in my little $1.80 a day hotel room across the street from the beach, I ventured out late one afternoon to sample the souvenirs and the citizenry. The souvenirs were the same silver-and-enamel vodka cups, the same lacquered boxes you find in any souvenir shop anywhere in the Soviet Union.

I walked through the outdoor bazaar near the wharves where the passenger liners dock, watching Soviet tourists surging around the stands. Like me, some from Armenia were buying color film. In the Soviet Union, film usually comes without a roller. You have to buy one and then wind the film on it in a dark room. In my search of every Sochi store by the boat terminal I could not find a roller. I finally gave up and, in the cool of the early evening, watched sunburned couples—boys in white open-necked shirts, girls in cotton print dresses—dancing to "Chatanooga Choo-Choo" in one restaurant. Then I strolled across the street to look at the port terminal building roof. It was trimmed with dolphins standing on their heads. On each corner stood a statue of a woman, with reindeer or other such oddities in her arms. This entire creation was bathed in blinding light.

"*Vee Polsha?*" a voice behind me inquired.

"No," I answered in Russian as I turned to face three young men, "I am not Polish, I am American."

That made them even more interested in striking up an

acquaintance. So we sauntered across the square to an ice-cream stand in a little park with tables and chairs. A girl in a white uniform weighed out 100 grams of ice cream in lovely mounds in a silver goblet for me.

First came the usual questions: "How much money do you make?" "Is London as big as Sochi?" (Sochi's population is 300,000.) "Why don't American rockets work?"

I was waiting for the inevitable U-2 questions such as those I had heard from taxi drivers and other Russians in Moscow, and I wasn't disappointed. "Your airplane, why did you send that over us?" demanded one young man. "Americans are aggressive and militaristic." "How would you feel if a Soviet plane flew over Chicago or New York?" "Eisenhower is a bad man to send the airplane." "Why do you want to spy on us?"

"Yes, perhaps the flight was ordered at a bad time, before the summit conference. Many Americans are sorry this happened," I told the young men.

This stopped their line of questioning. They appeared satisfied. Then I could not resist adding, "But you have spies in our country, too."

"That is not true," one of the trio said, laughing. "Never."

But the others said, "What? Who?"

I related all the details of Soviet spy history I could remember, from the Abel trial to Soviet trawlers prowling around U.S. shores. These boys reacted as if they had never before heard of Soviet spies.

Finally the waitress, who had been hovering around, told the boys to go away. Apparently she thought they were bothering me. We made a date to meet at the same place the next day.

By that time I had had the same conversation a dozen

times over with other Russians in Sochi. The first question a friendly Russian usually asks a foreigner is, "Where are you from?" When I replied, "The United States," the complaints, indignant outbursts, and hurt questions would begin. Almost every Russian I met, from taxi drivers and store clerks to other guests on the hotel beach, shared one common reaction—bewilderment and almost child-like naïveté about why on earth the Americans would want to spy on the Russians. Why are Americans afraid of Soviets? they wondered. Most Russians do not know how their country's foreign policy and speeches about the victory of communism affect people on the other side of their sealed-in world. As the word "peace" constantly rains down on Soviet people, many feel the socialist countries are the only peaceful ones.

Tired of the spy discussions, I retreated to the beach to brood in silence instead of meeting the three boys. Moscow Radio—the ever-present Big Brother—was broadcasting the latest commentaries on the "provocation" and "violation of our borders." I sat up and looked cautiously around me. I was the only American in Sochi at the time as far as I knew, and certainly the only one on the beach. I felt very self-conscious and alone.

But the Russians were ignoring "Big Brother" in favor of carefully applying sun-tan oil, white paper nose guards, and makeshift sun hats. I joined the few swimmers who ventured outside the stone wall marking the deep water. (Most Russians stay on the shallow side.) The next time somebody said, *"Vee Czechoslovakskaya?"* I answered, *"Da"* (Yes), and swam away.

Later, back in Moscow, some American students touring the country told correspondents they were in Yalta when the U-2 incident was broadcast over the "Big Brother" radios that hang on the streets. Everywhere the boys went —in parks, on street corners, in restaurants—groups of Russians gathered to argue, complain, or just talk with them about the U-2. To one large argumentative group the boys replied, "It was a government order, it was not our doing." Then one of the men in the crowd said to the other Russians, "Comrades, it was Eisenhower's fault, not these boys', so leave them alone."

The only truly hostile incident was reported by two American embassy wives. They said they were spat on at Gum by an elderly woman. Otherwise nobody was violent or wrote "Go home, Yankee" on our cars. Russians are too polite to foreigners for that.

One other trend was noticeable among Russians who talked to foreigners about the U-2 incident. Although they unanimously objected to the flight, they weren't quite so positive that their Premier should have walked out on the summit conference. Some Russians appeared extremely disappointed the meeting had not come off.

By August the constant campaign in the press over the U-2 and the downfall of the summit had whipped up excitement in Moscow to a fine pitch over the Powers trial. Word whirled round Moscow that the trial would be held in the House of Unions, an elegant dark green and white building near the Bolshoi Theater that had been a noblemen's club in czarist days. The building seemed logical as a trial site because it was being repainted. We figured that the Russians, who like to stage events to perfection, would want the building to be in ideal shape. Correspondents kept watch on the workmen in coveralls painting on their scaffolds. When the repair work was finished, we reasoned, the trial would be announced, which it was—August 17, 1960, a date on our calendars that few Moscow correspondents will forget.

Most of the foreign correspondents who covered the Powers trial agreed the event itself was not a trial in the western sense of the word. It was a well-staged show. It fittingly was held, not in a courtroom, but in the concert hall of the House of Unions. To us correspondents covering the event from the balcony, it was an odd sensation to see an American spy walk onto the stage of the hall where Rachmaninoff and Tchaikovsky had played. With his crew haircut, American accent, and simple way of speaking, he made me think of soda fountains and main streets and sport shirts and other symbols of ordinary American life—so very, very far from this very Russian room with its crystal chandeliers and marble columns. Yet there the American sat, listening intently through an earphone to the English translation, sometimes fiddling with a pencil, on the same stage where the Soviet political purge trials of the thirties had been held.

The Press Department of the Foreign Ministry and the Central Telegraph Office had reproduced our CTO setup in a hall outside the press balcony. Long-distance telephone booths, typewriters, tables, and even a battery of censors in all languages were provided. However, after the first day, correspondents dictated their copy on the telephone without even writing it first. The censors at first cut us off as we gave our running account to our offices in London, Helsinki, or Frankfurt. But after listening to what the correspondents reported, the censors let their cut-off switches alone.

Details of the trial, of Powers' confession, of his defense

that he was just a paid tool of the U.S. government, and of his eventual ten-year prison sentence are well known and need not be repeated here. But while the trial was going on, another drama, just as powerful but not so well known, was unfolding behind the scenes.

When Powers' parents and his wife arrived separately in Moscow before the trial, it was clear that the family for various personal reasons was divided into two camps. The father, Oliver Powers, or "Pop," as the correspondents casually dubbed him, had in his camp the manager of a dry-goods store from his town of Pound, Virginia; the senior Powers got to know the storekeeper, Sol Curry, by going across the street to use the store telephone. Oliver Powers also was accompanied on his long trip to Moscow by his own lawyer, a young fellow also from Virginia; and by his wife.

The parents were judged by correspondents to be unstudied folks who understandably did not know how to handle the publicity spotlight they found themselves in.

Barbara, the wife, arrived in a different airplane, her pretty face set with a determined look. She moved with poise and seemed more at ease in the glare of publicity than the rest of the family. One day I invited Barbara and *her* camp—two lawyers, a doctor, and her mother—to dinner at my apartment after they complained about the food at the Sovietskaya Hotel, where the entire Powers clan was quartered. One of her attorneys called to say with regret that they were too busy talking about the trial to come to dinner. The next day Barbara sent me a note on what stationery stores call "informals"—small note cards engraved, "Mrs. Francis Gary Powers." I was struck by the control the woman must have had to remember to bring "informals" to Moscow where she was going to attend her husband's trial that might result in his execution as a spy.

The Sovietskaya Hotel established Barbara's and "Pop" Powers' camps in adjoining rooms on the assumption it was all one big happy American family.

The few times this proximity was put to use was when "Pop" made some possibly inappropriate statement to the press that filtered back to Barbara. Soon afterward, reporters keeping vigil in the hallway could watch her stride to Oliver's room, where, we later learned, there was a discussion about what should be said to reporters.

From various comments dropped in each camp it became clear that one sore point was the fact that *Life* magazine was said to have sponsored the senior Powers' trip to Moscow in return for his first-person account of the experience. This reportedly was not to Barbara's liking because it risked putting a commercial stamp on the family's undoubtedly sincere efforts to help the pilot. Barbara's goal was to win sympathy and understanding in the U.S. for her husband. Yet she herself previously had given *Newsweek* magazine some of the love letters Powers had written her from Lubiyanka prison.

As the trial day drew near, press announcements fell as thick as li'l old magnolia blossoms from each family camp, and both sides obliged the clamoring reporters with press conferences. Every member of the family has a heavy southern accent, which made them almost unintelligible to Soviet and European correspondents who now and then joined the group. In fact, some of the American scribes needed a translation, too.

Barbara's lawyers held virtually daily briefings in the

third-floor lobby of the hotel for about seventy-five reporters, to the amazement of the Soviet hotel guests. TV
cameramen left their gear piled in the lobby overnight.
Some reporters camped until the small hours of the morning outside the family's doors or inside their rooms. Moscow never had seen anything like it.

After one of Barbara's press conferences in the third-
floor lobby, Oliver Powers and Sol Curry, the dry-goods
man, strode from their suite. Curry waved the news reporters and photographers over to the other side of the
lobby to hear what Powers had to say.

"Those people," said "Pop" Powers, indicating his
daughter-in-law and her lawyers, "have done more harm
than good. They came here without any permission from
me. Too much has been said in this case already," he
added darkly, while a female correspondent from *Izvestia*
scribbled notes (the Soviet press failed to print any of
them, however).

Finally, one of the American correspondents took Curry
aside and suggested that the elder Powers' speech was not
in his son's interest. As "Pop" was returning to his room,
Curry grabbed his arm and begged correspondents not to
print anything about the family troubles, for it might endanger the pilot's case.

Each day of the trial, the family sat in a special box in
the back of the Hall of Columns in the House of Unions,
like honored guests at a concert. During intermissions we
had to dog the family for their reactions and any word of
their expected reunion with the pilot. Then after an ex-
hausting day of covering the trial we still had to race to
the Sovietskaya Hotel to see what family camps Nos. 1
and 2 were up to.

Before long the strain caught up with the pretty army wife from the South. She was able to keep going with the help of correspondents, talking far into the night around a bottle of Kentucky bourbon to keep her mind off the trial. I remember one night while her doctor and lawyers drifted in and out of her room Barbara sat with her hair up in curlers, carefully applying red polish to her long fingernails. Each night she prepared for the next day's ordeal, pressing the black dress with the white collar that her attorneys had picked out for her in preference to "her cotton dirndl things," as they said. A Bible lay on the next table.

"Oh, she prays," put in her mother in response to a query. "This is my Bible. I brought it. But, oh, yes, Barbara reads it."

Next door I looked in on the opposing camp. Several correspondents were chatting with Oliver Powers and his attorney; in this room they drank Coca-Cola. "They make the best Coca-Cola in the world right in Virginia," "Pop" was reflecting, trim and dapper in his glasses and crew haircut. "It's that water, that wonderful spring water runnin' over those rocks, clear and cool. Yessir, sure do like that Coca-Cola."

Mrs. Powers, the pilot's mother, who was suffering from heart trouble, sat quietly in a chair in a corner of the room. She smiled now and then to a question and would answer with dignity, "I feel fine." She appeared to be in a daze. Her white marcelled hair made her appear years older than her perky husband.

As we prepared to leave the room, one of the correspondents, Joseph Michaels of NBC, impulsively kissed

"Mom" on the cheek. Later Michaels said sheepishly, "When I kissed Mrs. Powers, I meant it."

This family drama was not lost upon the Soviet journalists. During the trial I asked one what he thought of the family.

"The father's selling his memoirs to *Life* magazine is indicative of your sick, capitalist society," he replied. "Americans will do anything for money. Even when his son is on trial for his life. . . . The wife keeps dabbing her eyes with her handkerchief. Is her grief genuine?"

Meantime, the object of all these disputations was sitting in his cell in the Lubiyanka by night and in the courtroom during the day. He did not know how much the outside world knew of the incident, or of him. At first he was unaware of the press conferences at the Sovietskaya, the memoirs promised to *Life*, and the blazing spotlight on his family affairs.

Shortly after the trial began, his Soviet hosts handed him a copy of *Newsweek* magazine. It was the first western publication he had seen since he left his airbase. Inside, spread for all the world to see, were reproduced the personal letters he had written to his wife. Powers reportedly hit the ceiling.

When he had his celebrated first meeting with his family, I learned later, he appealed to them to stop the flood of publicity, well intentioned as it might be.

Later I happened to be in New York City on the UPI staff covering Khrushchev's second trip to America. Watching the Premier pound his shoe on the table at the United Nations were Oliver Powers and Sol Curry, the dry-goods man. Powers said sadly he wanted "to talk to Khrushchev about freeing my boy," but they were unsuccessful in winning an audience with the Premier at the U.N. Next they tried to corner Khrushchev at the Soviet embassy on Park Avenue. We reporters covering the embassy used to see Oliver standing on the corner, a block from the embassy, staring over the wooden police barricade at Khrushchev's headquarters. He looked sad and frustrated, an ordinary fellow from a small town caught in the confusing web of cold-war politics. "Pop" and Curry never were able to get by the New York police lines to even approach the embassy. Finally they went back home to Virginia.

Months after the trial, Russians still asked American acquaintances, "Did you think the trial was fair? Did you think Powers was brainwashed?"

Powers' guilt, of course, was admitted by President Eisenhower before the trial even began. So there was no question of his being "brainwashed" to extract a confession. But given his own personality and attitude, he apparently fit in readily with the Soviet theme that he was directed by his Pentagon bosses; that he was an ordinary fellow who wanted to live; that he had done something endangering peace; and that he was sorry.

In his defense, perhaps it should also be pointed out that he was in Soviet hands for three and a half months before coming to trial. During this period he spent his days and nights alone in a small cell, often at night with the light on, we later learned. He was cut off from any communication with his countrymen or the outside world. He was not allowed outside newspapers or magazines. He was not allowed to see anyone from the American embassy.

The RB-47 incident was different. When that American airplane was shot down by the Soviets over the Bering

Sea in July 1960, the faces of some Russians became dark with anger. "Not another one!" was a typical reaction. But, on second thought, the reaction changed to wait and see. It was not clear exactly who was in the right in this case.

One Soviet friend of mine summed it up neatly months after the Powers trial and the release of the RB-47 pilots: "Powers was tailor-made," he said. "If we had ordered to measure the kind of pilot we wanted caught in a spy plane, we couldn't have done better. But the RB-47 pilots, they were not the same."

16

The Case of the Forbidden Painting

"Be Vigilant!" cried the article in the Moscow newspaper. "We are happy to welcome foreign guests in our country, whether they come as tourists or diplomatic officials . . . but we shall chase spies out of our house, spies operating on the ground or in the air."

The Soviet press was peppered with high-pitched warnings during July, August, and September of 1960 to the Russian people that foreigners in their midst may be spies. The stories may have been part of a buildup for the Powers trial. They may have been stimulated by alarm over the partial success and size of American espionage efforts within the Soviet Union. Whatever the reasons, the new campaign strummed a centuries-old familiar melody: beware of foreigners.

Both before and after the Powers trial the din continued. Diplomats from all countries were favored targets. Three members of the American embassy were expelled, two men and one four-legged associate. After Henry Shapiro, our UPI bureau chief, discovered he was allergic to cats, the Shapiros gave their big red Siberian cat, Reezhie (Ginger), to Colonel Edwin Kirton, the air-force attaché at the American embassy.

On August 11 Kirton was ordered to leave on an espionage charge. He was accused of taking notes on a train. The Kirtons hurriedly packed their baggage and Reezhie and left for Washington. Thus Reezhie became the only cat ever thrown out of the Soviet Union on spy charges.

Russians were warned through the "Be Vigilant!" press campaign that tourists may be spies in sport shirts. One traveler was expelled for handing out Bibles. A student tourist was charged with recruiting Soviet boys to be spies by giving them jazz records, whiskey, and "anti-Soviet literature"—namely *Time, Look,* and *Life* magazines.

Many of the accused tourists probably were innocents abroad who acted so suspiciously one can't blame the Russians for sniffing danger. One tourist was questioned because he took notes and made sketches of railway equipment. He later told us correspondents he was writing a college thesis on Russian railways.

Two different groups of American students were detained and another group expelled for passing out hundreds of copies of *Amerika* magazine, the U.S. magazine in Russian distributed in the Soviet Union. Their behavior had nothing to do with espionage, but the expulsions heightened apprehension in the foreign colony.

Members of American and other foreign delegations; American exchange students at Moscow University; and members of visiting foreign entertainment troupes were accused in print of carrying on cloak-and-dagger activities. One by one the Soviet press picked off every category of American in the Soviet Union.

"They'll be after us next, and I have a feeling I'll be first," mused Carl Mydans, then *Life* correspondent.

He was right in a way. On August 14 *Trud,* the trade-union newspaper, launched what was mainly a blistering attack against *Life* for printing "caricatures" of the Soviet Union. Mydans also was accused of photographing a forbidden factory in Leningrad (which happened to be in the background of something else he was shooting.) No espionage charge was mentioned, but every detail of the factory incident was published—an indication of how closely our activities were documented.

Mydans' temporary visa, issued in three-month stretches to keep *Life* on its toes, expired about the time the article appeared. He had several days of worry, but the visa was reissued.

Despite the warnings and harassments, it was evident the Soviets wanted to continue tourism, cultural, trade, and journalistic contacts with foreign countries. The newspapers even warned Soviets lest the vigilance program turn into a spy mania.

We foreigners wondered if the watch on us would be doubled because of the U-2 and RB-47 incidents and the "Be Vigilant!" campaign in the press.

Most foreigners in 1960 believed their telephones were periodically tapped or hooked to tape-recording machines. Once during the vigilance period an American scribe picked up his telephone and heard his conversation of two hours before being played back! Often our telephone conversations would be suddenly cut off or would fade or be interrupted by static.

Our mail obviously always was opened and reglued with brown Soviet glue. Once my mail was mixed up with another foreigner's mail. Another time, inside one of my magazines I found a letter intended for an embassy. But all that was par for the course.

After the U-2 incident, I often looked in the rear-view

mirror of my car to see if I was being tailed. I felt disappointed never to see a car behind me. What was the point of coming to Russia if you weren't followed once in a while?

Other reporters noticed evidence of more thorough checking. Perhaps it was just ordinary procedure that we detected, just because we looked harder for it.

When Bud Korengold flew to Yalta to photograph the new Franklin Delano Roosevelt Street for UPI, he was followed by three suspicious uniformed policemen the minute he appeared with his camera.

That summer of 1960 another foreign correspondent used to come by my apartment often for supper. One evening the Moscow long-distance operator called my apartment to ask for this journalist. Apparently the operator first called his hotel and, although I had never been at the hotel, somebody there knew where he was spending his time.

It was during the spy hysteria that the Press Department took some foreign correspondents on a junket to Murmansk for a rare glimpse of how that city beyond the Arctic Circle was being developed. Four Murmansk "journalists," wearing green snap-brim hats and dark brown coats, joined our group. We soon decided they were security police. Each time a local citizen talked to me on the street or in the hotel lobby, "green hats," as we called them, would rush over in musical-comedy style to eavesdrop. The entire press corps—including correspondents from the satellite countries—bought the "green hats" drinks, snapped their pictures (which they adored), and cheered them on.

The vigilance campaign took effect with Soviet people.

Citizens stared so when I took photographs around Moscow that I finally stopped.

One week-end I went to Leningrad on a story. On the train I shared my compartment as usual with three Soviet men. One noticed my foreign magazine and asked where I was from.

"I am an American correspondent," I said, which usually brings a surprised smile and friendly questions.

But he froze and turned away. Across from me a Red Army officer lowered his copy of *Pravda* and carefully scrutinized me. The rest of the way I didn't look out the window for fear I might be peering unknowingly at a military installation.

In Leningrad I checked in at the Victorian-style Astoria Hotel. The only other westerner at the hotel was an American tourist with a big red mustache and a tape recorder and camera draped around his neck. He was the kind of tourist who has the security police promptly on the alert. He spoke some Russian. He said he was a former publicist and hoped to tape some interviews to sell to radio networks when he returned to New York.

"I don't think you should walk around with that machine," I said nervously. He buttoned his coat over the tape recorder. I thought that looked worse. As we walked down the wide, eastern European-looking streets of Leningrad, he kept fiddling with the recorder and his camera despite my protests. I was sure an army of men in green snap-brim hats must be following us.

At one point we stopped at an outdoor book stall. Two boys, about ten or eleven years of age, began to talk to us. My companion decided to interview them, since they spoke a little English. He pulled them aside to an alleyway. After a few minutes, one of the boys looked over our shoulders to the street beyond and said, "I must go now. *They* are watching."

That was enough for me. I did not want to endanger my visa by getting mixed up in a "Be Vigilant!" article. "I'm going back to the hotel. Meet you in the dining room at seven tonight," I said and walked back alone to the Astoria.

At seven he failed to appear. I ordered my caviar and watched a group of sixteen students from Leningrad University at the next table. The girls wore attractive (for Russia) cocktail dresses, make-up, and short hairdos. The boys were handsome and fairly good dancers. I was thinking how much more western Leningrad is in spirit and appearance than Moscow when I was called to the telephone in the lobby.

It was my new acquaintance. He was in the Peter and Paul Fortress, which contains the famous prison for revolutionists in 1917 and is now a tourist attraction.

"In case you never hear from me again, I want you to know I am in a building next to the voting hall," he whispered loudly. "I am being questioned by five men."

"Are they in uniform or out of uniform?" I asked quickly.

"Out."

"Oh, oh," I sighed. "You're in trouble." (A Russian acquaintance once told me, "It's the police out of uniform, not the ones in uniform, that you have to worry about.")

"I haven't done anything," the tourist whispered over the telephone. "I was sightseeing, and saw the voting place, with the signs and people going inside, so I went to do a story. As I was leaving, these men stopped me. I took no pictures."

"And the tape recorder?" I asked.

"It's under my coat. Oh, they haven't seen that. I'm also pretending I don't speak Russian. I've really fooled them."

I sighed again. "That's what you think."

I put an Intourist guide on the telephone to help rescue the tourist. After the security police examined his camera and tape recorder, they let him go.

A week later he turned up at the Puppet Theater in Moscow, still with the suspicious-looking tape recorder bulging beneath his raincoat. He waved hello to me. And right behind him, sure enough, was one of the boys in a green hat. We might read about that tourist any day now.

Even though I had escaped detention with him, I figured probably the security police had seen me with this suspicious-looking character. Nevertheless, I promptly forgot my Mata Hari nerves when a tourist said to me over dinner at the Ukraine Hotel, "I met a Russian artist who says he does modern, almost abstract art."

I was as excited as if somebody said Coca-Cola stands had opened on Gorky Street.

The tourist arranged for a poet friend of the artist to telephone me the following day.

"I will take you to the artist's home," said the poet, Yuri, speaking bad French in an attempt to sound on the telephone like a foreigner. "He lives 18 kilometers from the center of Moscow. Can you go that far?"

I assured him we could go 40 kilometers (about 25 miles) without asking permission from the Press Department of the Foreign Ministry. We made an appointment to meet in front of the Bolshoi Theater on Sverdlov Square Saturday at 11:00 A.M.

I had worked late on a rocket story and had had only

four hours' sleep when Saturday morning rolled around. The store at the corner was out of eggs again. I was hungry and tired but at eleven I eagerly arrived in a taxi, at Sverdlov Square, leaving my conspicuous car at home.

The minute I saw Yuri, the poet, I knew I had escaped from the narrow world of foreigners into the exciting stream of true Russian life. Yuri wore corduroy slacks and jacket, a turtleneck sweater, and horn-rimmed glasses. He combed his hair straight down his forehead in a sort of Julius Caesar style. He looked right out of the Left Bank in Paris, Greenwich Village in New York, or Grant Street in San Francisco. He was a real, live "Bolshevik beatnik."

Russia is so little like Soviet propaganda says. Each time I can scrape beneath the official veneer to find the real country underneath is a thrill. Discovering a Bohemian like those in the rest of the world made me want to hug Yuri with joy.

We climbed aboard a bus. While strap hanging, we discussed modern paintings and museums in America, much to the curiosity of our interested fellow passengers. At the electric-train station we walked through the crowd of *dachniki*, or *dacha* dwellers, coming in from the country with sacks of fresh eggs, yellow chrysanthemums, and fat cucumbers for their city relatives. Others were going home to the suburbs, their string shopping bags filled with trophies snared in Gum. Many passengers milled around the stands where *morozhenoe*, or ice cream, and *piroshki*, fried batter filled with meat or rice, were being sold.

Except for restaurant conversations with *stilyagi*, Yuri was the first Russian I had met who spoke no English and was far removed from the official scene. He said he worked in a publishing house. He was part of a group of writers and artists interested in abstract art and the "cool" type of writing exemplified by San Francisco's Jack Kerouac. He said they learned about these trends from tourists, the American Exhibition, and foreign magazines left behind by travelers.

After about twenty minutes we got off the train. He led me over the tracks and down a narrow dirt road that divided rows of frame houses and fields. I wore a black and white tweed coat, no hat, and flat shoes. I was sure nobody could tell I was foreign. I felt a part of Russian life, no longer an outsider isolated in diplomatic houses and the Central Telegraph Office.

The artist's simple wooden house was the equivalent of a three-block walk from the station. He met us at the door. We walked through a large bare room that apparently served as a studio, and into a smaller room. Some chairs and a table stood at one end. The other end was separated by a screen painted with an abstract design, behind which I guessed part of the family slept and cooked. The house was neat and clean. The wooden floor was painted dark brown. Some modern-looking paintings added color and interest to the walls.

The artist's wife, a *babushka* (grandmother), and two small children extended warm handclasps and a chair. Then for an hour the artist and the poet brought out the works of four painters of Moscow's artistic "underground."

"There are twelve of us in this group," the artist, whom I shall call L., explained. "We meet often to discuss painting. We work as illustrators on magazines but try modern painting at home."

One of the artists was attempting in vain to paint like Modigliani. Another did abstracts with an air brush. One of his paintings consisted of splashes of orange and white dots. A third tried various abstract designs. They were admirable attempts but rather mediocre, I thought.

Then L. brought out his own work. There, on canvas after canvas, was Moscow, but not the Moscow that *Pravda's* preachers of "socialist realism" would have approved of. L. appeared to be, like artists in many countries, a sensitive person who had some viewpoints concerning society. The colors were grays, blacks, and browns—unnoticeable in Paris or Los Angeles but anti-Party Line in Moscow.

One canvas showed a grocery store marked "closed," with a scrawny cat sitting in front of the barred door next to an overturned milk can. In the sky a sputnik whizzed toward the cosmos. Another painting showed vodka bottles stacked up against some electric power lines. Not many of the paintings were what *Pravda* would call happy. His style was slightly Disneyish and whimsical. It seemed to me to fit the Russia of peasant houses that don't sit straight, with its occasional air of an Alice in Wonderland country "run by slightly mad children," as author John Gunther put it.

I decided I wanted to buy some of the "underground" art. For the equivalent of $125 I acquired a painting of some new Moscow apartment houses, almost surrealist in his version, with a capricious orange streetcar in the foreground.

Then the poet, the artist and his family, and I gathered around the table to talk over glasses of steaming tea and big hunks of homemade bread and raspberry jam. They told me the artist sold his paintings to "friends, actors, theatrical people." He showed me a design he had made for a modern lampshade. It was pretty revolutionary for Russia but ordinary in the outside world.

"Why doesn't the Communist party like abstract art?" I asked.

"I don't know," he replied. Then, indicating he was a loyal Soviet citizen, he added confidently, "Not soon, but perhaps in two or three years, I will be allowed to exhibit my paintings in Moscow."

The family asked about my life. I told them about Missoula, Montana, and the university there that I had attended. I pulled out a torn photograph of my sister, her husband, and their four children taken on the back lawn of their house in Kansas City. The Russians examined the photograph as if it were a Rembrandt.

As I left, the artist snapped my photograph with his family standing in front of the door, almost overgrown with vines and bushes. Smiles, handshakes, thank-yous. I told them I might be back the next Saturday to buy another painting.

I was exhilarated. I had met an interesting artist like some I had known in New York and San Francisco and Paris and Rome. L. and his wife were not "beatniks" really, but what Americans call "upper Bohemians." They were quiet, pleasant, warmhearted, and well-mannered people.

"I bought a painting," I happily told the policeman in front of our apartment house when I stepped out of the taxi with my large canvas.

The next Saturday I tossed aside the rules and drove my car to the electric-train station. With Yuri was another poet, a short fellow who looked Armenian to me.

I had brought along two copies of *Amerika* magazine which contained layouts on American abstract art. If I had given them a trip to Paris they couldn't have been more delighted. The sight of two beatniks and a foreign woman looking at modern paintings in *Amerika* magazine must have been an oddity. Half the crowded train's passengers clustered around our seat and peered over our shoulders.

"Groups of young people read modern poetry together in Moscow," said the Armenian. "Some fellows in Leningrad came to Moscow with a big sackful of the new poetry last week."

He handed me a copy of one of these examples of the "underground" poetry circuit of Leningrad. Roughly translated, it sounded like this:

They drank they ate they
Smoked
They sang they danced they howled
Sorokin crept up to kiss
Julie
Sokhorov dozed on his chair
Sidorov threw up.

Summer, an open window
On the table wine in its bottle
On the street children squeak
Women squeal
A crumpled envelope in a hand
March comes to mind
My wife left me then
I don't love you, she answered
Now she writes I'll come back soon
I'm glad and not glad

> Such is her habit
> She's hysterical
>
> Well, they buried Maria's body
> We didn't get married
> They say we didn't care
> She had 22 abortions
> Toward the end of her life
> She looked like hell.

I was gleefully copying what I thought was probably the first Bolshevik beatnik poem to meet western eyes when I happened to glance up. Coming down the aisle was a young man with a gentle, open face. Underneath that nice face was a familiar navy-blue uniform with red epaulets. He seemed to take forever to thread his way through the crowd blocking the aisle—like that memorable scene in the Russian silent film *Potemkin,* in which the director, Sergei Eisenstein, showed over and over again a baby carriage bouncing down the Odessa steps, to stretch time and prolong the agony of the infant's descent.

He's coming after me, I thought.

He was.

"*Vee inostranka?*" (Are you a foreigner?) asked the policeman.

"*Da,*" I said faintly.

"This is a closed area. You are violating the law by being here. You must get off at the next stop and return to Moscow," he said pleasantly but firmly in Russian.

"But I am allowed to go 40 kilometers," I retorted.

"Ask your embassy where you can go. Some areas are closed."

By this time the entire carload of passengers crowded

around us. They stared at me, their earthy Slavic faces watchful and quiet. I could see "Be Vigilant!" articles dancing inside those kerchiefed and capped heads.

I stood up and crawled over various knees to reach the exit. I hoped my two beatnik companions would stay behind and pretend they weren't with me.

The Armenian did. But the Russian poet Yuri hurried behind me and gallantly took my arm. We stood by the door, the crowd staring, while the policeman continued to lecture me until the next stop.

"*Mir i druzhba*," I said in frustration to the policeman as we climbed off the train.

Once seated on the return train to Moscow, I was so frightened I began to cry. Yuri watched me in apparent unconcern. "It's all right," he said.

He was only about twenty-five and, I thought, probably did not know about the bad days just a few years before when Russians were questioned for even talking to foreigners.

"No, it isn't all right," I sobbed. "We both are in trouble. You may wind up in Siberia. I may lose my visa and have to leave my job here."

When I returned to my apartment house, the policeman was in his little house on the telephone, checking me in, I supposed. I usually gave him a cheery "Good day." But this time I marched unsmiling by.

I was so upset I could not sleep.

Two days later Yuri called. He said the secret police had arrived at his apartment and checked his documents. I was appalled but he insisted everything was all right.

"As you cannot go to L.'s house, I will bring you the

second painting at Sverdlov Square tonight at 7:30," he said.

I was distraught with indecision. Sverdlov Square was not closed to foreigners. But Yuri and L. perhaps were going outside the law to sell paintings to foreigners, let alone the unapproved variety. During these U-2 days was no time to be adventurous.

But the thought of another painting from the "closet school" was too much for me. Feeling the eyes of our policeman piercing my back, I took a taxi to Sverdlov Square, wondering if the phone-tapping security police would be there, too.

I was freezing cold and worried. By eight o'clock Yuri had not shown up. What could have happened to him, I wondered. Then I spotted them, two of them, in dark green snap-brim hats and scarfs, hanging around the Bolshoi Theater steps long after the audience had drifted inside for the ballet. I flagged a taxi and went home.

After a nervous conference with some friends I decided to telephone the Press Department to tell them what had happened before the police did.

But I could not incriminate L. by mentioning him. So I told the Press Department I had started to the suburb of —— to look for icons in the market and a policeman had stopped me.

"You must always get permission before going any place," was the chilly reply. "That suburb is closed to foreigners."

For several days I nervously expected every newspaper to carry a "Be Vigilant!" article about my adventure. And every telephone call I feared would be a summons to the Foreign Ministry. Not only had I entered a closed area, possibly one housing armament factories, in the wake of the Powers incident, but I had bought an officially unacceptable painting and contacted what the regime regards as anti-Soviet elements.

Various diplomats in our building heard of the incident and dropped in to the office to "console" me. They told me of a French diplomat beaten by the "tails" who followed him, of a British embassy wife seduced by her husband's chauffeur and urged to be a spy, etc.—not exactly consolation.

Henry Shapiro was out of the country during my adventure. When he returned to Moscow, he hurried to the office to inspect my painting. After one glance he said, "I don't think you should see those poets and artists any more."

Henry decided to send me to Stockholm for a few days to get over the jitters. At the airport, the minute I showed my passport, two customs officials marched out and searched every crevice of my baggage. Since this happens seldom to tourists or correspondents, it was probable they were looking for paintings. I judged this as a warning I should not try to take that picture out of the country.

When I got back to Moscow, I saw an acquaintance from the Foreign Ministry at a reception. I decided to get it over with and inquire if he knew what would happen to me.

"I am in trouble," I began. "On a train two Saturdays ago a policeman told me to get off—"

He raised his hand to interrupt me. "You first went on the train the Saturday before at 11:35, with Yuri ——, a writer. You arrived in —— at 11:58. You went to a house and stayed five hours. You bought a painting of some buildings and an orange streetcar. Then you returned to Moscow and went home by taxi.

"The following Saturday you met Yuri —— at the station in your car and again boarded the train and entered the closed area."

I was so startled I could only say, "But there was no-body following me. How did you—how did the police know?"

"In America if you steal something in a store, you think nobody is watching you, but before you leave the store they catch you," he said.

Had I been followed by police, in or out of uniform, who watch that closed electric-train station? Or had the secret police heard me make the appointment on the telephone and followed me there? I never will know.

"I suppose those people were anti-Soviet and spoke English because they hang around foreigners," the Soviet official said.

"They spoke only Russian. They are nice people and loyal to their country," I retorted. "What's wrong with modern art? Why don't you Communists accept it?"

"Because it may excite the people, and we don't want elements that agitate them," he said.

"So that's it!" I said. "They can't be excited! That's why you frown upon jazz and spontaneous meetings. This artist is so loyal he is sure his work will be accepted soon officially," I argued. "You are so reactionary! Your country is being liberalized and you won't admit it. I wager in five years you will see nonobjective paintings in the Moscow galleries."

"If there are, they will not be in your western style but our own Soviet style," he concluded, a patriot to the last.

"Wait," I said. "What about Yuri and L.? Are they in Siberia?"

"They do not send people to Siberia any more, Miss Mosby," he said. "They have been told not to contact foreigners any more to sell paintings."

"And what about me? Am I to be expelled?"

"I suppose you were only interested in paintings, not vital factories," he said. "I suppose you will remain here."

And he walked away.

Some diplomats were convinced that although I was safe from expulsion the painting incident would wind up in the Soviet press. The newspapers are fond of printing violent attacks against foreign correspondents.

"You haven't heard the end of this," one diplomat predicted.

For weeks I nervously watched the newspapers. And I fervently vowed never again to stray from the beaten path to talk to any "ordinary" Russians that people back home often complain correspondents don't know: official types are safer. As one Soviet acquaintance jokingly remarked to me, "After this, Alinutchka, when a Russian wants to talk to you, ask to see his Party card first."

Sure enough, a Soviet newspaper one day printed a blistering attack against me in connection with the painting incident, but it was not a "Be Vigilant" article. Instead the story stated that I consorted with odd characters to buy abstract paintings—a clear warning to foreigners to beware of man-on-the-street contacts.

"But they didn't even get the name of the artist right!" I cried to Korengold as we pored over the article.

Instead of fingering L ——, the Soviet newspaper reporter accused another artist of selling me the painting.

I had never even met the man, let alone bought a painting from him!

To the poor innocent artist the story was not funny. Later I heard he stomped in righteous rage to the newspaper office to complain.

We decided the secret police who recorded my visit to the artist's house may not be as frighteningly efficient as foreigners seem to think.

One American friend came to my apartment after the attack to examine my painting, which by now was famous in the foreign colony. He told me a Russian joke that pokes fun at Soviet inefficiencies and seems to fit the occasion.

First Russian: Is it true that the secret police have installed microphones in the rooms at the Hotel Ukraine?

Second Russian: Yes. But you know how things are around here . . . they hardly ever work!

Later some official-type Russians happened to be in our apartment building at a diplomatic reception. I invited them to drop in to our office. We walked back to my apartment and they spotted my painting. They stood in silence, looking at the picture, which represented such a shocking change from the approved style.

To show his opinion of it, one of the Soviets reached out with his little finger. "I will put on the mark of Glavlit," he announced jokingly and carefully drew on the painting the crooked arrow in a circle that was the "brand" of the now defunct Soviet censor.

The mark is still there.

17

Around the World in 89 Minutes

The day John Kennedy was inaugurated as President of the United States, I listened to the news on Moscow Radio at the apartment of a Russian friend.

"Do you think Kennedy will want to negotiate?" he asked. "We don't want to give up the ground we've gained. We've seen foreign movies and orchestras and now Hemingway is published here. You've no idea what that means to us! We want to be closer to the West."

On that day, the *mir i druzhba* train found itself back on the tracks again, headed in the direction of friendlier ties between the Soviet Union and the West. Practically overnight, relations between the U.S.S.R. and the United States began to climb back to the peace and friendship of less than evil days.

The "Be Vigilant!" campaign died from the newspapers and I stopped worrying that any spy alarm would catch up with me and my painting.

The autumn after the U-2 trial was one of marking time in Moscow, waiting for the new American administration. That September, Henry Shapiro and I, along with several other Moscow correspondents, flew to New York to cover the second chapter of "N. S. Khrushchev in America," his visit to the United Nations.

Although I was home for the first time in more than

two years, I didn't have much time to look over the United States. It was almost as if I'd never left Moscow. Most of my time I spent chasing the indefatigable Mr. K. from one diplomatic cocktail party in New York to another. And week-ends I parked with a contingent of reporters across the road from Khrushchev's week-end retreat at Glen Cove, Long Island.

Soviet correspondents sought me out at the U.N. building to complain they were followed. They sounded like American correspondents lamenting in Moscow! One Soviet scribe said he found a microphone in his hotel room and said into it, "I don't like the Dulles-Eisenhower bankrupt policy," proving he had learned his *Pravda* lesson for the day. Almost all the Soviet correspondents objected that they were restricted in New York, even as to which side of the street they could walk on. Two young Soviet journalists were astonished when I told them that "all foreign correspondents are restricted to a 40-kilometer radius in Moscow."

Russians are usually friendly, no matter what job they have. One of Khrushchev's security policemen whispered to me, "How are you, Miss Mosby? I remember you from Moscow." Even the Premier himself pumped my hand in the U.N. lobby and noted I was part of his "sputnik" contingent from the Soviet capital. And, to indicate what a "small town" the Moscow "in" group is, when I returned to the U.S.S.R. in October a Soviet journalist said he had already heard how I shook the iron gate of Khrushchev's Glen Cove hideaway when the Soviet security police let a competitor into the yard and not the rest of the press corps.

The change in American presidents at first brought

some happier stories for us correspondents in Moscow. One day Bud Korengold and I were just wandering around the American embassy. But we didn't go to the offices on the ninth floor because the elevator was marked "out of order." Late that night we learned why: upstairs were the two RB-47 pilots, preparing to leave the Soviet Union in secret, according to a Soviet-American agreement. That was one story we missed.

But the following month we had ringside seats on a story I'll remember as the most exciting I have covered in Moscow, or yes, even in my life: the first flight of a human being into outer space.

The first tip about the real Columbus of the cosmos came on Saturday, April 7. I learned that eastern European communist correspondents had been alerted to listen to the radio. But all was quiet. Sunday, nothing.

Then Monday afternoon into the Central Telegraph Office marched some Soviet television cameramen. They set up their gear, just as they habitually do to film "bourgeois" journalists sending news of a Soviet rocket achievement around the world.

"What's up?" CBS's Marvin Kalb asked one of the Russians.

The cameraman pointed to the sky.

We at UPI reasoned that Soviet TV crews operate under most carefully considered instructions. They would not be ready to photograph reactions to a launching unless an announcement of one was planned.

Usually secretive Soviets seldom give tips to "bourgeois" reporters, but suddenly all over Moscow foreign correspondents got friendly hints from communist sources to listen to Moscow Radio.

When nothing happened that night or Tuesday, our Soviet translators shook their heads doubtfully at these "crazy" western journalists. At midnight the drama grew wilder when some Soviet sources said the cosmonaut had been launched and returned in "ill health."

I went to bed at 1:00 A.M. At 2:00 A.M. another source telephoned with the rumor that the ill cosmonaut might be Vladimir Ilyushin, son of a well-known Soviet aircraft designer. I got out of bed, padded into the UPI office in my bedroom slippers, and sat down at the desk. I began to dig out piles of ancient files, trying to find photographs and stories on Ilyushin—just in case Tass said he was the cosmonaut.

Fifteen hours later, I was still sitting in my nightgown and slippers with our male staff bustling around me. I hadn't once been out of the chair.

The announcement had come at 10:00 A.M. We had been alerted four hours beforehand by Tass in London —another almost unprecedented occurrence in Soviet journalism.

"*Vnimanie . . . Vnimanie . . .* (Attention . . . Attention . . .) boomed forth the announcer's voice in deep tones over Moscow Radio. It was one of the great moments in the history of man's life on earth. And there I sat, clutching the telephone, still with cold cream on my face and my hair up in curlers.

Shapiro dictated over one telephone to London. I dictated to Frankfurt over another. Korengold raced around Moscow, getting comments from scientists and quotes from exuberant citizens. Our rival, the AP, sent out the flash that the cosmonaut had gone up and come down, as Tass erroneously reported to all agencies in

London. But our story was saved when Shapiro cried to our London office, "No, no! He's still in orbit!"

Not anyone, not even eager Soviet journalists who were tipping off western correspondents, dreamed the Soviets would announce the launching while the cosmonaut was said to be still in outer space.

And his name wasn't Ilyushin but Yuri Gagarin!

We worked with no sleep and little food through the next hectic four days: the airport welcome for Gagarin, cool and poised as if he had coasted around the block on a bicycle instead of whirring around the world in 89 minutes. The Kremlin reception. The demonstration on Red Square with Russians surging to break through the police lines, women ill and fainting. Never had we seen Moscow so jubilant. That week a meat shortage plagued the city and housewives had to trudge to several stores before finding any. The milk bottles arrived at my door with bits of white paper stuffed in the top. The dairy apparently ran out of tin-foil caps.

But the genuine joy on Russians' faces! All the shortages, the sacrifices, the consumers' goods and gadgets they gave up so that their country could have a man in space—the Russians we saw thronging through Red Square glowed as if it was all worth it. Strangers kissed one another, old women did jigs, young people cheered, students walked out of their classes.

In some ways it was altogether different from covering such a story in another country. We never could get near Gagarin's wife or children. The family lived in a military area closed to foreign correspondents. When they came to Moscow to welcome home Gagarin, they were kept away from hotels and the press with more care than if they had been Khrushchev himself. The closest we were allowed to Gagarin was at a press conference, where only written questions, screened by both scientists and Press Department officials, were given him to answer.

When the smoke had cleared, rumors and doubts still plagued some correspondents. Because the Russians have a centuries-old reputation of being mysterious and secretive and sometimes not presenting the truth, a few scribes figured a shot had been made when we first heard the rumors on Saturday, only with a dummy inside the *Vostok* spaceship. Others insisted Gagarin made the trip himself on that Saturday, and, four days later, when the shot was announced, only a dummy sat inside the ship as it circled the earth.

But most correspondents finally decided the flight happened exactly as the Soviets said it did.

It was wild and wonderful. I'll never forget it.

Gagarin's feat was followed by many other noteworthy front-pagers—the 22nd Party Congress and the macabre snatching of Stalin from his tomb; the strained Soviet-West relations and the frightening late-1961 Berlin crisis. The tensions of a seven-day forever-exciting work week burned me out. With the end of the Party Congress, I applied for a transfer from Moscow, and a few months from this writing my tour of duty in the Soviet Union will end.

No matter in what city I live next, I doubt if I will find such an odd mixture of the zany and the serious, or of warmth and suspicion, of lies and sincerity, as among the Russian people. They are what I will remember.

They can be maddening and frustrating at times, admirable and lovable at others. But they are here to stay, and they can be fascinating. They are peasant-shrewd, argumentative, talkative, emotional, dramatic. As is well known, they are always right, you are wrong. An American tourist after a two-week visit to the Soviet Union said the other day, "Why, this society operates on a different wave-length from the rest of the world."

One of their most intriguing traits, stemming back to old Russia, is that they tell each other—and foreign strangers—exactly what they think. Everybody's business is theirs to mind. They argue spiritedly with strangers in stores and tell off salesgirls. Once in the Old Believers' Church (a branch of the Russian Orthodox Church) I was surrounded by *babushki* (grandmothers) who traditionally wear heavy scarfs wrapped around their heads. Nothing would suit them but that I should take off my green angora beret and put my wool scarf around my head!

Russian housewives often stop foreigners' wives on the street because their children are wearing lightweight fleece-lined nylon snowsuits. A Russian thinks, how could the child be warm unless he's bundled to his eyes in furs and woolens like a little overstuffed teddy bear?

"Put your child's hood over his head. His ears will get cold," a Russian woman will scold a foreign mother.

If a correspondent is snoozing at the Central Telegraph Office with his feet up on a chair, a Russian invariably will march over and berate him for soiling socialist property. Often children will beseech foreigners around hotels for chewing gum. When I hand out a few pieces, a Russian usually will stick his nose in to see what's going on, to scold the child, to ask me why I gave him gum, etc. One night a correspondent, felled by that Russian secret weapon, vodka, had no choice but to stop his car and be

sick. He happened to fall ill on Red Square—right next
to the most sacred spot in Moscow, the tomb of Lenin.
And what's more, the clock in Spassky Tower was
just striking 2:00 A.M. Out marched a platoon of Red
Army soldiers for the traditional "changing of the guard"
around the tomb. My friend might have gone unnoticed
in front of the Arc de Triomphe or Buckingham Palace.
But not in Moscow! An army officer and a civilian followed him home and complained indignantly to him about
what they considered a desecration.

Generalizations about the Soviet Union are dangerous.
But there is one thing I have tried to show in these pages
—and that is that underneath the propaganda, the Russian people are very, very human. One takes comfort in
discovering they do have a sense of humor, even about
their society. The other day I asked a Russian why psychoanalysis is not practiced in the Soviet Union.

"What's the good of going to an analyst with your
problems if his prescription is: 'What's wrong with you is
that you're sharing an apartment with six other families'? "
he said drily.

In the winter of 1961 in Moscow, both Russians and
foreigners turned downright giddy with a flood of "Armenian Radio" jokes about Laos, Cuba, and all. These jokes,
which spread from Russians to foreigners and back again,
concern an imaginary question-and-answer program on
the Armenian radio station.

Some samples:

Question to the Armenian Radio: Why is communism
like the horizon?

Answer: Because it is an imaginary line between heaven

and earth; and the closer you get to it, the farther away it goes.

Or, Question to the Armenian Radio: Could Switzerland ever be a communist country?

Answer: Yes. But what a pity!

Or, Question to the Armenian Radio: What does peace and friendship mean among peoples?

Answer: It means all the Russians, all the Uzbeks, all the Ukrainians, Armenians, and Tartars, will all get together—and beat up all the Georgians.

Recently in Moscow a conference was held by the Ministry of Communications. One speaker was introduced as Comrade So-and-so, "head of the Armenian Radio." The Russian audience broke up laughing.

Through other jokes one senses the feeling of security the Bolshevik regime has acquired. Recently I told a Soviet communist friend a Russian joke I'd heard about Khrushchev talking to a peasant while touring the farm country.

"Do you have any complaints?" inquired Khrushchev.

"Oh, no. The crop is harvested ahead of schedule, we have plenty of tractors and seed and lots of food and shoes to buy," said the peasant.

"Wait a minute! Don't you know who I am?" demanded Mr. K.

The peasant peered at the Premier and exclaimed, "Oh, it's you, Comrade Khrushchev! At first I thought you were an American correspondent!"

My communist friend did not laugh after I finished the joke. He mused, "Hmm. That's interesting. Two years ago, the joke would have been the other way around. The peasant might have been afraid to tell the truth to a Soviet official. It shows our Leninist party and its leaders are accepted and that Mr. Khrushchev is popular."

Russians laugh at "shortage" jokes, too, such as: "A Soviet man came home from work and found his wife in bed with another man. The husband flew into a rage. 'There are oranges and new chairs for sale on Petrovka Street today,' he snapped. 'Why aren't you over there standing in line to buy some?' "

Russians smile more as their lives improve. In fact, it's difficult to write about the country because it is changing so quickly. As I write this, I think of how different Moscow is from when I arrived in 1959. Two big modern-looking shoe stores have opened up on Lenin Boulevard with Czechoslovakian shoes—some with almost pointed toes—in the windows. In the new apartment buildings all over Moscow are bright new furniture and food stores. At last Vnukovo Airport has been remodeled. Tourists who saw it before 1961 might not recognize it; the waiting room is decorated with lavendar plastic walls, chrome trim, modern furniture, and a snack bar.

Moscow is becoming quite a city. New hotels are planned, the subway is to be lengthened. Russians talk eagerly about grandiose plans for the 1967 World's Fair in Moscow and the influx of foreigners it will bring.

Many other aspects of Russian life have not changed during my years in the Soviet Union. Perhaps they never will. After the November 7, 1961, usual demonstration in Red Square, Bud Korengold and I left the Central Telegraph Office to join some Russians singing and dancing on Gorky Street at 1:00 A.M., which is the custom. One boy was playing an accordion, others were doing fast folk dances. When the Russians started to saunter home we tagged along.

"Isn't that your hotel over there?" asked one of the girls. "It's time to say farewell."

They were friendly but they weren't about to take us home to supper. We dropped out of the group, shunned foreigners once again. I think that incident will be repeated for many November sevenths to come, cold war or no.

Another aspect of the Soviet Union that has not changed in some years is that the Marxist-Leninist club still is in business, and the Bolsheviks still are pushing their international membership drive. As long as this country adheres to its driving expansive philosophy, the non-communist world will be in conflict or competition with Soviet Russia in one form or another in virtually every field.

Russian pride and sensitivity date back to many years before the Bolsheviks seized control, and these traits may go on even after the Russians reach their goal of producing as many, let's say, ice-cube crushers as the United States. A British correspondent the other day took an English friend in the hospital the usual sick-bed gift of fruit. The nurses immediately brought to the patient's room an even bigger basket of fruit, apparently to indicate the Englishman was not being starved to death. A Russian workman, his eyes wide with appreciation, inspected one of the newly furnished apartments in our new diplomatic apartment house on Kutuzovsky Prospekt. Then he shook his head and said proudly, "Our sausage, furniture, and paintings are better."

I will remember centuries-old rites in Russia that still

have that mystic, long-ago aura despite the social up-
heavals the country has undergone. One December day in
1960 I attended the funeral of the head of the Old Believers' Church. There was no public announcement of
the funeral time, let alone of the death, and *Pravda* had
just delivered its usual Christmas message that "Christ is
a myth." Nonetheless, more than a thousand Russians,
mostly elderly, turned out on a dark, drizzly day for a
three-hour funeral service which dated back to the tenth
century when Christianity was introduced to Russia.

For two hours the mourners stood in the yellow and
white cathedral, their tapers flickering light over the 1,600
ancient icons that decorated the walls and columns. About
twenty priests with long hair, beards, and stiff golden
robes stood around the body. Sometimes they stopped to
kiss the face of the deceased. Often the "old believers"
standing in the church vigorously crossed themselves,
followed by abrupt little bows. In the funeral procession
down the muddy road, the chanting priests carried icons
atop wooden poles as Russian priests have for centuries.

Even the Soviet funerals of the new era retain some of
that Russian mysticism. Five thousand mourners walked
slowly across the cobblestones of Red Square for the
state funeral honoring a Soviet scientist, Igor Kurchatov,
the father of the Soviet hydrogen bomb, in February of
1960. They carried large photographs of the bearded
scientist—the icon tradition of old Russia. Each photograph was trimmed with red and black, the traditional
Russian funeral colors. Pallbearers followed with a small
flower-covered bier containing the scientist's ashes. It was
20 degrees below zero Centigrade, and the wind brought
snow flurries swooshing across Red Square, the flakes so

white against the gray sky and black mourners' coats. A band played Rachmaninoff's "Funeral March," its slow "da . . . da . . . da . . ." echoing across the gold domes of the Kremlin churches. Government and party leaders climbed to the top of the Lenin tomb, the semi-mystic center of important Soviet rites, for the reading of the eulogy. A three-gun salute barked through the snowy stillness and then President Voroshilov placed the ashes in a niche in the Kremlin wall.

Some of this ingrained Russian-ness that stays on despite the changes was evident on the last trip I made to Moscow from the outside world.

After two and a half months "outside," I was vacationing in Vienna, alleged city of intrigue, which lived up to its advance billing for me. My last day there I had lunch in the old-world Red Bar of the Hotel Sacher. A man was playing "The Third Man Theme" on the zither, and furtive-looking characters glided in and out. My companions, two Austrian correspondents, repeated rumors of the big "coup" in Russia that had shaken Khrushchev from power. They said an Austrian who worked at the Soviet embassy in Vienna reported it.

"Nonsense," I said, laughing. "Russians are too secretive ever to employ anyone at their embassies except Russians."

But, concerning the Soviet Union, one is never sure. I was anxious to get back to Moscow to see what the then existing censors were cutting out.

That last day the inevitable telegram arrived from the Moscow UPI office: "06140 alinotchka bring saccharine tablets antihistamines blue plaid scarf volkswagen fuses bulbs tire patches caps for tire air nozzles two chamois cloths and several fashion magazines stop unlet shopping interfere leastly two good meals on us stop love stop also six toilet deodorizers regards korengold and shapiro"

I was told to be at the Soviet Aeroflot office the next morning at 6:40 to catch their bus to the Vienna airport for the plane to Moscow. I arrived breakfastless and sleepy at 6:30. The Russian chauffeur didn't arrive with the bus until 7:20. We pulled in to the airport at 8:00 and the plane didn't leave until 9:30. I didn't realize until later the chauffeur never did collect my fare for the bus.

"Paris" . . . "London" . . . the loudspeaker called out, and finally, "Passengers for Moscow," which never fails to make me feel cut off from one world and heading into such an alien one.

An Austrian television cameraman and I were the only passengers aboard the silver TU-104 120-passenger Soviet jet. We settled down in seats around a little table holding a small lamp with a parchment shade. Overhead, hangers for coats swung from baggage webbing. The Russian stewardess said she had no pillows or blankets to give us. She passed out copies in Russian and German of *New Times,* one of the Soviet Union's many propaganda magazines sent abroad.

Dinner was served: fried chicken, the usual peas and carrots in a heavy white cream sauce served in a pastry shell, apple juice, fried potatoes, and a mixture of chopped herring and egg.

"Russian!" said the Austrian, picking up the heavy brown bread.

After we crossed Hungary there was no mistaking the great Russian steppe below us—snow-covered in early November, the flat forests of birch and pine stretching on and on like a silent ocean.

Then, Sheremetevo Airport, the usual red banners flapping in the freezing wind: "Long Live the Great Communist Party of the Soviet Union." Photographs of Nikita Sergeievitch flanked the slogans.

"Well, I see he's still in power," said the Austrian photographer.

Inside, the airport was the same old melee. Baggage, short Russian porters in quilted jackets, the usual young Intourist officials looking officious, bewildered passengers. In the noisy throng I spied an old acquaintance, Paul Coates, a columnist from the Los Angeles *Mirror*. His face was almost gray. Like many first arrivals to Moscow, he was experiencing some shock.

"I can't figure it out, it's so confusing," he said. He added that he had been waiting an hour for an Intourist guide to find him.

Going in the other direction was a British correspondent, who had just completed a month-long tour of Soviet collective farms. He wore the air of the tourist who knows the country now. Or does he? "The more I saw, the more confused I became," he said, "but I will say after seeing the farms that this country is being dragged, kicking and screaming, into the twentieth century." He added with a laugh, "You may not like this, but, you know, Russians and Americans seem a little alike. The same boasting about building the biggest this or that, the same naïveté, the same pioneer spirit . . ."

Victor, our office chauffeur, who was supposed to meet me, was nowhere to be seen.

"Alina!" cried Slava, one of our translators, when I telephoned the UPI office. "I called the airport and they said the airplane was arriving two hours from now. Victor is coming right out."

Well, that figured. It was just like old times.

The Austrian photographer's Intourist car, due him on the $35-a-day plan, was nowhere to be found. Will Intourist ever change? I offered him a lift. Although a mass of formalities is required to bring camera equipment into the Soviet Union, he neatly spirited his away from the usual easygoing customs that may never change, either.

Our office car was loaded to the fins when a passenger from the Brussels plane ran over and tapped on the window. "I see you are foreigners. Can you take me to town? There are no taxis," he said.

We squeezed him and his three suitcases into the front seat and skidded off down the icy road.

"Drab, but such building activity. A new city in the making," said the excited newcomer, a Belgian exchange student, repeating what countless arrivals had said before him.

When we turned into No. 13 People's Street, I saw that the old Taganka prison stockade had been torn down. In its place was a new prefabricated apartment house in the making. The old shack tacked onto our "garden" entrance was also gone. But in its place in the yard were three empty bathtubs littered with assorted refuse.

Inside, our smiling Soviet translators were waiting with "welcome" signs and little gifts. Tonya, the maid, had hot *blini* waiting. The Tass teletype was clacking away as usual, "The might of the socialist camp is determined by the fact that it is the standard-bearer of social progress and is defending a historically righteous cause which will inevitably achieve complete victory . . ."

The bedbugs were back in the bedroom, some Russian partygoers were singing to the accompaniment of an accordion down the street, and a girl friend from the U.S. embassy was sitting in my bathtub.

"The embassy's hot water is turned off for fourteen days for repairs, so I'm borrowing your tub," she explained.

I put down my heap of baggage and laughed. I knew I was back in Moscow.

Now, as I write this, I know I'll soon be leaving. The other day instead of answering the phone by saying, "United Press International" I said, "United States." I think it's time to go home.

I will miss Russia. I will miss my Russian friends.

One devout Communist I know, one of the group I call "the Rover boys," soon takes off for Brazil as a "missionary" to spread the faith. I wish him the worst of luck.

Slava is about to become a father for the first time. Arthur, the senior interpreter, has just acquired a private two-room apartment for himself and his family, and he is a happy man. A London newspaper published a photograph of one of L.'s paintings recently. I hear that twenty of his works, somehow transferred to England, will go on exhibition in London soon.

Mikhail has a better life now, too. He is remarried and has been transferred to Kiev, where he has a new private apartment, two rooms for the family of three. I traveled there to visit them recently.

"When you leave could we have your modern dishes and drapes?" said his bride. "We want to have an American-style apartment."

Mikhail looked younger and happier than I had ever seen him. "Here I am almost fifty, and only now I feel that

I'm beginning to live," he exclaimed. "It was not having a private apartment that depressed me so. Now to have a toilet of my own! It was sharing the bathroom and lavatory with other people, that's what I hated."

Dmitri, my ex-Russian friend who "defected" to the West, wrote from England, where he is attending Cambridge University, "I offer Grandma's recipe for your cockroaches. 'Lasso them, step on their toes, and put some salt on their tails.' Or expose them to the sheen emanating from that white MG of yours. They will be dazed and die. So will the Russians . . .

"I face a 15-year prison sentence if I come back, but I would like to return, once, just to walk up Gorky Street and hear Russian spoken again."

The other day I received a letter from an American correspondent who was stationed in Moscow during the early fifties.

"I saw that Russian film, *Ballad of a Soldier*, in New York," he wrote. "I thought I had left Russia behind me, but as I watched the movie it all came back. . . . Does one ever get over Russia?"

Mikhail once told me he heard that most foreign correspondents complain and turn cynical while working in the Soviet capital. "But, you know, it's a funny thing," he said. "After they leave, there's something about Russia— they look back on their years in Moscow with a bit of nostalgia.

"You'll never forget Russia," he said, and he's right.

About the Author

ALINE MOSBY was born and brought up in Missoula, Montana. Since graduating from the University of Montana she has worked as a journalist in various parts of the world, both with the United Press International and as a free-lance reporter. Miss Mosby has also written for radio and magazines, and in the course of her work has traveled extensively. She is currently with the Paris bureau of the UPI.